# Unbroken Circles for Schools

## Restoring Schools one Conflict at a Time

# Ken Johnson

Published by:
Southern Yellow Pine (SYP) Publishing
4351 Natural Bridge Rd.
Tallahassee, FL 32305

www.syppublishing.com

The contents and opinions expressed in this book do not necessarily reflect the views and opinions of Southern Yellow Pine Publishing, nor does the mention of brands or trade names constitute endorsement. No attempt has been made to verify facts presented by individual authors.

ISBN-10: 1940869161
ISBN-13: 978-1-940869-16-2

Front Cover Design: Jim Hamer

Front cover photo credits as follows:
Shutterstock
Image ID 1883598 Copyright Tad Denson
Image ID 168691196 Copyright Zurijeta
Image ID 2199895 Copyright OLJ Studio
Image ID 176554478 Copyright Claudia Paulussen

Images page 36 & 39; Thomas R. Fournier, Sr. with ©2012; purchased by Ken Johnson

Printed in the United States of America
First Edition
August 2014

# Dedication

I dedicate this book to the hope of a better future for our nation's children where schools can once more be a place of learning and a safe-haven for those needing the valuable skills being taught. It is my sincerest desire that the community-minded, restoration-focused methodology of this program will finally allow our children the opportunity to be children without fear of being arrested and tried as adults for trivial offenses and dreaded "crimes of the future."

For my wife, you have always stood by me and understood my heart when seemingly no one else could. You alone know the drive that I have for Collaborative Justice and the passion that I have for protecting the future of our youth. Few men are so fortunate to seek out their dreams and visions. Even fewer are so blessed to know such a deep and profound love and have that love returned. You make me want to be a better man.

*The little world in which children have their existence, whoever brings them up, there is nothing so finely perceived and so finely felt, as injustice.*

-Charles Dickens

*To raise up and to restore that which is in ruin*
*To repair that which is damaged*
*To rejoin that which is severed*
*To replenish that which is lacking*
*To strengthen that which is weakened*
*To set right that which is wrong*
*To make flourish that which is insecure and underdeveloped.*

-Dr. Maulana Karenga, *Selections from the Husia: Sacred Wisdom of Ancient Egypt*

## Table of Contents

# INTRODUCTION

First, I want to thank you for purchasing this book. Unbroken Circles is a new way of thinking about conflict. It combines pieces of Restorative Justice, Collaborative Justice, and my own experience. A great deal of time, years in fact, were spent pouring over research, interviewing professionals, evaluating existing programs, and gathering data to develop a program that is easy to use, reliable, and most importantly, highly effective. Not only does this book represent my life's work but also it marries my training, as a culturalist (a.k.a. Social Scientist) and M.B.A., with my career, in the criminal justice and Conflict Resolution sectors, to make an effective program that is a paradigm shift in how school-based conflicts are resolved.

Sadly, the present system of handling juvenile and youthful offenders offers no remedy to the issues at hand. Nor does the present system offer any voice to the victims, community, and even offenders. Unbroken Circles [SM] is a remedy to alleviate further misery to society by giving voice to the victim and the benefit of atonement and re-assimilation to the offender through the inclusion of a community of care.

No other commercially available program on the market marries the concepts and practices this way. As a friend of mine, and a leader in the mediation field for the First Judicial Circuit of Florida, once said about Unbroken Circles [SM], "it is Conflict Resolution at its best!" Additionally, the programs and practices are something that do not require you to buy additional CDs, computer programs, booklets or study guides. I merely offer up the plan and give suggestions to best implement, run, manage, evaluate, and grow the program. In the end, I leave it all up to the school, or school system, to determine what is best for them and to tailor-make a version of my program that will deliver what they need

**The Background**

When I tell people about this program, they always seem to ask why and how it all got started. Once we get past that, it is like some special "key" that opens a doorway in their minds. From there, people seem to be hooked on the idea and are supportive of this paradigm shift.

Briefly, I originally came up with the idea for this program while I was attending classes at the University of West Florida (UWF). I started college at age sixteen. After graduating from the local junior college, I spent some time as a substitute teacher trying to get my life started on a career path. I was deeply troubled with how things were going with this country. Everywhere I went, I saw unresolved conflicts or conflicts made worse by ineffective methodologies. Society was doing the wrong things repeatedly and somehow expecting different results. It was distracting to say the least!

Ironically, I took a criminal justice job to clear my mind and help me find grounding I needed to gain perspective. It was my hope that the constant bombardment of conflicts would desensitize me—much like an allergy shot. To the contrary, I began to notice patterns and commonalities with the various types of conflict.

When I realized I could not run away from the conflicts, or become desensitized to them, I came up with a different game plan. I would work to resolve conflicts. In no time, it became apparent that I needed more education if I was to find the skills and resources needed to fix the problems that I saw daily.

I guess you could say the rest was a bit fortuitous. You see, by the time I was at UWF, working on trying to find solutions to those perceived problems, I already had years of experience working in the criminal justice system, special certification as a County Court Mediator through the Florida Supreme Court, and past experience in the public education field. Somehow, some way, all of this gelled for me at UWF. I attribute part of it to seeing weekly hoards of juveniles enter the criminal justice system. Many of those I taught in school were charged for trivial offenses (most tried as adults for trumped-up misdemeanor and felony level charges). Likewise, I saw graduating high school seniors denied admittance to the military for similar types of criminal activities. Indeed, my heart became burdened. I needed to come up with a viable and lasting solution to an epidemic problem—how America mishandles juvenile-based conflicts and crimes.

Trying to find a more direct solution, I remembered Dr. Rosezetta Bobo, from the Florida Supreme Court. As a mediation trainer, she told me how Restorative Justice allowed victims to be actively involved in the prosecution of justice, how it allowed criminals a way to atone for their actions, and how it allowed the community to heal by re-assimilating both victim and offender back into society.

I soon found a learning resource at UWF's College of Professional Studies while looking for a means to study this fledgling system of dispute resolution. There, I started my journey by enrolling in a Restorative Justice class taught by Dr. Cheryl Swanson.

Dr. Swanson served as my mentor into the field of Restorative Justice (RJ). I admit that we often differed in opinion on how best to provide RJ-based services to society. She focused primarily on prisons and law enforcement while I focused on schools, places of worship, etc. Despite these differences of opinion, we both appreciated the benefits that Restorative Justice posed to the parties involved and the promise of making "whole" that it offered society. In addition, using my mediator background, it was not long until I was on the fast track to the development of a meaningful dispute resolution program for our ailing school system.

**The Development**

When thinking about how this program would best work, as well as what to call it, I became obsessed with rubber bands. Some rubber bands were small and could not take a lot of force when stretched beyond the limits. Others allowed for more give, but they also allowed for so much slack that sufficient force could build up from the inside and burst through the band. It fascinated me how each size had its own benefits and limits. After a while, I further developed my gedankenexperimenten—German philosophical term for "thought experiments" first taught to me by my philosophy professor, Dr. Raymond Wolf of Pensacola State College. I continued to play with the bands to see how I could maximize their benefits by playing off their limitations. Next, I reflected on how I could use this knowledge in my own life in other, seemingly unrelated situations.

Over time, I took multiple rubber bands and pulled against them. It was with these rubber bands that I noticed certain key characteristics. For instance, when tugged from the center, I noticed that the rubber bands leant strength to the other bands as opposing force was exerted. Even when a rubber band broke, the other bands, working in conjunction with each other, kept the system whole and the opposing force from fully breaking through.

I spent years investigating multiple Conflict Resolution methodologies (i.e., peer mediation, circles, panels, etc.); therefore, I noticed how each methodology was like a given type of rubber band with benefits and limitations uniquely inherent to it and it alone. After some time of re-arranging the programs on a hierarchy of community support, the program of Unbroken Circles [SM] was conceived.

## Initial Public Reception

Initially, I tried to have the local school district use the program. Drug Abuse Resistance Education (D.A.R.E.), the law enforcement-based drug and crime prevention program used in the local schools had seemingly escalated the number of convictions in juveniles for my county. When public discourse took place over this, the law enforcement officials only wanted to talk about how grant money was funding everything and how they increased the number of convictions—as if that were a good thing to do with our community's youth. When the public officials spoke out, the message was surprisingly in favor of this punitive agenda where many community leaders called for a need to increase the number of convictions. The goal was to "send a message" to a youth-base that was perceived and portrayed as becoming increasingly violent and out of control. Yet, when it came to the actual youths and families affected, there was almost no opportunity for their voice to be heard.

I knew something desperately needed to happen to change the tide. It seemed like every week there was a D.A.R.E. or other school resource officer program related story with school kids arrested for incidences of little harm. For instance, there were numerous accounts where elementary-aged children held up a French fry, tater tot, or even a chicken nugget, saying "bang!" to a teacher. This resulted in the child's arrest for assault with a firearm and other charges. The stories became ludicrous, and overwhelmingly saddening to hear.

While researching material for my program, I learned of a local youth arrested on felony bomb-threat charges for drawing a cartoon picture of a bomb at school. Authorities told me that the child was bored and drew a picture that was reminiscent of Bugs Bunny-type bombs rather than actual hard schematics. According to the authorities, the student was drawing on a piece of paper when it fell to the ground. Another student picked it up, handed it to a teacher, she screamed, the D.A.R.E. school resource officer was called in, and the child was cuffed and arrested. Months later, the prosecutor's office finally lowered the charge from felony-level bomb-threat charges to falsely pulling a fire alarm. This was portrayed as an act of benevolence. That story of a local child hit home with me, and I proceeded to go about my work trying to stop this from happening to other youth.

Initially, presenting the program to teachers and schools was both challenging and rewarding. Verily, I did find a good number of public school teachers who saw benefit with the program. Many heralded it as a new way of thinking. However, difficulties arose when the local teachers' union representative stepped in and wanted the school board to pay teachers twice their pay to learn the program on school time. The request was viewed as so over the top that the program was dropped from consideration.

This became a common theme as I tried employing the program in neighboring counties within the district. In reality, from a political perspective, one understood why the program was failing to gain ground even with the support of teachers. After all, it was well apparent that the teachers' unions were unreasonable with their demands. Concurrently, federal grant money was pouring into the state and counties to arrest students on frivolous charges. The Governor's Office came out with a "Blue Ribbon Panel Study" claiming the need to incarcerate seven percent of the state's youth each year. The news media was totally focused on the illusion that more arrests meant that the student population was more violent and dangerous to the public. The elected members of the school boards were heralded as tough on crime and education-focused. The only "losers" in the process were the students, and we all know that minors do not vote or pay taxes.

## A Smoldering Ember—A Renewed Flame

Outraged at how entire communities could turn their backs on their youth, I focused my efforts on working with Restorative Justice International, an internet-based collection of Restorative Justice Professionals. Here, I was able to review the latest data and books soon to be published, etc. Using other Conflict Resolution and mediation based groups, I kept up with how other methodologies were developing. This allowed me to publicly speak and write, gaining awareness for the program while also keeping abreast of the political landscape.

Those efforts were not in vain. If anything, the down-turned economy was a blessing in that grant monies for youth-incarcerating programs dried up. In fact, the same agencies that were funding these aforementioned, onerous programs are now funding programs that evaluate and promote Restorative Justice based initiatives because of their high success rate and cost savings to the community.

It is my goal to make this program available to as many schools as possible. The political landscape is now right for a program of this kind to succeed. The need has never been greater! Moreover, since this program was built off the successes of so many other working programs, it is possible to use certain base elements and still have a functioning system that will do more for the students, staff, parents, and community than what the status quo presently offers.

Ultimately, this book serves as a dynamic, education sector-based Conflict Resolution module that melds proactive and reactive measures together. The purpose is to change the retributive nature of social responses, in regards to student misconduct, utilizing the centuries-old, tested techniques found in Restorative Justice. The Unbroken Circles [SM] program is intended to unify schools, build character, espouse good citizenship, improve grades in low performers with a history of disciplinary issues, and reduce recidivism rates. The skills and lessons espoused by this program give the students the tools they need to diffuse problems both at school and at home.

The program covers a wide array of tactics and methods that run the gamut from simple daily class circles, to peer mediation, conferences, and other forms of Circle Justice. The plan slices through every aspect of a child's life, whether in the classroom, on the playground, on school grounds, or even in the juvenile justice courts. A community of care is created. This is a veritable unbroken circle that will hold the offender accountable and seek for the child to make things right when wrongs have been committed.

**Layout of the Book**

For you, the reader, the book is broken up into traditional chapters and into sections. This improves the progression of better understanding.

Section 1 is the educational aspect of the book backed up with research and proven practices. The intention to afford a basic understanding of the approaches and methodologies that best comprise the Unbroken Circles [SM] program, as well as the research-based evidence and supporting theories needed to comprehend fully what the program is about and how it works. Think of Section 1 as a crash course.

Section 2 is the operational side of the equation. It is one thing to know something but quite a different matter to implement that knowledge in a functional way. Section 2 uses business expertise, education, and practical Collaborative Justice skills to lay out a guide that is flexible enough to employ in any given school setting and specific enough to obtain the results desired from the program.

There is also a Conclusion and Appendix section. Unlike a lot of "how to" books I see on the market, I wanted the Appendix section to be something that is functional for you. It is comprised of suggested forms and guides. It is not meant to be all that you need to carry out an individualized program successfully. Rather, this section offers tools school officials will need to get a program up and running until they can hone their own program and develop the format that best meets the needs of the individualized program of the school or district.

I should warn you that any program of this nature is a large undertaking. Such a program necessitates expert guidance by professionals trained and certified to handle the methodologies employed by the Unbroken Circles [SM] program. It also requires appropriate pairing of the best-qualified people with a job that best fits their desires and personalities. The "years in service" promotional system must be abandoned and the school, or district, should look at every candidate based on their personality, motivations, drive, abilities, and background, to place them where they can best excel in the program.

Above all else, always be mindful of why you are embarking on the journey. It is my hope if you share the same angers and frustrations, and have a similar drive to thwart further harm, you will consider this program. From a professional and personal standpoint, I can honestly say I am tired of watching my generation, and my parents' generation, waste away the future of up and coming generations by clouding their past and coloring their character with frivolous arrests and questionable convictions. According to a federal report titled *Prevalence of Imprisonment in the U.S. Population, 1974-2001,* an African American male has nearly a 17% chance of going to jail or prison. Over 5.6 million Americans were incarcerated in 2001 alone! Moreover, the sad news is that incarceration rates are increasing almost exponentially. (Source: US Department of Justice, August 2003, Publication NCJ 197976)

When our children are school age, we are best able to turn the tide of this horrific trend. This is because they are of the right age and mindset to learn and apply the tools set forth in this book. This nation should be embarrassed to send our school-aged children to jails and prisons rather than teaching them how to atone responsibly for wrongful actions, in a nurturing environment. It is my sincerest hope that as a reader of this book, you will feel the same way. That is why I started this introduction by thanking you for purchasing this book and why I will end it thanking you—because I want you to take the contents of this book and change things in the life of a child for the better!

# Section 1

# 1.1

## Background

We, as a nation, are on the brink of a national travesty. At the heart of this issue is the future of our children. Ultimately, it boils down to whom we view as dangerous and how we seek to punish those offenders. In an ironic turn of events, community after community, all across America, now see our youth as being heinous criminals.

While I would like to think this is a new concept, brought on by bad science and media hype, the truth is that this issue has been a near four decade-long era of bigotry and hatred geared exclusively towards our nation's youth. The culprits of this movement have been numerous and range from academics to politicians, teachers, law enforcement, the judiciary, and beyond. Notable within this movement is the tone and pattern of the rhetoric employed. In most cases, juveniles are portrayed as evil and as an endangerment to society. Faulty research is presented as proof of illogical correlation to youthful behavior and crimes of the future. Media attention is solicited and provided to build sufficient hype; professionals are assembled to tout the media hype and flawed research as proof of the baseless assertions. A public push is made to rile the masses and get anti-juvenile laws passed; programs are instituted on multiple levels so the policies are not easily removed. Any sound evidence to refute the rhetoric is denied media attention until the resulting policies have been used a decade.

Case in point, since the 1960s, psychologists and criminologists have heralded the "MacDonald Triad" as a way to predict potential serial killers and serial rapists in juvenile offenders. The triad of bed wetting, playing with fire, and mistreating animals is now a predictive labeling aspect of the justice system that adults do not have to endure. When arrested for a crime, the court system evaluates a juvenile to see if he or she fits into the MacDonald Triad. Such an association colors the trial, treatment of the defendant by officials, plea bargains offered, the judgment, and the sentencing. Moreover, it stigmatizes the child for the rest of his or her life because of "crimes of the future" that they have never or may never commit. At the same time, they are denied constitutional rights and freedoms that their adult counterparts are given as being "owed to any

US citizen or person charged with a crime in America." MacDonald later wrote that he could not replicate his findings. He also stated he did not believe in the validity of the triad. Despite the fact that it has repeatedly been found by the psychological field to be something that cannot be duplicated—it is still somehow seen as an irrefutable, predictive tool embraced by the courts.[1]

Since that time, both the government and the media have launched a campaign, especially at young boys, to vilify juveniles and to hold them as being more feared, and therefore more criminally accountable, than adults are. Starting in the 1990s a flood of new laws were passed by states, removing protections for juvenile offenders based on the belief that juveniles were becoming particularly dangerous. In particular, preteen and teenage boys were portrayed as murderous thugs and rapists who dealt in drugs and had no remorse. Sadly, the facts of the matter were not investigated. If they had looked, the lawmakers, the media, and the educators would have found that ninety-two percent of all murderers are over the age of 18. Only four out of every 100 juvenile arrests ever had anything to do with a violent crime—less than half that of adult arrest ratios. Of that violent crime arrest-rate ratio, only one-quarter of one percent (0.0026) of all juvenile arrests accounted for crimes of murder or rape.[2]

The result is that several states have gone well past the MacDonald Triad, creating mythological "super predator" criminals due to the fear that juveniles are evolving into dangerous criminals. These predicted criminals are so heinous that it would make the Columbine High School shooter look like a Boy Scout. While officials openly admit that such an "ultra criminal" has never been arrested or convicted, these reports—from special panels and special committees—call for extraordinary measures. This often results in more arrests and juvenile offenders tried as adults. In my home state of Florida, law enforcement has been called upon to arrest the state's youth on misdemeanor and felony offenses by as much as seven percent of the youth population per year.[3]

If one looked at historical arrest statistics only, an argument exists that our nation's youth have turned into a cesspool of hell-spawned beings who would gladly cut their own grandmothers' throats for a video game system or new pair of sneakers. Yet, when we look at the backroom meetings that set the standards for the statistic gathering practices, quite a different picture emerges. With outdated concepts and theories that cannot be replicated, no supportive empirical data of mention, and a flagrant disregard for the Constitution and due process of law, one can see there is a clear and present objective being perpetrated against our nation's youth. At best, it is a shameful and misguided attempt to by-pass the inalienable rights of a voiceless segment of our socio-political culture. At worst, it is an onerously established, draconian methodology meant to gain financial funding, power, and social/political accolades by enslaving and ripping away the futures of a vulnerable and unprotected segment of the community, with little to no true political and social representation.

As a community, we rightfully seek to teach our youth that life is full of choices. Solutions to problems are in abundance if one looks hard enough. However, sometimes what we say is not necessarily, what we do as a society. In the case of juvenile disobedience, the justice system focused on the retributive side of the equation. The situation is exacerbated by charging offenders for crimes not perpetrated, over charging (in the hopes to reach a plea bargain rather than following true due process of law), and stigmatizing the defendant with labeling that (whether found innocent or guilty) will have lifelong consequences. In a sense, they offer one solution for handling an issue while saying that there is a plethora of solutions for any one problem. Indeed, this conflict can and does lead to outcroppings of a myriad of issues that are counterproductive and unhealthy for all involved.

## SNAPSHOT        *Taking a look at the facts*

*Approximately every 20 years, the number of juvenile offenders being housed in US detention centers doubles. If we were becoming a more violent, out-of-control society, like the so-called "experts" contend, then logic says we'd also see corresponding spikes in adult crime similar to what we see with juvenile crime. However, with non-violent crimes removed (including drug offenses), we do not see this spike at all. In fact, academic surveys of court proceedings indicate it is easier for a juvenile to be arrested and charged for a felony level crime than it is for an adult carrying out the same actions. Once arrested and charged, a juvenile's chances of a misdemeanor or felony conviction is far greater than that of an adult participating in the same actions. Such a conviction follows a juvenile for the rest of his or her life and ultimately affects his or her ability to enter into military service or get a job. The stigma alone causes many not to be able to find gainful employment. When one also takes into account the fact that he or she is losing time from school to battle such charges and serve time, the juvenile is at a serious disadvantage. The top reason a juvenile leaves the Juvenile Justice System is he or she reaches the age of 18 and transitions to adult prisons to finish out his or her sentence. A growing percentage of prison inmates now attribute their criminal occupation to a singular juvenile offense. One event held them back educationally, stigmatized them socially and economically, while also subjecting them to a subversive criminal element where they learned how to commit greater crimes just to make it in a hostile and broken correctional system.*

### Juveniles in US Public Detention Centers

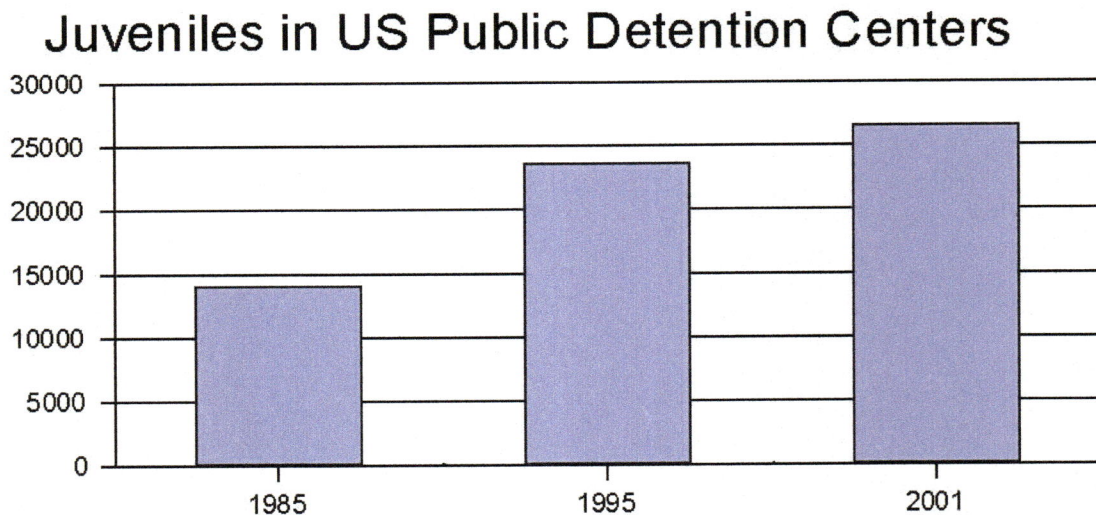

**Table 1** *Source:* **January 2008 Florida Department of Juvenile Justice Blueprint Commission showing the number of Juveniles in U.S. Public Detention Centers using a one-day census.**

When a wrong has been committed and the offender punished, what has truly been done? When offenders do wrong, we punish them. America has used this retributive system of jurisprudence since its inception. However, besides the obvious, what is happening with this sort of justice dealing system?

Essentially, what usually happens is that the system steps-in. The victim's voice, as well as the victim's needs, are removed from the equation; the offenders are usually forced to deny their misdoings, and the community is still hurt by the unmet needs of the victim, the offender, and society. When we do not address these needs, we do not solve the problem created by a rift in the community, but instead we make the rift larger.

For juvenile offenders, there are compounding issues that further complicate matters since they may be overcharged for a relatively trivial offense. They may fit a profile that changes how they are afforded basic Constitutional rights. As minors, they often do not have the right to or knowledge to properly lodge an adequate defense. Whether or not they wish to atone for their crimes, the juveniles become locked into a "conveyor belt" like system of justice, which aims to destroy their future. This harm is then carried over to future generations where the juvenile's future offspring are denied proper resources. The juvenile becomes economically hampered because of the socio-economic stigma of the offense and labeling. Thus, communities are denied taxes on future income and sales.

Luckily, there is a different style of justice. One style gives victims a voice, communities a voice, and seeks to repair the wrongs through the offender seeking atonement. Restorative Justice seeks to repair the harm by reassimilation of both the victim and the offender.

With that said, it is of special importance to note that Restorative Justice professionals oft times compare their style of justice with the aforementioned status quo system by pointing out how traditional justice practices tend to replace the victim and community with that of the nation or the state. The contention is that making the nation or the state a surrogate victim leaves a host of unmet needs for all parties concerned. Alternatively, as Eduard A. Ziegenhager wrote, "The state itself has taken the role of a surrogate victim thus effectively excluding the expression of interests which comprise part of the social control."[4]

Under this premise of the criminal justice system, victims are considered "blocked out" of the process by having no voice in the matter or any form of fruitful engagement with the alleged offender. The community, like the victim, is barred from any meaningful say or engagement. In addition, the offender is portrayed as being left to the devices of a pre-determined, "conveyor belt-like" justice system where a judgment is ordered and a sentence is carried out. The offender is then forced to try to find a way to assimilate back into a community that traditionally ostracizes those with a criminal background.[5]

All levels of society—from the schools to the prison systems—have experienced massive increases in socially undesirable behaviors. This is due to rifts caused by ineffective handling of misbehaviors and crime. More saddening is that we often fail to see the harm caused; therefore, we keep trying to combat wrongful behaviors the same old way. As result, this alarming trend appears to get worse in return. A vicious, tornado-like societal vortex is thus started that can easily spiral a youthful offender up the ladder of criminality to thief, drug dealer, batterer, and worse, in just a matter of a few years. Still, without a second thought, we fight these misdeeds with ineffective methods. If society were a person, psychologists would say we are misguided to keep employing the same broken methods that make matters worse rather than better.

What if there was a better way that could heal the wounds? What if there was a way that classrooms, schools, and the juvenile offender-related courts could be improved and strengthened? What if there was a method to make the offender accountable, address victim's needs, address the needs of the community, address the needs of the offender, and essentially put things back in a state of all-rightness? The truth is, there is a better way. The book will help an individual school system solve the woes that plague our great nation's educational system.

## An Old Idea Revisited

Before explorers first landed on the shores of "Turtle Island," what many Native American tribes have historically called North America, there was an existing system of justice. The thousands of American Indian tribes had different systems and rules; however, they were all similar in that the goal of justice was to restore balance. Today, in many parts of America, we call their form of justice "Circle Justice". As Ben Mikaelsen wrote in his book (p. 241), *Touching Spirit Bear*, "Circle Justice has been practiced by native cultures for many centuries. Only recently has the concept been given a chance to work within some modern U.S. judicial systems. The strength of Circle Justice, however, comes from the creativity of the individual members within each Healing Circle."[6]

Of course, American Indians do not have a "fix" on the market when it comes to justice practices that heal. Indeed, there are countless other cultures such as the Maori of New Zealand and the Hebrews chronicled in the Bible, that indicate how mankind's original view of justice was to repair the harm done by injustice.[7]

Over the years, parts of Canada, communities in America, portions of Europe, segments of Africa, as well as Australia, and all of New Zealand have replaced the standard retributive systems of modern society for the restorative practices of the past. These practices vary from simple circles to peer mediation to full-blown conferences and Circle Justice.[8]

If you think of it as being like a flow chart, all of these various practices ultimately fall under a main category heading called either "Conflict Resolution" or "Alternative Dispute Resolution." From there, a branch forms known as "Restorative Justice" and from here comes what we know today as "Restorative Practices."

Thus, Restorative Justice is a form of Conflict Resolution that is akin to, but different from, other forms of Conflict Resolution found in Western society. Some other forms are mediation, expert determination, and arbitration. For this reason, multiple forms of non-Restorative Justice-based Conflict Resolution practices are effective with Restorative Justice since they have similar ideologies inherent to their classification and purpose.

To put things in perspective, Hank Robert, an accomplished martial artist of the mid-1900s, decided to form a martial art that would be undefeatable. According to his book titled *Defend Yourself! Ketsugo: Complete Self-Defense,* Robert found a way to merge "the striking and kicking methods of Karate and Savate, the twists, locks and joint-breaking art of Aikido, the pressure points used in Yawara and Ate-Waza, and the devastating throws of Judo and Jiu Jitsu." He called this art *Ketsugo,* which is Japanese for combination. Robert teaches the reader to start with a daily routine of practicing the common skills used by all of the arts that Ketsugo embodies (e.g., kicking, punching). From that base, the student switches from one art form to the other as the situation deems. Moreover, Robert contended that learning just some of the basic skills of Ketsugo made one more likely to properly defend oneself in the event of a physical attack.[9]

Using Robert's idea of combining the best of various practices to make a new and stronger practice, one could say that the *Unbroken Circles*[SM] system is similar to Ketsugo. It uses circles, mediation, conferences, and other Conflict Resolution practices to make one art form. This deals with injustice in a myriad of ways with the ultimate goal being restoration to all parties concerned. In addition, like Ketsugo, there are common elements that comprise all of the Conflict Resolution practices of the *Unbroken Circles*[SM] system. Therefore, practicing one or two Restorative Practices is enough to have a noticeable impact on the student, the class, and the school. Moreover, like Ketsugo, the art of Restorative Justice—and Conflict Resolution as a whole— only get better when there are multiple arts and practices to draw upon that can be tailored to the needs of a situation.

## Synopsis of the Success of Restorative Justice Practices

What does the research have to say about Restorative Justice concerning the school system and juvenile offenders? There is a significant amount of research saying quite a lot about this subject! Probably the most startling revelation is not what the research reports state but rather what they are repeating, over and over again, in independent and unrelated studies, books, and interviews.

Implementing restorative practices in a school system is found to greatly improve grades, significantly lower discipline referrals, boost self-esteem, and increase attendance by a remarkable margin in poor performers. Moreover, chronically persistent problems entrenched in the school culture (i.e., bullying, fights, and theft) are reduced when the school embarks on a conflict resolution program that embraces Restorative Justice Principles. As with the schools, studies concerning the juvenile court systems of New Zealand, Australia, South Africa, England, Canada, and America have found remarkably lower recidivism rates, with some reporting lesser-level repeat offenses in those offenders that do recidivate back into the system.[10] Graham Robb—a head teacher who worked multiple years with the Thames Valley Police in a Restorative Justice-based "Whole School" program—said,

> Restorative Justice practices are now being used in England to, manage behavior in classrooms, deal with significant problems such as bullying, theft and damage, resolve playground, social areas and school community issues, resolve conflict between adults within the school community or conflict between the school and families, inform circle time, PSHE (personal, social and health education), citizenship and other curriculum activities, and develop democratic processes of a school—e.g., school councils.[11]

# References

1.  Franklin, K. (2 May 2012). *Homicidal Triad: Predictor of Violence or Urban Myth? Psychology Today. Witness* Blog. Retrieved on 5/5/2012 from http://www.psychologytoday.com/blog/witness/201205/homicidal-triad-predictor-violence-or-urban-myth

2.  Kappeler, V. E. & Potter, G. W. (2005). *The Mythology of Crime and Criminal Justice (4th Edition).* Long Grove, IL: Waveland Press

3.  Florida Department of Juvenile Justice (January 2008). *Florida Department of Juvenile Justice Blueprint Commission Report.* Retrieved on 5/5/2012 http://www.djj.state.fl.us/blueprint/documents/Report_of_the_Blueprint_Commision.pdf

4.  Schneider, H. J. (1982). *The Victim in International Perspective.* France: Walter de Gruyter

5.  CliffsNotes.com (12 September 2011). *Which Model? Crime Control or Due Process.* Retrieved from http://www.cliffsnotes.com/study_guide/topicArticleId-10065,articleId-9911.html

6.  Mikaelsen, B. (2001). *Touching Spirit Bear.* New York: HarperCollins Publishers

7.  Zehr, H. (1990). *Changing Lenses: A New Focus for Crime and Justice.* Scottdale, PA:Herald Press

8.  Bazemore, G. and Walgrave, L. Eds.(1999). *Restorative Juvenile Justice: Repairing the Harm of Youth Crime.* Monsey, NY:Criminal Justice Press

    Bazemore, G. and Schiff, M. Eds. (2001). *Restorative Community Justice: Repairing Harm and Transforming Communities.* Cincinnati:Anderson Publishing

    Bazemore, G. and Schiff, M. (2005). *Juvenile Justice Reform and Restorative Justice: Building Theory and Policy From Practice.* Portland:Willan Publishing

    Hayden, A. (2001). *Restorative Conferencing Manual of Aotearoa New Zealand: He Taonga no a Tatou Kete (A Treasure From Our Basket).* Wellington, NZ:District Courts of New Zealand

    Johnstone, G. Ed. (2003). *A Restorative Justice Reader: Texts, Sources, Context.* Portland:Willan Publishing

    McLaughlin, E., Gergusson, R., Hughes, G. and Westmarland, L. Eds. (2003). *Restorative Justice: Critical Issues.* London:Sage Publications

    *National Evaluation of the Restorative Justice in Schools Programme* (2004). United Kingdom:Youth Justice Board for England and Wales

    Roche, D. (2003). *Accountability in Restorative Justice.* Oxford:Oxford Press

    Strang, H. (2002). *Repair or Revenge: Victims and Restorative Justice.* Oxford:Clarendon Press

    Zehr, H. (1990). *Changing Lenses: A New Focus for Crime and Justice.* Scottdale, PA:Herald Press

    Zehr, H. (2002). *The Little Book of Restorative Justice.* Intercourse, PA:Good Books

9.  Robert, H. (1961). Defend *Yourself! Ketsugo: Complete Self-Defense.* New York:Magnum Publications

10. *Bronx Community Solutions.* Center for Court Innovation website. Retrieved 5/3/2006 from http://www.courtinnovation.org/index.cfm?fuseaction=Page.ViewPageID=597

    Chmelynski, C. (17 May 2005). *Schools Find "Restorative Justice" More Effective Than Expulsion.* Retrieved 7/7/ 2006 from http://nsba.org/site/print.asp?TRACKID=&VID=58&ACTION=PRINT&CID=682&DID=35966

    Elliott, S. (June 1995). *The Responsive Classroom Approach: Its Effectiveness and Acceptability.* Retrieved June 29, 2006 from http://www.responsiveclassroom.org/pdf_files/rc_evaluation_project.pdf

Elliott, S. (February 1999). *A Multi-Year Evaluation of the Responsive Classroom® Approach: It's Effectiveness and Acceptability in Promoting Social and Academic Competence.* Retrieved 6/292006 from http://www.responsiveclassroom.org/PDF_files/final_report.pdf

McCold, P. (12 November 2002). *Evaluation of a Restorative Milieu: CSF Buxmont School/Day Treatment Programs 1999-2001.* Restorative Practices E-Forum. Retrieved 6/28/2006 from http://fp.enter.net/restorativepractices/erm.pdf

Mirsky, L. (20 May 20 2003). *SaferSaner Schools: Transforming School Culture with Restorative Practices.* Restorative Practices E-Forum.Retrieved 5/27/2006 from http://fp.enter.net/restorativepractices/ssspilots.pdf

Morrison, B. (22 October 2002). *Restorative Justice and School Violence: Building Theory and Practice.* Restorative Practices E-Forum. Retrieved on 7/3/2006 from http://fp.enter.net/restorativepractices/morrison_bullying.pdf

Morrison B. (2005). *Restorative Justice in Schools: International Perspectives.* Retrieved 6/28/2006 from http://hamfish.org/pub/conf2005/Morrison%20883%20Paper.pdf

Youth Justice Board for England and Wales (2004). *National Evaluation of the Restorative Justice in Schools Programme.* Retrieved on 6/25/2006 from http://www.youth-justice-board.gov.uk/Publication/Downloads/nat%20ev%20of%20rj%20schoolsfullfv.pdf

Robb, G. (10 November 2005). *Restorative Approaches in Schools: A Perspective from England.* Retrieved on 8/10/2012 from http://canada.iirp.edu/uploads/article_pdfs/man05_robb.pdf

Strang, H. (2002). *Repair or Revenge: Victims and Restorative Justice.* Oxford:Clarendon Press

11.     Robb, G. (10 November 2005). *Restorative Approaches in Schools: A Perspective from England.* Retrieved on 8/10/2012 from http://canada.iirp.edu/uploads/article_pdfs/man05_robb.pdf

# 1.2

## Before We Get Started

By now, you have realized this approach to Conflict Resolution has profound affects, and effects, on the lives of children and the communities they live in. The intense impact this program has is directly attributable to the pure simplicity and interlocking flow of the foundations and core understandings upon which it was built.

Indeed, as a colleague of mine commented about this program, Unbroken Circles <sup>SM</sup> incorporates the best of what Conflict Resolution has to offer. Verily, it is like Ketsugo in that it marries the best of multiple practices and schools of thought to make an art form that is stronger and better than its individual constituent parts.

However, it does no good as a Conflict Resolution program if the persons doling out the program do not understand what conflict is. By far, it will be the longest chapter of the book because it is the groundwork the other constituent foundations are built upon. If the program were a finished house, this chapter would be analogous to the bedrock upon which the house is placed.

Verily, there are a wealth of books, which cover conflict in one form or another. However, very few make an attempt to tackle an understanding of what conflict is and how it works. This chapter details a history of conflict, shows the evolution of conflict, tries to dissect conflict, portrays conflict in multiple forms, and ultimately puts everything in a readable and condensed version for easy reference.

Today's society is the product of centuries of cultural evolution. Base concepts that we take for granted are the culmination of centuries of evolution. Because of the all-encompassing nature of this chapter's subject matter and the historical evolution of basic concepts, some examples and references are not school based when talking about conflict. Example: A property crime where a student breaks a window and owes money to the school. This concept of justice, in the form of repayment, came from a time when people were paid if a family member was wrongfully killed. Therefore, if I do not relate a conflict fact to schools, take a moment to consider how it connects to conflict in contemporary American society.

## A Brief History of Unmanaged Conflict Handling Practices in World Societies

As long as humankind has existed, there has been unmanaged conflict in some form. According to anthropologists and paleontologists, the first forms of conflict for early human society most likely revolved around the scarcity of resources. Things such as hunting grounds, water, and mates would be the issues that scientists posit as primary sources of conflict for early man. The conflicts resulted in disputes that often culminated in violence, a primary conflict-resolving tool. Fossil records shows that hostile disputes were commonplace for early man with many losing their lives due to injuries and the resulting complications received. Over time, as society evolved, it ultimately changed how people saw and handled unmanaged conflicts.

Some cultures, especially those that were theocracies, adopted the proverbial "eye for an eye" mentality. A given harm was matched by an equal harm. The problem with this mentality is that in a world crying out "an eye for an eye," the logical progression of thought is everyone ends up "blind." In other words, the harm created by the retaliation never repaired the harm caused, and the society was left worse than before the conflict happened.

For this reason, other civilizations, which were ironically theocracies as well, developed a variation of "an eye for an eye." Resolution to conflicts occurred in "token." We see this in Native American history with tribes like the Aniyvwiya (Cherokee), the Muscogee (Creeks), and others of the Southeastern Woodlands tribes. A good example of this is observed concerning how wars were handled. The Native Americans knew the harm of war and tried their best to stop it at all costs. They invented the game of stickball. Ironically, translations for the tribal names of this game mean "War's Little Brother" or the "Little Brother to War." Indeed, it is still a brutal sport with players being sent to the hospital. However brutal it was, it allowed whole communities in conflict to join in a game and battle out their differences without the deliberate taking of human lives. This is not to say that players did not die or become maimed on occasion due to the severity of their injuries. Nevertheless, the lives damaged or lost paled in comparison to the lives that would have been lost in a true war. Indeed, when the Unega (Europeans) arrived, the sport's merits were so self-evident that the Europeans refined the game into what we know today in contemporary society as lacrosse—a game played in high schools and universities across America and Canada.

Naturally, a societal war-like game does not handle individual, or even familial, conflicts. For this reason, tribes developed clans. With the Cherokee, there were seven clans in each village. Each clan had its own distinct role For instance, the Blue Clan were the apothecaries of the tribe. The Paint Clan were the tribal doctors. The clan got its name from the healers "painting" the oft-toxic remedies onto the patient's skin so it could be safely taken in by the body. From there the Wild Potato Clan were the tribe's farmers. The list went on to include all aspects of life within the Seven Clans. Unlike the Judeo-Christian/Nordic/Eurasian cultural structures, the Southeastern Woodlands tribes usually were matriarchal societies. A group gained their clan identity from their mothers and not their fathers. In fact, an old joke of the Cherokee is that "we know who your mother is, but your father is just rumor." Giving women sole power resolved conflicts of who had the heirship rights to a given heritage of a clan. Women had the right to divorce men, they had total ownership of the home, and the resulting children of the union were the property of the mother and her clan. Each family had a "Beloved Woman" that was over the clan. The eldest brother of the mother was entrusted to teach the children the ways of the clan—taking the place of the father in many ways should the union ever fail between the child's parents. Ultimately, any clan member was accepted as family. A Bird Clan member in one city was seen as family when visiting a different city. In cases where a major harm or death occurred, the clan could even elect the "Blood Law" in which the offender's own family would hand over the perpetrator, or sometimes a stand-in, for the victim's clan to kill.

While amazingly complex, and contrary to traditional Western culture of contemporary society, this structure resolved a host of conflicts revolving around domestic, role and inheritance disputes. Blood Law, however you may feel about it, further settled conflict by making sure that there was peace between the families. If anything, it was a grim reminder of how harmful unmanaged conflict can be. For this reason, any law or decree made by the Seven Clans was sacrosanct.

In far less civilized cultures such as that of the Scandinavian and European cultures (i.e., Vikings, Norman, Anglo-Saxon, and early Germanic Tribes), war was commonplace. Usually, wealth was created by directly causing conflict with a weaker group. The exception to such a rule was when a crime took place within the tribal or community unit. For these groups, death of a person had a financial value, much the same way that the theft of chattel had a value. Over time, the general concept of "wergild" was acknowledged as standard practice for handling virtually all crimes of property loss and homicide. The term wergild also referred to as weregild and wergeld, actually means "man payment."

While it may seem a bit barbaric for contemporary Americans to acknowledge wergild as a valid and justifiable way of handling homicide, it is important to note that our Criminal Justice system still uses this concept today. The entire concept of "restitution," also called "compensatory damages" in civil trials, is ordered by courts every week for crimes that have been committed. In criminal cases, restitution is intended to give monetary compensation back to the victims for the harm and financial cost that they received by being burglarized, raped, assaulted, and such. In civil cases, compensatory damages are handled in a similar way, but the court is not burdened by "proof beyond a reasonable doubt", and compensation can even be given to families for the actual death of a person. In addition, both criminal and civil courts can also award "punitive damages" as a way of further financially punishing the offender for excessively horrendous actions against the victim. In some cases, a person can go to court twice, once in criminal court and then again in civil court, for the same crime. As Wendy McElroy noted in her article, "Criminal Versus Civil Remedies for Intentional Wrongs," McElroy talks about how O.J. Simpson, a famed sports figure, was tried both in criminal and civil court for the death of Ronald Goldman. Simpson was declared innocent in the criminal case but was found guilty in the civil case—to the tune of a judgment award of $8.5 million for compensatory damages. Under American law, the two trials did not constitute "double jeopardy," a spelled out protection of citizens found in the US Constitution. [1]

In the Roman Era, and later Medieval Europe, the issue of unmanaged conflict was taken away from the people, and the unmanaged conflict became a crime against the state (government). Essentially, the ruler claimed anything and everything. In English literature, we know that Robin Hood was charged with the crime of taking the king's deer to feed the hungry. The deer were wild, but the king claimed all game for his own hunting enjoyment; therefore, hunting was deemed illegal. When a murder was committed, it was a "crime against the crown." The victim was taken out of the equation and the "state" was supplanted as a type of surrogate victim. There, the "actus reus," or "guilty action," was hopefully looked at in balance with the "mens rea," or "guilty mind." Since a crime against the state had to be an intentional wrongful action, the state looked at the case to make sure that the perceived crime had both elements of a guilty action that were predicated by a guilty mind. Over time, this concept evolved where "civil infractions" could be penalized for lower level crimes that had actus reus elements but no apparent mens rea tied to it.

Like with wergild, it should be noted that we see the concepts of mens rea, actus reus, and civil infractions in our contemporary Criminal Justice system. We also observe, in criminal cases, instances of victims being supplanted with the state. Misdemeanor and felony level crimes often require that there be both a mens rea and actus reus component before a person can be found guilty. In circumstances involving errant chattel, speeding, code/ordinance violations, etc., the state can come along and "fine" someone without a question of a mens rea component to the wrongful action. The only times that these civil infractions escalate to actual misdemeanors or felony level crimes is when the offender has demonstrated mens rea by consistently engaging in the same wrongful actions after being repeatedly cited and fined by authorities and/or refusing to pay their fines and penalties for said multiple infractions. In some states, there are laws, the "Good Samaritan" laws, where a witness can be charged with a crime in the event that he or she sees a crime or accident happen and fails to either get help or render assistance. In these cases, the guilty mind and the guilty act both are the witness' essential refusal to take action to mitigate the harm caused by the crime or accident.

Using the "state as surrogate victim" concept—Robin Hood's crime of illegally taking game—wildlife-related crimes are the second-most common committed crimes in the world. Although many states see game as the property of the person holding the game, people are arrested and fined each year and their property seized for taking game and fish in illegal or inappropriate ways. Many of these people are merely trying to get the game and fish for food or clothing, defend life and property from harm, and/or pay bills. Some claim that these laws are onerous do nothing to protect the wildlife, and that their use is to incriminate the citizen. For instance, in Tennessee, fishing for trout on a Thursday will land the offender with a hefty fine and seizure of his fish, tackle, and any other item of value. Meanwhile, in Florida, one can fish for multiple species using lures with multiple treble hooks, yet it is illegal to catch these same fish using live or dead natural bait with multiple hooks. This results in the game officer seizing the fish, tackle, and any other item of value.[2] Conversely, while it is legal in Florida to view deer at night with a light, in Alabama, shining a deer with so much as a two-cell flashlight is sufficient crime for the game warden to arrest someone. The warden can then seize anything of value the individual may have, including, but not limited to, one's vehicle. In one case, two boys were walking along the road, saw something move, shined a light on it, and were ultimately fined and their property seized—it was a group of game wardens and a fake deer meant to catch poachers.[3]

Indeed, game laws can be very easy to break and are a major reason why adults and juveniles have misdemeanors, and even felonies, on their record. For this reason, proponents of fair and reasonable game law revisions posit the capricious nature and unconstitutionality of game law arrests using current laws and practices in its "state as surrogate victim" rationale. In particular, they note how American wildlife officers have ultimate arresting authority that allows them to search and seize evidence in places and ways forbidden to other branches of law enforcement. Often, poverty-stricken juveniles are involved. This further complicates matters where not only is property seized and a fine enacted, but there can be criminal charges as well due specifically to the fact that a juvenile is involved. Such seizures, fines, and criminal charging of alleged perpetrators often denies a person of his or her constitutional rights. A good example of how crazy matters can become easily inflamed can be seen in the July of 2011 truTV's "Rednecks & Riches" episode of *Storage Hunters*. This is a reality television show involving the auctioning of storage units. The auctioneer sold bidders, Brandon and Lori Bernier, a unit that had a mounted, and allegedly extinct, hartebeest—that the game officer ultimately seized. Indeed, the game warden verified that all but two of the mounted animals were legally taken. When Mr. Bernier asked the officer a question about the situation, and for his credentials, the officer notified the Berniers he could arrest them and seize all the animal mounts, which could lead to prison time and a $10,000 fine.[4] The problem with this situation is the hartebeest in question is not extinct. It is legal to hunt them on ranches in Africa, New Zealand, the United States, (including Louisiana), and other exotic game ranches all over the world. In fact, it is because of hunters actively working to conserve the animal that the hartebeest is not extinct. Had the Berniers taken a child with them to the bid, it is conceivable that both they and the child could have had further criminal charges to face just because a child was present—based in part on a British legal concept called "parens patriae." Thus, this historic evolution of the "state as surrogate victim" chronicles how conflict has actually been created between the "state" and its "constituency" by robbing the "constituency" of its natural rights to not only victim-identity and community justice dealings but also to basic Constitutional rights.

Yet, this travesty of justice is not something new. In Medieval to early Renaissance England, the notion of "surrogate victimization" by the "state" created a glut of new criminals. The need to keep track of violations, and subsequent actions by the court, became paramount as the number and diversity of "criminals" in society increased. Soon, villagers cried out for justice as people were given different punishments for a crime. Neither the king nor the courts could afford to have verdicts continue to run contrary to each other for similar cases since this would further rile the masses with cries of "injustice!" Certainly, things needed to be fair if there was ever to be any sort of peace. Therefore, there was a concept created called "Common Law," which was based in part on "Case Law," where certain base concepts were recognized by the court. For instance, a given concept of real estate Common Law is that there must be a written agreement with spelled out "consideration" (exchange of money or services) in order for a contract to be valid. Therefore, in areas which use British Common Law, one will see property deeds say "for one pound (or dollar) and other valuable consideration." This does not mean that the property sold for that amount, but rather it implies that monetary consideration of some kind took place. In Florida, one might even see "Love and Affection" on a deed between family members since the state sees such as being valuable consideration.

Case Law worked in conjunction with, and ultimately expanded on, Common Law by allowing the law to evolve with the times. A "chess game" of sorts set of rules emerged where one court would not trump another court of the same level. However, a higher court could always overturn a lower court. The verdicts from these higher-level cases ultimately became law for the areas that the higher courts presided over.

Again, we see this all the time in the American judicial system where British Common Law, as well as Case Law, is commonplace. In Florida's own constitution, it specifically says that any issue not covered by the laws of the land shall revert to British Common Law. In our society, as well, we find issues where monumental court cases are cited as law. For instance, there are laws in many states which make it a crime to abort a fetus, but these laws are made moot by the historic Supreme Court case of "Roe v. Wade" which ultimately gives the woman the legal right to abort a fetus. While legal scholars note that the Constitution allows Congress powers to limit what the Supreme Court can rule on, as a practical matter, the Congress usually stays out of the affairs of the Supreme Court and gives them carte blanche. It is for this reason that President Thomas Jefferson expressed a tremendous amount of mistrust and disdain for the judiciary's ability to review the constitutionality of laws, essentially reinterpreting and making up their own laws, and using Case Law to uphold such rulings and findings. Jefferson reportedly even went on to say that the US Constitution, and any other constitution, should only be valid for 19 years; then be rewritten in its entirety so as not to entrap or enslave future generations with the actions of the present generation.

While many of the Founding Fathers, like Jefferson, were deists who saw God in nature rather than focusing on a truly Biblical version of God. Early Christian groups modified the American system of law and government to offer possible solutions for conflict issues. These perceived solutions involved having the offender afforded ample opportunity to revisit and study the Bible. Sadly, not only did these practices fail miserably, often driving the offender to the point of insanity, but they also set a system in place, which has become nearly impossible to eradicate. Most notably, before Quaker reforms took place, early prison systems were not a primary punishment for criminal acts. Instead, capital crimes were often handled by corporal punishment, public humiliation, and even banishment. However, this changed when Quakers took positions of power. While some good was first seen when they eradicated the death penalty for theft, burglary, and all capital offenses other than first-degree murder. They also created and established what we know today as the historical penitentiary model for American prisons. Here, the goal was initially to rehabilitate criminals by giving them a "safe" setting to focus and reflect upon God while paying penitence for the harm trespassed upon His people. Ultimately, this was seen as a good thing, which led to numerous writings and historic works. However, demand outpaced supply once the prison became the ultimate form of handling offenders of crimes. Overcrowded prisons quickly allowed more malfeasant behavior to develop while giving no benefits of rehabilitation to the offender or the community. This resulted in the refinement of the program by other Christian groups to allow prisoners to serve what we know today as solitary confinement—a practice known by criminologists and psychologists to drive many people insane.

Later, secular efforts in the Northeastern United States led to treating children offenders differently from adult offenders for the same types of crime. In 1825, the first juvenile detention center, called the New York House of Refuge, was established by the Society for the Prevention of Juvenile Delinquency.[5] Later, juvenile justice advocates, such as Jane Adams, of the Hull House in Chicago, lobbied lawmakers to create a separate set of laws for juveniles dealt with by the courts. Hull House lobbyists, as well as Ms. Adams herself, argued that juvenile offenders needed a separate area for confinement because of mental and emotional differences between children and adults. In 1899, the first exclusively juvenile court was created in Chicago. Under a British legal doctrine, it was called "parens patriae"—which translates into "the state as parent."[6] While such actions and reforms became wildly popular in other states across America, many legal scholars point out that this concept initially ran in strict opposition to the US Constitution and ushered in a new paradigm shift concerning how Americans saw crime. In essence, a juvenile was not fully able to appreciate the harm created by their actions and, therefore, should not be treated as adults in the prosecution of crimes. Special prisons were made for juvenile offenders with the intent of reforming their behavior. Ultimately, this paradigm shift in the law became known as the Juvenile Justice System of present day. Under juvenile laws that resulted, the state could arrest children on special crimes geared only to youth as well as try juvenile offenders as juveniles. The offenders often have to serve out a given sentence, pay back restitution to the victim, and meet other court ordered requirements. In exchange, their crime(s) were not made publicly known and/or publicly held against them as adults.

Over time, the approach to handling juvenile offenders waxed and waned from juveniles being treated as juveniles to juveniles being tried as adults. For instance, two former directors over the Office of National Drug Control Policy, as well as a former Princeton University and University of Pennsylvania professor, came out with a book in 1996, titled *"Body Count: Moral Poverty and How to Win America's War Against Crime and Drugs"*. On page 27 of this book, one can further understand the stark contrast of how Americans see juvenile offenders. The authors wrote,

> America is now home to thickening ranks of juvenile 'super-predators'—radically impulsive, brutally remorseless youngsters, including ever more pre-teenage boys, who murder, assault, rape, rob, burglarize, deal deadly drugs, join gun-toting gangs and create serious communal disorders. They do not fear the stigma of arrest, the pains of imprisonment, or the pangs of conscience.[7]

This book helped set the stage for a host of legal debates where juveniles were increasingly treated as adults. With the help of Professor John J. DiIulio, Jr., this book, and the research the book was based upon, hit the national stages of television shows and a *Time Magazine* interview. DiIulio made claims that ran in stark contrast to actual federal reports on juvenile crimes. In support of DiIulio's work, others such as Susan Estrich

28

and Professor James Alan Fox came out with similar rhetoric. Susan Estrich, in a 1996 *USA Today* article, warned of a "tsunami" of juvenile crime looming in the future for America.[8] In the same *Time Magazine* article featuring DiIulio, Fox said; "So long as we fool ourselves in thinking that we're winning the war against crime, we may be blindsided by this bloodbath of teenage violence that is lurking in the future."[9] Naturally, such arguments and calls for legal reforms were based on perceived "future crimes" rather than actual present-day data.

In truth, for some unknown reason, preteen boys were singled out as being particularly heinous to the culture with lobbyists calling for laws imprisoning these young males for any minor violation or infraction of school policy, animal ordinance, curfew ordinance, etc. At around the same time, other critics, such as Franklin Zimring, had their voices stifled by the media. Zimring claimed that proper scrutiny had not been given to the facts and wording that DiIulio used. For instance, DiIulio seemingly confused the term "chronic delinquent" with the term "violent" to make his findings work. DiIulio also seemingly made assumptions, which Zimring found to be false. Specifically, using DiIulio's assertions, Zimring concluded that, by 2010, the majority of violent juvenile criminals would have to be under age 6 rather than over age 13 (the standard age break-over point for violence in juvenile-based crimes).[10] By 2001, some five years after DiIulio's initial assertions were made, the U.S. surgeon general declared the "super-predator" theory a "myth."[11] However, as Professor Steven Drizin noted, in 2001, despite a reduction in juvenile crime, polls were showing as high as 62% of the American population still believed in the "super-predator" myth, and they believed that crime was on the rise. Such a belief caused the doubling of youths in adult correctional institutions and an exponential increase in the number of children tried as adults under the premise that they are budding sociopaths.[12]

Indeed, this conflict between myth and reality has caused a host of conflict issues. Some legal scholars hypothesize that it is now easier for a juvenile to be convicted of a crime than an adult doing the same wrong deed. Additionally, with the waxing and waning of thought on this subject, a number of additional "diversionary" methods have now been enacted, including such things as Teen Court. Here, juveniles act as adults in a quasi-judicial setting and render out verdicts and punishments that the offender is then required to fulfill. Such quasi-court settings cause for a host of legal and moral issues such as how can it be legal under our Constitution, as well as morally and legally ethical, for non-adults to try to convict another non-adult even with adult supervision helping in the process.

While the debate brews in academia over such topics of inequality and constitutionality, a few jurisdictions in America, such as Vermont, have undertaken a different route by enacting Restorative Justice practices to address juvenile crimes.[13] However, the creation of laws and application of said laws have not always gone hand-in-hand. Some children's rights proponents claim that the "state" refuses to follow the very principles of Restorative Justice it enacted as law. This is evidenced in Florida where 985.155 of Florida Statutes enacted Neighborhood Restorative Justice Centers. However, the State Attorney offices of each circuit, which are charged with creating and regulating such centers, refuse to establish and use them as an alternative means of handling juvenile crime.

## Understanding How Unmanaged Conflict Works

Knowing the history of unmanaged conflict is important. Now, we must try to understand what unmanaged conflict is and how it works. Common sense tells us conflict has always been around, but little is taught about how unmanaged conflict works and operates. An individual is expected to understand that conflict exists; then he is told how to handle unmanaged conflict. There should be more care devoted to this subject if people are to understand the nature and modality of conflict. While this is a brief explanation of the complexities and modalities of unmanaged conflict, a clear perception of the nature of conflict is necessary for a full understanding of it. Understanding knowledge is as much about one's frame of mind and background as it is the actual content delivered for academic mental assimilation. A grasp of conflict resolution can be drawn from several life circumstances, including my own. My father was a firefighter of notable reputation in my community. Some said he could put out a fire when no one else could. I once saw my father jump out of his truck and beat down a fire, which was consuming several acres, with nothing more than a bush that he broke off. In my mind, he was a giant who had knowledge that I wanted to learn. Eagerly, I listened to him and even induced him to recount tales of his training and experience.

I am reminded of how Daddy talked about fire in various situations. For him, fire was a living, breathing creature, which could be herded, diverted, and corralled, like any other beast. He also said that, like any living creature, fire had three fundamental requirements: heat, fuel, and oxygen. If any part of the triangle were broken then the fire would ultimately die. Recounting the day of a brush fire, he told me how he used the wind, previously burned ground, and the green brush limb to tear apart the "triangle" so that fire was dispatched in a seemingly miraculous way. He taught me how intimate knowledge of something gained one power. He taught me fire was neither good nor evil; it was our loss of control that caused harm.

It should come as no surprise that I see conflict much like my father did fire. Conflict is indeed a living element that is active and reactive. In addition, like fire, it is neither good nor evil. In a controlled setting, conflict can actually be beneficial—known as "anabolic conflict" because it builds and improves upon a given situation. However, if uncontrolled and unmanaged, conflict can leave travesty in its wake as it consumes all around it while it endeavors to suck out the life, heat, and nourishment of any setting that it is in—this is called "catabolic conflict." The field of mediating conflict that I primarily work in is like my father dealing with uncontrolled fires.

To understand the concept of uncontrolled conflict, school behavior modification specialists like to use what is known as an ABC Chart or ABC Methodology. The ABC part of the name stems from a belief that any action is based off an antecedent, a given behavior, and a resulting consequence. Using this understanding, uncontrolled conflict is the antecedent matched with a wrongful, or inappropriate, behavior to create an undesirable consequence. Unlike the fire triangle that my father often referred to, the ABC Methodology for understanding unresolved conflict does not offer a way to remove any one of the three elements and have that action alone extinguish the conflict. Instead, the logical solution offered is changing the wrong or inappropriate behavior, which can be a prolonged and sometimes ineffective manner of handling conflicts. This is a primary source of why most school-based behavior modification programs do not work. The students lack the tools and resources to appropriately handle and distinguish catabolic from anabolic conflict.

## SNAPSHOT | *Taking a look at the facts*

Did you know that unmanaged conflict has a cost associated with it? Professionals in both the fields of Human Resource Management and Conflict Resolution have historically contended there is an actual "dollar and cents" value that managers, supervisors, board members, and others in authority often overlook. It takes away from employee performance, takes away from administrator performance, diminishes the quality work produced, and continues to increase costs as the unmanaged conflict spirals out of control with grievance filings and acts of retaliation and sabotage. For a school, the costs are realized in teacher performance, administrator performance, staff performance, referrals, lower student performance, absenteeism (both teachers and students), tardiness (both teachers and students), the development of non-beneficial "factions," and a host of other undesirable behaviors—behaviors that cost time and money. In states, like Florida, where schools get their funding based on FCAT test results, low-test results, due to unmanaged conflict, can actually lead to terminating programs altogether from the school curriculum.

Like any accounting issue, the cost must be identified and accounted for before benefits and expected returns can be projected. Once a cost has been identified, how then do you figure out the Return on Investment (ROI) and the payback period to determine if the solution is viable? According to Cynthia Barnes-Slater and John Ford, of MGH Consulting, LLC, the ROI and payback period can be calculated as follows[*]:

### ROI Calculation Formula
*(NOTE: PI = Performance Improvement in $$$)*

ROI = (PI - Cost) / Cost
($2808 - $300) / $300 = 8.36%

### Payback Period Calculation Formula
*(NOTE: PI = Performance Improvement in $$$)*

Payback Period = (Cost X 52 weeks) / PI
($300 X 52 weeks) / $2808 = 5.6 weeks

[*] *Source:*

Barnes-Slater, C. & Ford, J. (2012). *Measuring Conflict: Both the Hidden Costs and the Benefits of Conflict Management Interventions* (Web Article). Law Memo. Retrieved on 7/24/2012 from http://www.lawmemo.com/articles/measuring.htm

**Lohman Cabbage Conflict Model**

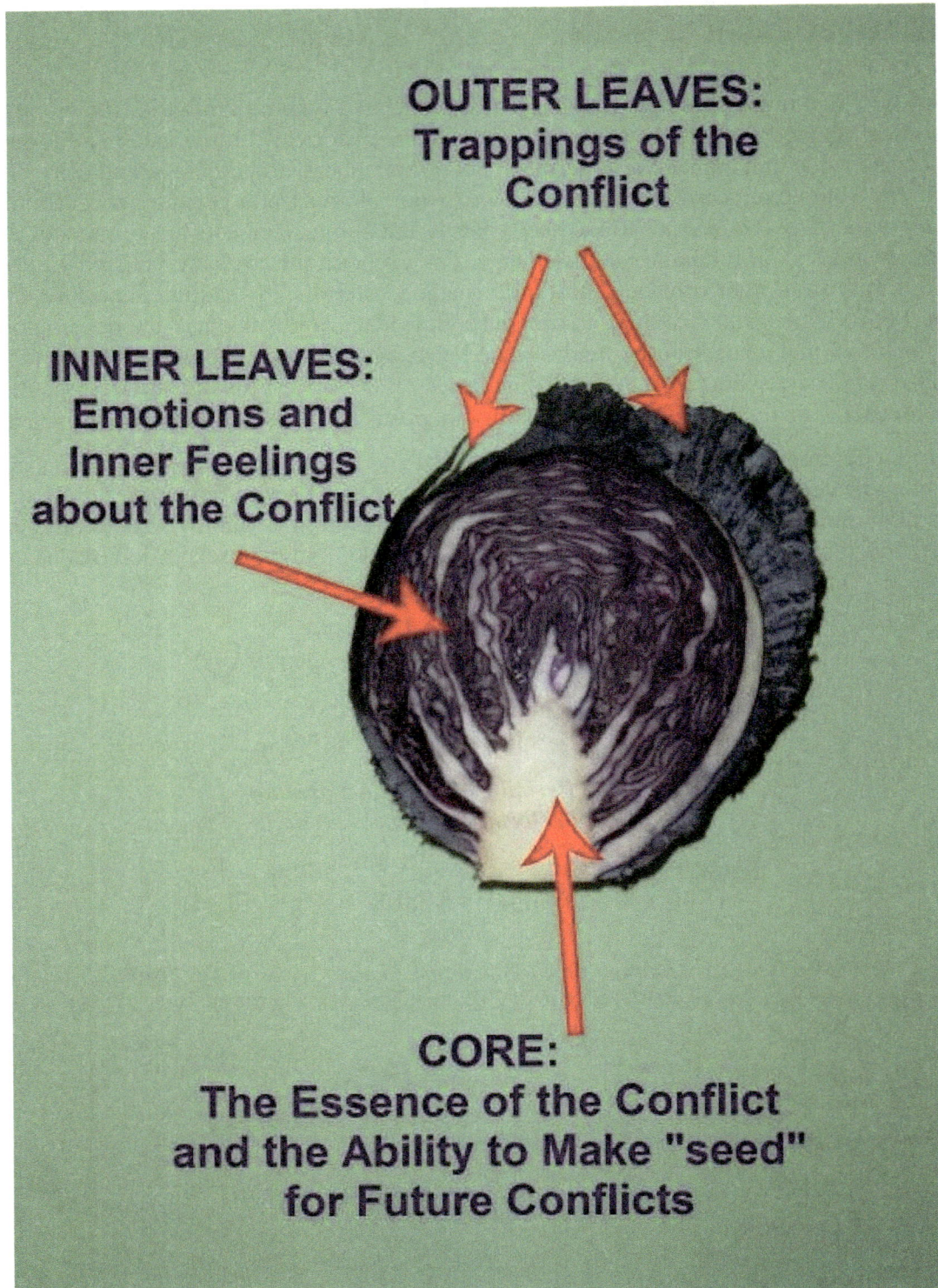

**OUTER LEAVES:**
Trappings of the Conflict

**INNER LEAVES:**
Emotions and Inner Feelings about the Conflict

**CORE:**
The Essence of the Conflict and the Ability to Make "seed" for Future Conflicts

*Photo and Diagram ©2012 by Ken Johnson*

In the Netherlands, Alexander F. de Savornin Lohman developed a methodology of understanding unmanaged conflict, using a cross-section of a head of cabbage as a point of reference. This model, called the "Lohman Cabbage Conflict Model," only has three essential elements. The "outer leaves" of the "cabbage" represent legal interests, rights, and obligations that the conflict has caused or requires— essentially what a mediator, arbitrator, or judge would see in a civil court case. The "inner leaves" of the "cabbage" are more fragile, delicate, underdeveloped, and hidden. Therefore, they are representative of the emotions, agendas, expectations, and even power games at play—ultimately what a mediator, arbitrator, or judge would hear as the case progressed and each side told their version of the truth. The "core" of the "cabbage" is the true conflict. It is the living part of the plant, which has the potential to grow, form seed, etc. Like a cabbage, all of the other "leaves" are attached to the "core." They act as a hedge of protection for the "core" as it endeavors to live and reproduce.[14]

The problem with Lohman's model is that it merely attempts to explain the makeup of unresolved, unmanaged conflict and the function of each part. Lohman does not address harm or offer solutions. In truth, Lohman is an advocate (an attorney), and, therefore, his model does not and would not work to show how to resolve conflict. Instead, his primary intent was to show how unresolved conflict is structured so that a legal professional can understand and be more respectful of the purpose, usage, and functioning of each part. However, as limited as it may appear to be, the model does have tremendous use for understanding a little of how unresolved conflict is structured.

To understand further the formation of unresolved conflict, one should look at the works of Ron and Roxanne Claassen. In their book, *Discipline That Restores: Strategies to Create Respect, Cooperation, and Responsibility in the Classroom,* the couple demonstrates a model of conflict that they call the "Unmanaged Conflict Cycle." The model has five stages. Though the model depicted in their book varies from the "shark" model of this book, the core stages and overall cycle are identical. While the Claassens used simple arrows and text to illustrate their point of view, I feel sharks give a better understanding of the program and add a visual example.

**Stage I**
Change/
Confusion/
Tension

**Stage V**
Adjustments

**Claassen Unmanaged
Conflict Cycle**

**Stage II**
Role/Dilemma

**Stage IV**
Confrontation

**Stage III**
Injustice Collecting

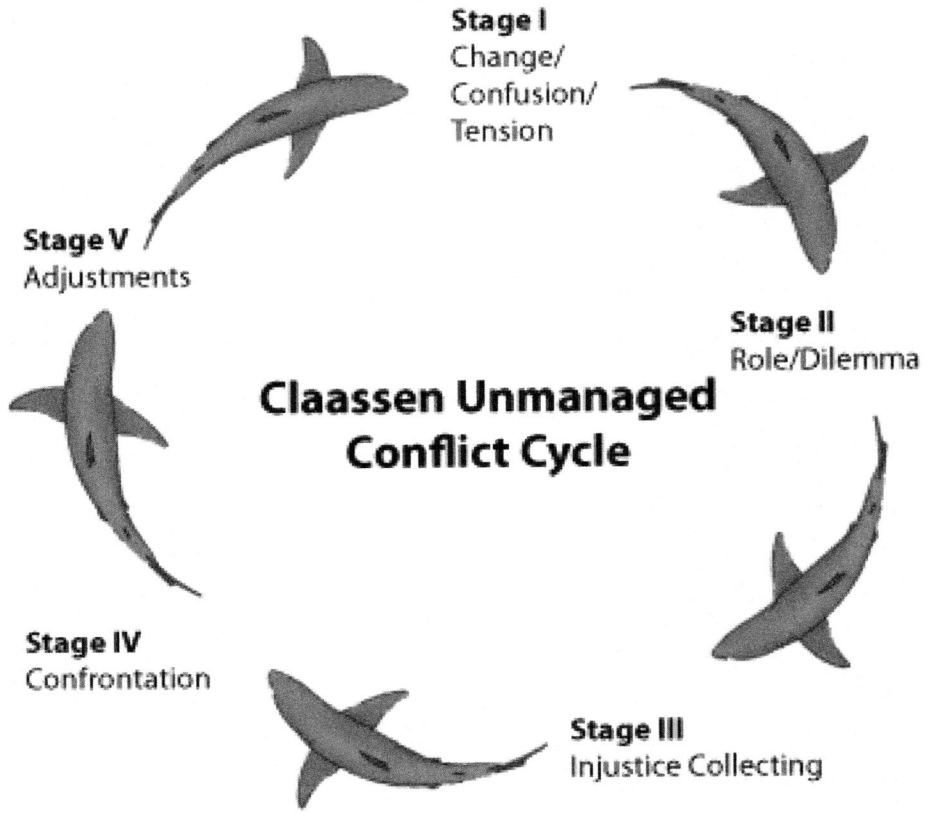

Graphics Design by Thomas R. Fournier, Sr. with ©2012; purchased by Ken Johnson

Under the original Claassen model of the Unmanaged Conflict Cycle, the first stage involves issues of unresolved tension and confusion. The second stage involves the issue of role dilemmas. From there, the third stage encompasses an aspect called "injustice collecting." Ultimately, the fourth stage embodies confrontation while the fifth stage results in adjustments. Clearly, this model shows a more dynamic modality of conflict where simple unresolved issues can cause dilemmas and confusion as to one's purpose, role, and identity (both individually perceived as well as publicly perceived). As the cycle gathers momentum, the conflict turns on the person, causing him or her to take inventory of all the ways that her or she has been wronged, used, abused, and ultimately mistreated. This naturally colors the person's perceptions as he or she seeks to confront the perceived cause of the conflict and adjust accordingly to how the outcome of that confrontation played out.[15]

Indeed, the Claassen model of the Unmanaged Conflict Cycle does a far better job of explaining how conflict forms and operates on its own and how it affects the person, or persons, dealing with the conflict. Unlike fire, the Claassens depict unresolved conflict as evolving and even "thinking" to some degree—though never outright saying so in their book. After all, why would a person start collecting and chronicling acts of injustice unless the conflict was evolving and, therefore, exerting forces that played with the mind and emotions of the individual dealing with the conflict? Indeed, the model does not give a direct methodology for actually battling the conflict, but it does give one a good idea of how the conflict works, grows, evolves, and plays out. Whereas the Lohman Cabbage Conflict Model gives a rudimentary understanding of unresolved conflict, the Claassens' Unresolved Conflict Cycle model gives people a more sophisticated and holistic understanding.

Working from the model provided by the Claassens, I decided to take a deeper look into how conflict works. With the model as a reference base, I realized how out of control conflict could become. Using research into Organizational Psychology, it became apparent that both Lohman and Claassen were on to something. For me, it was like a half-finished sentence where one gave the start, another picked up a different section, and now it was time for me to finish the expression.

Lohman, I contend, is right in his assertion that conflict produces "seed." While Lohman did not overtly ever contend that unresolved conflict wishes to reproduce, he did at least allude to it in his expression of how the "core" of his model had the potential to produce "seed."

By the same note, I contend that the stages of the Claassens' cyclical model are also sound. However, as I told Dr. Claassen in my review of his book, I feel that the nature of unresolved conflict is not so much a cycle as it is something that grows, expands, and builds. After all, as Dr. Claassen inferred in his model, unmanaged conflict exerts a force that seemingly wishes to grow the conflict rather than extinguish or positively transmute the conflict.

For these reasons, I created a model of unmanaged conflict using an avalanche as a metaphor. The "Avalanche Model of Unresolved Conflict" depicts the five stages of the Claassens' "Unmanaged Conflict Cycle," progressing, cycling, and gathering momentum as other people are brought in. Those five stages are Unresolved Confusion/Tension, Role Dilemma, Injustice Collecting, Confrontation, and Adjustments. This continues until it negatively evolves into other forms that cause far more harm than the original conflict ever would have, if it had been resolved earlier.

## Avalanche Model of Unresolved Conflict

Stage I: Change: Confusion/Tension

Stage III: Injustice Collecting

Stage II: Role Dilemma

Stage V: Adjustments

Stage IV: Change: Confrontation

Stage II: Role Dilemma

Stage III: Injustice Collecting

Stage IV: Change: Confrontation

Stage V: Adjustments

*Graphics Design by Thomas R. Fournier, Sr. with ©2012 purchased by Ken Johnson*

Unlike other models, the Avalanche Model of Unresolved Conflict allows for a more dynamic and holistic element to be carried further along a continuum of understanding. Thus, unresolved conflict can grow, produce seed that grows in others, and expand the scope and nature of the conflict. This seed is most commonly, but not always, generated in the "Adjustment" phase of the cycle. The problem is that people see Adjustment as being positive rather than seeing it as a modality, or function, of how people find coping means to deal with a problem. In fact, one of the key ways that the Avalanche Model of Unresolved Conflict differs from Claassen's Unmanaged Conflict Cycle is in the additional development, understanding, and depiction of how Adjustment can produce seed. The result is a precipitation of the catabolic conflict's evolution demonstrated across cultures, communities, and organizational structures. It also harkens to the destructive nature of unresolved conflict and how improper handling of the conflict can carry over, having drastic consequences over time.

To look at this matter in detail, we must first look at common perceptions, and misperceptions, as well as the modality that actually takes place. As stated before, most people see Adjustment as being a positive phase. Without reason to believe otherwise, and no logical basis making any assumptions to the positive, people wish to assume that everyone is of the same mind, and that they will use the Adjustment phase as a way to cool down, look at options, re-evaluate the situation, and review differing sides to gain knowledge and understanding. This misconception further carries the belief that the person will ultimately allow "cooler heads to prevail" and that the subject will find a peaceable way to resolve the conflict. Contemporary humankind, additionally, with all of our brutal sports and wars and violent content entertainment media, is supposed to abhor catabolic conflict and wish to find peace at all times. Again, such misperceptions are not founded in logic or fact.

In truth, America, as well as most of the world, usually revels in catabolic conflict and seemingly disparages the growth, development, and ultimate educational assimilation in people that allows them to handle conflicts calmly and properly in an anabolic manner. Because they lack the knowledge, acumen, and functional application experience, people usually choose poorly when handling a conflict-saturated situation. Besides the lack of knowledge and acumen, which is critical to properly diffusing a conflict-ridden issue, people also tend to take action, more oft than not, when they are stressed and/or angry. When a person is stressed or angry, his ability to think rationally and gather information to resolve a conflict is narrowed. The focus, instead of understanding, becomes an adversarial mindset where the brain goes into a "Me/Us" vs. "Him/Her/Them" mentality. Many, but not all, of the ways that a person may negatively, or improperly, adjust for a situation, are to engage in the "Nine Common Functions of Negative Adjustment."

## Nine Common Functions of Negative Adjustment

**STORMING**

This is primarily seen with youth and in people who are vested in something and care deeply about it. For young children, storming is their "blowing up" or "throwing a tantrum" because they love the person dearly and have so many unrefined emotions that they often know of no other way to express their feelings. With adults, being so close to another person, a group, a job, etc. can cause one to have such deep, intertwining emotions that any hurtful action causes him or her to be nearly unable to respond in any other manner than like a small child "storming off," "blowing up," and/or "throwing a tantrum." Usually, depending on one's age, this stage can go from a few minutes to a few hours. Do not overlook storming. It means that a person loves something, and therefore cares for something, very deeply. Storming is an indicator of profound hurt. Sadly, once the hurt subsides, it is replaced with rage, and a person can escalate his or her actions in a number of ways so that the perpetrator feels that same level of hurt.

**VILLIFYING**

The person in the conflict sees one's self as the "victim" and the other party/parties as the "offender." The result is the victim seeks to make the offender out to be worse than what he or she truly is. Usually, the offender is referred to as a "demon" or "evil" person out to "destroy" the seemingly "innocent" person(s) being victimized. The phase of Injustice Gathering is now done to prove that the person is "evil" and "out to get" the victim. Subsequently, anything and everything that the offender does, whether positive or negative, is perceived as occurring for nefarious reasons. The whole purpose is as a primary, psychological modality, by the victim, giving himself or herself the reason to engage in another confrontation with the offender in an attempt to right perceived wrongs. It should be noted that multiple cycles of unresolved conflict can result in the victim adjusting his or her perceptions and portrayals of the offender. Most commonly, a victim will begin by portraying the offender as mean and uncaring. Later, as the unresolved conflict continues to cycle multiple times over, the victim may use words like "evil," "heinous," or "criminal" to give a particularly reprehensible overtone to the offender. Ultimately, the victim may undergo so many cycles of unresolved conflict and Adjustment that the human aspect may be removed. We see this occurring primarily when the victims starts to uses words like "devil, witch, demon," monster," etc. to depict the offender. By using such inhuman descriptive terms as identifiers, the humanity of the offender has been obscured by the problem. It is in this phase alone that word usage gives a vital clue to the nature and longevity of the unresolved conflict. In addition, it is important for conflict resolution specialists to note that once a victim starts depicting the offender as a "demon" or "monster," there is invariably very little room for the modality to progress without negatively transmuting into a stronger, more harmful phenomenon.

**ARMY BUILDING**

Conflict can result in a victim feeling the need to gather the support of others. The purpose is one of two things: getting ready to launch another engagement against the offender or further "vilifying" the offender in a manner that

41

uncovers the "misdeeds" and establishes an unfriendly climate to the offender. The hope here is that the wrongdoer's actions are identified publically and that they will be "dealt with" by "others." Perhaps, they will feel ostracized and leave the negative climate of the group. If one uses the concept that multiple cycles can grow conflict, then one of two things can be said. Army Building can either be a resulting action from the Adjustment phase of unresolved conflict, (a secondary cycling of unresolved conflict), or it can be an evolutionary function, an Adjustment after the act of vilifying has failed to resolve conflict (a tertiary, or greater, cycling of unresolved conflict). Those studying unresolved conflict should to note that Army Building, as a secondary cycling of unresolved conflict is a far different animal than the Army Building derived as an Adjustment, or evolutionary incarnation of vilifying. Most importantly, the former is less dire than the latter and has fewer destructive qualities since the desired outcomes and modalities are far more innocent in nature. Remember, as a course of human nature, armies, are more likely to treat perceived "wrong-doers" humanely if they see the offender as a person who has different points of view, motives, or objectives. This is not the case when they think that they are dealing with a "monster" or "demon." Repeated cycles of unmanaged conflict result in altered perceptions of the individuals involved. The offenders may be seen as something different or harmful, even less human.

**ENTRAPMENT**

Sometimes, there is a perceived need that justification, or further action, is needed in order to handle the matter of the offender being able to further victimize people and engage in nefarious behavior. The victim will sometimes engage in the activity of setting the offender up, laying out various "traps" so the offender's misdeeds are noticed by a group or persons of higher authority. This can be from simple surveillance footage gathering and/or manipulation, to evidence gathering and/or manipulation, to actually "setting up" the offender in a given scenario, etc. The whole purpose is rarely ever to get rid of the offender but rather to catch the offender so as to get him or her to stop his or her activities... coerce them. For this reason, Entrapment can be either a secondary or a tertiary cycling of unresolved conflict.

**DRAGON SLAYING**

Akin to Entrapment, the Dragon Slaying form of Adjustment uses sabotage and entrapment against a perceived offender. However, unlike Entrapment, Dragon Slaying is not a quasi-benign activity merely done to foil and uncover the despicable actions of a perceived offender. Nor, does one see Dragon Slaying as being a way to get the offender to leave of his or her own volition—which is an intended function of Entrapment. Instead, Dragon Slaying is the willful entrapment and sabotage of a perceived offender for the sole purposes of getting him or her arrested, fired, expelled, or otherwise forcibly removed in a disgraceful and emotionally-wrecking way. Dragon Slaying is in no way kind. It is highly calculated and evidence of deep-rooted hatred resulting from multiple cycles of long-standing unresolved conflict. If anything, it is the act of Entrapment cycled, until it has evolved into a heightened, aggressive action of similar modality and thought.

**CHAMPION FINDING**

Using the same thought of how multiple cycles of long-standing, unresolved conflict evolve into heightened, more aggressive, methodologies, "Champion

Finding" is yet another manifestation of this phenomenon. When a victim cannot, or will not, successfully entrap or forcefully cause the perceived offender to leave; the victim may opt to engage in the action of "Champion Finding." "Champion Finding" is typically an evolutionary aspect of unresolved conflicts that comes from "Army Building." Here, the victim looks to a singular person, or group of people, who are either more powerful or brash than the victim. The purpose is to take on and vanquish a perceived offender by causing the offender to leave due to force, collusion, disgrace, etc. In some circumstances, "Champion Finding" can be a secondary, or tertiary, cycle evolving from "Dragon Slaying" where the victim feels too weak or too ill equipped to carry out the perceived goal and therefore needs an outside force.

**BURNOUT**

In some countries, such as Germany, the term for this is better known as "Reactive Embitterment" or "Post Traumatic Embitterment Disorder."[16] However, in America, this term has a less formal name associated with it. Like the name implies, this is when the victim has engaged in multiple cycles of unresolved conflict and choose to do as little as possible with the associated group or community. Fuming and festering of emotions is the hallmark of this negative "Adjustment" phenomenon. "Burnout" phenomenon is most commonly the result of a very old and extremely long-lived cycling over of conflict where numerous other negative forms of "Adjustment," have failed. Here, the only hope that the victim now has is that time will afford them an opportunity one day to "strike back" at the offender for one final engagement opportunity. The person at this stage of the game is consumed with hatred to the point that they can breed hate and discontent in the others, regarding the offender, without trying. They have sufficient history and knowledge, as well as an ample and varied history of "Injustice Gathering" to quickly and effectively posit a negative argument as to the offender's character, actions, thoughts, intent, and even heart. Such a person is dangerous to the organizational architecture of a group, because they are usually deeply entrenched in the organization with a whole host of people who may share the same points of view about perceived injustices. A person of this type is like a burning coal that slowly smolders, waiting patiently for a new day in which conditions are right to ignite properly.

**RETREATING**

The "Retreating" phenomenon may outwardly look similar to "Burnout" to the casual observer. However, it is really an evolution of the phenomenon of "Adjustment," where the victim has finally decided to resolve the conflict by evading the presence of the offender and anyone associated with the offender. Ironically, this person can feel like such a social pariah that everyone within the group, including former friends and colleagues of the victim, are now seen to be associated with the offender. In an adversarial context, the victim is saying that the offender has "won." This can lead to a whole host of problems since the victim can engage in self-destructive behavior (since no one is perceived to care about him/her). They can stop trying to better or enrich their life, they can stop undertaking key duties or functions, and they can even engage in activities, which are onerous and/or destructive to the group or organization. Another way of looking at this is that the victim can easily decide to become an offender since they rightly, or wrongly, have engaged in so much victimization that they feel justified in their actions and immune from the consequences of such actions.

**LEAVING**

Another way that "Adjustment" can evolve is the person decides to leave the group or community. This is the ultimate evolution in negative "Adjustment." It is both fleeing from the conflict and resigning to the belief that no resolution can be found. Like the phenomenon of "Retreating," the victim stops undertaking in any key duties or functions that better the group or community. Because people have different tolerances, "Leaving" can be a secondary cycling of unresolved conflict, or it can be an evolution from multiple cycles of unresolved conflict.

## Psychological Indicators vs. Psychological Initiators of Unmanaged Conflict

Knowing the history, structure, and modality of unmanaged conflict is fine. However, it is not enough, in and of itself, to understand conflict and how it works.

It is time to add another level of psychology to the dynamics of conflict by talking about the difference between psychological indicators and psychological initiators of conflict. The examples are only a brief sampling of the wealth of knowledge available concerning conflict. Consider what is said to be a start rather than a "go to" reference of absolutes. Indeed, there is more at play than what can ever be placed in this book.

For many, a psychological indicator of conflict is almost identical to an initiator of conflict. After all, if conflict still happens then it all is the same thing—right? Nothing could be further from the truth!

An indicator of unmanaged conflict is symptomatic. It is the individual acting out in a given way so that one can understand that unresolved conflict is going on. Already, we have talked a little about this with the "Nine Common Functions of Negative Adjustment." To add upon this, think of the functionalities of negative adjustment as the holistic phenomenon of a dispute. Indicators are specific psychological phenomenon that are happening within a person then manifesting in an outward way.

Prime examples of psychological indicators of conflict are issues involving vandalism, mood swings, dissociative behavior, defiance, back talk, and acting out. These are symptoms of an inner, catabolic conflict eating away at a person until he or she has festered out in violent and erratic ways. Therefore, symptoms, like vandalism, are a child's outward struggle to show another how they have been hurt or oppressed. Similarly, mood swings and dissociative behavior are reflective of a person who feels so hurt and violated that he or she no longer knows how to fit in with a group. Even defiance, back talk, and acting out are said to be a way of fighting back against perceived oppression to keep self, or others, from being further hurt. However, I am not a psychologist and, therefore, do not suggest that such correlations be made without the assistance of a trained professional.

It is my hope that you see such wrongful actions with a therapeutic lens of understanding. Such behaviors often are not acts against authority. Look past the act itself. Under the expressed bad behavior, or mannerism, there is a root cause at play, which has manifested itself. The unresolved, catabolic conflict at play may not even be at the school. Indeed, the conflict may not be known to anyone other than the offender. In this circumstance, while the school, another person, etc. may be a victim of said actions—the offender is also a victim of predicating, catabolic conflict. Until that conflict is addressed, any action that one takes to stop or address the wrongful action will be nothing more than "adding fuel to the fire."

Psychological initiators of conflict are different. They are not a symptomatic phenomenon of an unresolved inner conflict. They are a psychological understanding of how catabolic conflict is allowed to grow. For the purposes of this chapter, I will talk about "Low Impulse Control," the "Palo Alto Car Experiment," and "Broken Windows Theory." Please keep in mind that there are other schools of thought, and various theories, out there. These three merely surmise the most popular.

Let us begin with "Low Impulse Control." Kent A. Kiehl is probably the most recently cited researcher in the field. In his paper, *"Pre-motor Functional Connectivity Predicts Impulsivity in Juvenile Offenders,"* published in the *Proceedings of the National Academy of Sciences* (Summer 2011), a number of subjects, aged 13-55, were scanned using magnetic resonance imaging. The test results were compared to incarcerated juveniles. Kiehl's findings concluded that impulse control issues are developmental in nature.[17] Low Impulse Control, also known as "Low Impulse Gratification," has historically been debated by psychologists and criminologists as a root cause of juvenile recidivism. Historically, there has been a divide with one side contending that Low Impulse Control is a mental disease that needs careful treatment. The other side suggests that Low Impulse Gratification is symptomatic of our diminishing culture where children are not taught delayed gratification. For the former, the matter is totally psychological, and juveniles afflicted with this "disease" are in need of treatment rather than incarceration. For the latter, this "disease" is really a "condition" caused by environmental and cultural stimuli. Thus, a change in environment and cultural stimuli can have a profound, transformative change if addressed head on.

Kiehl seemingly straddles the fence on this issue. He notes how the brain is behaving (giving credence to it being a mental health issue). Then he suggests that changes can be made to change the brain's pattern of thinking (giving credence to it is a sociological condition that can be handled with a change in environment and stimuli). In this, Kiehl was extremely wise to urge for testing first to ensure that the juvenile had the condition before treatment, or lack of treatment, ever took place and to determine which protocols be considered

A strong argument can be made that this condition is caused by our culture. To shine further light on this issue, I would like to tell a little story from my past as it relates to this issue.

In the late 1990s, I had a column, called *The X-Factor*, where I talked about sociological issues concerning the various generations (i.e., Baby Boomers, Generation X, and Generation Y). In one column, I recounted the story of a very heated argument between my father and I. My father said that he wanted his children to have it better than what he had—to want for nothing. I remember calling my dad "a fool." A serious man, brought up in the old school of corporal discipline, he was not used to having his grown son say such a thing. Quickly, I reacted with my explanation—Low Impulse Gratification was killing America's youth. As I explained it, he, being a Baby Boomer, grew up in a one-income family where children had to delay gratification in order to get what they wanted. This created a sort of sophistication and higher-function mental process that benefited the growing child as (s)he developed. In today's two-income society, the economy has adjusted to the point where there is no longer a benefit, but rather a demand for both parents to work in order to make the same family income (adjusted for inflation). Because of this, as well as high divorce rates fueled by financial issues arising from the increase of the two-income family, and the fact that we are so nomadic, children are essentially raising themselves with little to no adult interaction. These children are called "latch key" children. They became identifiable with Generation X; the numbers are exponentially increasing in numbers with each subsequent generation. The problem is that parents naturally feel a sense of guilt and instinctively replace "trinkets" (i.e., video games, new clothes, and new shoes) for their lack of parental involvement. This, I contend, has a negative mental effect on juveniles if their only source of insight comes from other "latch key" juveniles and love and discipline are supplanted with material goods. Over time, the juveniles risk becoming emotionally stunted—unable to handle more sophisticated elements of culture.

Proponents of a culturally derived origin of Low Impulse Gratification contend that conflicts in juveniles can stem from this aforementioned emotional stunting. The need for new sneakers, a new computer gadget, etc. circumvents traditional cultural controls of morality and responsibility. Thus, in handling a student offender, it is important to spot whether or not (s)he has this condition so that appropriate actions are taken to keep down the recidivism of wrongful actions.

In a different line of thought, we should next look at the "Palo Alto Car Experiment" —a precursor to, that somewhat re-enforces, the "Broken Windows Theory." The Palo Alto shows how deliberate actions to lower perceptions of care can provoke crime to happen. Moreover, it harkens to a notion in criminology that people react differently in groups than they would individually. In other words, one is more likely to commit a crime when (s)he is in the presence of a group of people with criminal behaviors than (s)he would be as individuals.

The "Palo Alto Car Experiment" is both simple and complex in its application and findings. In 1969, a psychologist, named Philip Zimbardo, took a 1959 Oldsmobile and placed it in front of the Bronx Campus of New York University. He then took another car, of similar make and model, and placed it in Palo Alto,

California near Stanford University on the outskirts of a rather affluent community. In this experiment, the only difference was the neighborhood that each car was in. Bronx was identified as a high crime, ghetto area whereas Palo Alto was identified as an affluent, low crime area. Both cars were missing license plates, and the hoods were raised to stimulate a mental/behavioral trigger that Dr. Zimbardo called a "Releaser." After a week, the car in Palo Alto was still untouched while the car in Bronx had suffered 23 separate acts of vandalism and was totally stripped down. It was only after Dr. Zimbardo, and some graduate students, took a sledge hammer to the Palo Alto car that he noticed not only how the community, but also his graduate students, began to embrace the act of bashing in and destroying the car.[18]

Since that time, many researchers have both proved and disproved Dr. Zimbardo's findings in individual field experiments. In Criminal Justice classes, however, the "Palo Alto Car Experiment" is taught as gospel. The crucial point of Dr. Zimbardo's findings, however, was not how the "Releaser" worked or didn't work, or even the fact that the cars ended up the same once sufficient lack of care was exhibited. Instead, the vital element of Dr. Zimbardo's findings was in how even well-educated and affluent individuals were willing to engage in seemingly immoral and unethical behavior once the group had established that it was acceptable to act in such a manner.

One way people notice cues, indicating that certain behaviors are acceptable, is by looking at the state of the facilities in which one operates. "Broken Windows Theory," developed and posited first by James Q. Wilson and George L. Kelling implies that crime is, at least in part, based on the lack of care exhibited by a community. Communities with unfixed, broken windows in buildings and homes also tend to have higher levels of crime. When the windows are fixed, and the appearance of care by the community is demonstrated (i.e., new paint on buildings, grass cut, etc.) then the level of crime experienced goes down.[19]

Like with Zimbardo's "Palo Alto Car Experiment," "Broken Windows Theory" harkens to a belief that crime, at least in part, is cultural and that groups of people will behave according to what the cultural controls are of the area. Thus, if adults and students engage in inappropriate behavior—the whole school community will degrade and start acting accordingly. If the building and grounds are not properly kept up, or if acts of vandalism are not immediately addressed and cleaned up—the whole school community will degrade and act accordingly. Call it "monkey see, monkey do" or whatever else one likes. This trend is seen in field experiments repeatedly. Therefore, it is a trend that must be addressed.

For the Conflict Resolution professional, it is important to note not only where catabolic conflict starts, how it functions, and how people react—one has to be intimately familiar with conflict at all levels and understand the various schools of thought and theory. Then, and only then, can a full appreciation be gained for the negative affects, and effects, of unresolved and unmanaged conflict.

## Conflict's Good Side

On January 1, 2008, an academic article was published about the good side of conflict. Despite the fact that hundreds of scholarly articles are printed every year on the field of Conflict Resolution, this particular article was a rarity since human nature, especially in contemporary society, finds conflict to be abhorrent rather than beneficial. However, as the authors noted, William Ellery Channing said, "Difficulties are meant to rouse, not discourage. The human spirit is to grow strong by conflict." Using this understanding, anabolic conflict can be a fuel source that spurs on adaptation and change. The authors contend that higher quality decisions are made using "Devil's advocacy" techniques to create controlled, beneficial conflict that eradicates "group think" mentality. Conflict, based on continual adaptation, learning to change, and deviations in a larger system, can also create an autopoietic system that allows the organization to continually create and renew itself in the face of adversity. Thus, conflict is the essential catalyst for growth and development—the hallmarks of a sound educational system. [20]

Indeed, for all of the talk in this book, as well as the whole field of Conflict Resolution, it is important to note the difference between "good" conflict and the unmanaged and disruptive conflict that causes fights, low morale, etc. It is like stress in many ways. A body can be stressed by lack of sleep, lack of proper nutrition, verbal assaults, and more. The body can also be stressed by swimming, hiking, bike riding, jumping rope, getting a kiss from a sweetheart, getting a good grade. One type of stress hurts, is believed to cause cancer, can cause mental and emotional instability, and is believed to cause an early death. The latter form of stress, sometimes referred to as "eustress," is considered both healthy and beneficial and is even believed to cause one to have a long life with less disease and more mental/emotional stability.

## Perception-Based Conflict

Probably one of the most often cited quotes about perceptions of crime is from Nils Christie. Christie is a Norwegian criminologist and sociologist who has worked diligently to change the views of conflict. According to Christie, "A warrior wears armor, a lover flowers. They are equipped according to expectations of what is to happen, and their equipment increases chances that their expectations will prove right." [21]

If Christie is right, part of the outcome that we see in situations is not how things truly are but rather, how we expect them to turn out and, therefore, how we modify the situation, sometimes very subtly with our behaviors and reactions, so that the end result is expected. This is a profound line of thinking since it strikes to the heart of the subjective elements of our society such as how schools address disciplinary issues, how officers handle suspects before and after an arrest, how the judicial process handles court cases, and so on. Indeed, Dr. Howard Zehr has further expanded upon Christie's contentions with his comparison of how outcomes are contingent upon perceptions.

Aside from being the "granddaddy" of American-based Restorative Justice Practices, a leader in the Mennonite community, a noted lecturer, and advocate for victims and offenders, Dr. Zehr is also a photographer. Using his photography background, Zehr proposed his "Understandings of Justice" in his book, *Changing Lenses: A New Focus for Crime and Justice.* For the sake of brevity, and initial understanding of the core concept, I will only cite seven of his thirty-four comparisons.[22]

## *Zehr's "Understandings of Justice" (Abbreviated)*

| *Retributive Lens* | *Restorative Lens* |
|---|---|
| Blame-fixing central | Problem-solving central |
| Focus on past | Focus on future |
| Harm by offender balanced by harm to offender | Harm by offender balanced by making right |
| Focus on offender; victim ignored | Victims' needs central |
| State and offender are key elements | Victim and offender are key elements |
| Outcomes encourage offender irresponsibility | Responsible behavior encouraged |
| Process alienates | Process aims at reconciliation |

Naturally, others in the fields of Conflict Resolution and Negotiations have latched onto the notion of perception-based outcomes in issues of conflict. More recently, Robert Mnookin, a law professor at Harvard University, talks in his book, *Bargaining with the Devil: When to Negotiate, When to Fight,* about traps that people fall in based on their perceptions going into a conflict. To understand more, let's look at Professor Mnookin's observations. [23]

## Mnookin's "Reinforcing Prisms" Traps Theory of Conflict Understanding

| NEGATIVE TRAPS (FIGHT) | POSITIVE TRAPS (NEGOTIATE) |
| --- | --- |
| Tribalism | Universalism |
| Demonization | Contextual Rationalization and Forgiveness |
| Dehumanization | Rehabilitation and Redemption |
| Moralism/Self-righteousness | Shared Fault and Responsibility |
| Zero-sum Fallacy | Win-Win |
| Fight/Flight | Appeasement |
| Call to Battle | Call for Peace/Pacifism |

As Mnookin notes in his book, these paradigms are truly reinforcing forces that distort one's judgment. For instance, the trap of Tribalism involves the notion that the group is reliable because it is known, while other groups are not reliable, or even evil, because they are unknown and not a part of the group. By contrast, Universalism falsely assumes that everyone is the same and, therefore, cannot understand differences related to divergence of cultures and history. The trap of Demonization is essentially seeing people as truly evil rather than humans with flaws. Contrasting that, the trap of Contextual Rationalization and Forgiveness assumes that all bad behaviors are due to external forces and, consequently, are forgivable.

Dehumanization is like the trap of Demonization in that it sees the opposing party as being less than human; however, it does not go so far as to frame the person as "evil incarnate." Indeed, the justification can be made that the opposing person can be treated more as an object than a person. Again, contrasting this trap is the snare of Rehabilitation and Redemption which believes that people are always worthy of redemption even if they show no desire for rehabilitation or redemption. Self-Righteousness views one side as innocent while the other side is totally wrong. Conversely, Shared Fault infers that everyone is at fault for something and that no one is "clean." Saying it is okay not to be "clean," the trap of Zero-Sum says winning by any method is perfectly fine so long as the enemy does not benefit. The opposite trap of Win-Win naively states that no matter how resources and opportunities may be depleting, there is always a way for both sides to benefit without hurting the other or taking from the other.

Considering the line of Freud, the Fight/Flight trap infers that one can thoughtlessly charge into battle or run away from a battle based on perception and circumstance. Along similar lines, the thinking trap of

Appeasement sees the opposite side as too powerful to fight or run away from, and, therefore, concessions must be made to keep the opposing side happy.

Finally, the Call to Battle versus the Call for Peace carries the previous notions up another degree. Call to Battle has a leader gathering forces in order to attack the other side, while the Call for Peace has a person stepping in and saying that peace at all costs is better than war. As Mnookin notes, the negative traps are an encouraging force, causing people to exaggerate and inflate the costs of resolving conflict while negating any benefits. The positive traps are the inverse of the negative, where the price of conflict resolution is irrationally underestimated while also overestimating the benefits.

## Putting the Pieces Together

This chapter included many rather distinguished academics and practitioners. We examined the history of how the world has handled unmanaged and unresolved conflict and looked at ways to understand conflict using diagrams, patterns, and psychosocial theory. What does it all mean if one cannot use it in a practical application?

In truth, while the Conflict Resolution professional uses the tools and knowledge talked about in this chapter on a near-daily basis—my sole goal was to inform and make you aware of "conflict" in every way imaginable. I wanted to elevate the understanding of this subject and give it the due diligence that other professions demand of their field of expertise. I also wanted to make you keenly aware of how diverse and dynamic both conflict, and the understanding of conflict, can be in achieving an outcome.

To put things in perspective, I would like to refer to a documentary that I saw on color and how it affected the human brain. In one experiment, Taekwondo fighters wore blue and red in a match. Scientists then took video from the fight and altered it so that the colors were switched. These scientists next had two groups of judges rate the fight, with one group seeing the fighters as they really fought and the other group seeing the fighters using the re-touched and edited video where the colors were swapped. The result was that judges in both groups scored the red fighter as winner of the match. In another experiment with the Himba tribe of Namibia, Africa, scientists evaluated how the tribesmen distinguished and perceived colors (see the following diagrams). In this test, a series of green squares were shown with all but one being the same color of green. In another test, a series of green squares were shown with an obvious blue square in the group. In the test with just green squares, the Himba test subjects were easily able to distinguish the off-color green square from the rest without fail—something that would be hard for a Westerner to do since the color is just slightly different from the other squares and, therefore, not easily apparent. In the test with the blue square, the Himba test subject had a great deal of difficulty and oft failed to find the blue square. The reason, the researcher contended, was that our words play on how we perceive colors.

The Himba had different names for the different colors of green, so they could easily see them. However, the word for blue is the same word for green, consequently, they could not see a difference in color because they had no differentiation or understanding that the color blue is a different color from green. Scientists took this experiment to other parts of the world including Wales, where the Welsh only have five colors in their native tongue; here, they found similar results. It was concluded that it is only by our shared experiences that we can develop and grow our frame of reference to understand and perceive differently—even things like colors. [24]

# Himba Color Perception Test

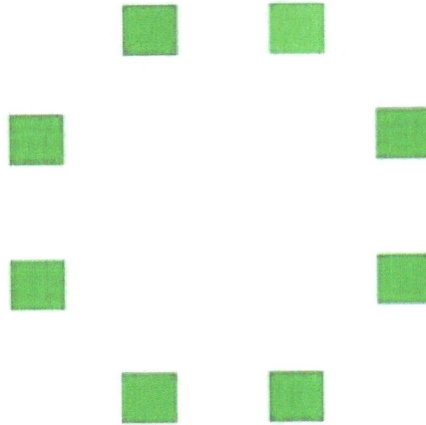

*In this test, one color tile is different from the others. Can you tell which one is which? The Himba can! That is because they have a different word for the different shade of green—therefore a different understanding and frame of reference allows them to easily see that the colored tile in the top right is a totally different green from the rest.*

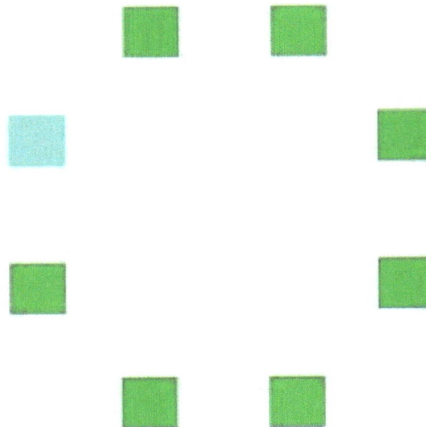

*Is seeing believing or is understanding a base of core perception functions? In this test, most Himba tribal members would likely be unable to find the blue tile in the top, left hand, second row. However, for most Westerners, such a distinction is rather easy, and the blue square is obvious. Scientists believe that our understanding of what something is allows us to perceive that thing. Since the Himba have the same word for the colors blue and green, it is believed by scientists that they actually have a basic framework that prohibits them from being able to perceive the different colors.*

I bring this up because our shared experiences and understandings have a profound impact on how we perceive things. As you go through the other chapters of this book, reflect upon everything that you learned in this chapter about conflict. Also reflect upon how perceptions and frame of reference have a profound affect, and effect, on what is seen. What is elementary to one, like the difference between blue and green, can be nearly indistinguishable to another. How then do we make one aware? The answer is simple—change the shared experiences and frame of references so that what was unseen is revealed.

In many ways, a Conflict Resolution professional is the opposite of an illusionist. An illusionist will take a carrot, hide it, use tricks of mental diversion, and tell you that the carrot is really a thumb. They can then trick and amaze you into actually believing that a needle is passing through his/her thumb without harm or pain.[25] This is what illusionists do—trick people for money and attention. A Conflict Resolution professional, to the contrary, sees that the parties involved are failing to see the conflict's catabolic nature. Therefore, (s)he works to reveal what was unseen so that all understand and are made better. An illusion is in many ways like the experiments on color done with the Himba. We think that what we see should be obvious and self-apparent to all. However, given the improper frame of reference, a person can be made to see what is not there and conversely, not see what is right in front of their eyes. Keep this in mind as you continue learning about the theories and methodologies contained in this book.

# References

1. McElroy, W. (13 August 2004). *Criminal Versus Civil Remedies for Intentional Wrongs.* The Future of Freedom Foundation. Retrieved on 3/6/2012 from http://www.fff.org/comment/com0408f.asp

2. Taken from the published game regulations (2009-2012) for the States of Tennessee (trout fishing regulations only) and Florida (saltwater fishing regulations only).

3. Taken from the published game regulations (2009-2012) for the States of Alabama and Florida (deer harvesting only) as well as a review of case history in local courts of counties in South Alabama and Northwest Florida.

4. Time Warner (2011). *Rednecks & Riches* (Television Reality Show). *Storage Wars,* Season 1, Episode 4. truTV (a Time Warner company):New York, NY

5. PBS (30 January 2001). *Frontline: Juvenile Justice* (Public Television Show). Public Broadcasting Service (PBS):New York, NY

6. Kappeler, V. E. & Potter, G. W. (2005). *The Mythology of Crime and Criminal Justice (4th Edition).* Waveland Press:Long Grove, IL

7. Bennett, W., DiIulio, J., & Walters, J. (1996). *Body Count: Moral Poverty and How to Win America's War Against Crime and Drugs.* Simon & Schuster:New York

8. Estrich, S. (9 May 1996). *Immunize Kids Against a Life of Crime. USA Today,* p. A15. Gannett Company:McLean, VA

9. Zoglin, R., Allis, S., & Kamlani, R. (15 January 1996). *Now for the Bad News: A Teenage Time Bomb. Time* Magazine. Time Warner: New York, NY

10. Zimring, F. (19 August 1996). *Crying Wolf Over Teen Demons. Los Angeles Times,* p. B5. Los Angeles Times: Los Angeles, CA

11. Kappeler, V. E. & Potter, G. W. (2005). *The Mythology of Crime and Criminal Justice (4th Edition).* Waveland Press:Long Grove, IL

12. Drizin, S. (19 January 2001). *Super-predators or Just Naughty? Chicago Tribune,* p. 19. Tribune Company:Chicago, IL

13. Vermont Department of Corrections (2012). *Restorative Justice.* Agency of Human Services. Retrieved on 02/27/2012 from http://www.doc.state.vt.us/justice/restorative-justice

14. De Savornin Lohman, A. F. (2011). *Lohman Cabbage Conflict Model.* DynaLaw:The Netherlands.

15. Claassen, R. & Claassen, R. (2008). *Discipline That Restores.* BookSurge Publishing:South Carolina

16. Rotter, M. (2009). "Reactive Embitterment: Conceptualization, Relevancy and Differentiation." Dissertation. Retrieved on 6/23/2012 from http://opus.kobv.de/tuberlin/volltexte/2009/2193/pdf/rotter_max.pdf

17. Wentworth, K. (17 August 2011). *Examining How Lack of Impulse Control Afflicts Juvenile Offenders. UNM Today.* University of New Mexico. Retrieved on 03/13/2012 from http://news.unm.edu/2011/08/examining-how-lack-of-impulse-control-afflicts-juvenile- offenders/

18. Florida State University (2012). *Philip Zimbardo.* Retrieved on June 23, 2012 fromhttps://www.criminology.fsu.edu/crimtheory/zimbardo.htm

19. Wilson, J. and Kelling, G. (March 1982) *The Police and Neighborhood Safety: Broken Windows. The Atlantic Monthly,* pp. 29-38. Atlantic Monthly Group:Washington, DC

20.     Andrade, L., Plowman, D., and Duchon, D. (1 January 2008). *Getting Past Conflict Resolution: A Complexity View of Conflict.* University of Nebraska —Lincoln. *Management Department Faculty Publications.* Paper 62. Retrieved on 3/13/2012 from http://digitalcommons.unl.edu/managementfacpub/62

21.     Christie, N. (1986). *Images of Man in Modern Penal Law. Crime, Law, and Social Change,.* pp. 95-106, Vol. 10, Issue 1. Springer:Netherlands

22.     Zehr, H. (1990). *Changing Lenses: A New Focus for Crime and Justice.* Herald Press:Scottsdale, PA

23.     Mnookin, R. (2010). *Bargaining with the Devil: When to Negotiate, When to Fight.* Simon & Schuster:New York

24.     BBC (8 August 2011). *Do You See What I See?* British Broadcasting Corporation (BBC): United Kingdom

25.     YouTube. (2009). *Needle in Thumb! (Magic Trick).* Retrieved on 7/21/2014 from http://www.youtube.com/watch?v=KvSE72R6eMc

# 1.3

## Program Basics - Perspective

Thus far, the text has detailed a wealth of knowledge about how society handles issues of catabolic (destructive) conflict, critical problems with established educational and juvenile justice systems, harms caused from these problems, and the history of how society has dealt with these problems. You have received information about a better system, which seeks to repair harms and bring healing. Until now, everything was an overview. In academic terms, the first couple of chapters were introductory courses. This chapter's intention is to go a step further and be an intermediate level exposure both to the concepts of the program as well as the program itself. Remaining chapters in Section 1 of this book will be full-on chapters that expressly talk about key elements used in the program. While Chapter 1.2 is the most important chapter for building a foundational vantage point to understand Conflict Resolution, Chapter 1.3 is the most critical chapter for the practitioner in establishing his/her practice and establishing effective programs. Keep this in mind as you read on.

## Forms of Conflict Resolution

We have mentioned Conflict Resolution a number of times. Let us take a look at the definition. In its most basic form, Conflict Resolution can be defined as a deliberate intervention to mitigate, alleviate, eradicate, or positively transform the harms and impact of catabolic (harmful, out of control) conflict by having all parties come together, share their understanding of the conflict, and peaceably try to come to a joint solution. A neutral third party—specifically trained to help in these kinds of situations—usually facilitates this process. These neutral third parties are referred to as Neutrals, Mediators, Ombudsmen, etc. In areas where parties may be subject to litigation or prosecution, the term Alternative Dispute Resolution (ADR) may be used. Thus, in today's complex society, it is common practice for professionals to use ADR and Conflict Resolution interchangeably.

There are multiple forms of Conflict Resolution with multiple functions. According to the Association for Conflict Resolution, there are nine different forms of Conflict Resolution commonly found in the school systems of America. The forms we will discuss are listed in the following chart.

## CONFLICT RESOLUTION FORMS

| | | |
|---|---|---|
| 1 | Negotiation | Where two or more parties reach an agreement through a "give and take" process. |
| 2 | Mediation | Parties meet with a neutral third party to confidentially discuss and deal with the conflict at hand. |
| 3 | Arbitration | Opposite of Mediation. Parties meet with a third party who acts as a quasi-judge in the matter, rendering a binding settlement agreement. |
| 4 | Mediation-Arbitration | Lesser-known and utilized hybrid form of ADR. With Mediation Arbitration, parties agree to start with mediation but allow the mediator to settle the agreement as an arbitrator if agreement is not reached. |
| 5 | Early Neutral Evaluation | A very rare and underutilized form of ADR where an attorney will review a case, try to resolve the matter between the parties, and then give information as to how to proceed with litigation and what the expected outcomes can be. |
| 6 | Community Conferencing | Community Conferencing, which many claim to be a functionality more aligned with Restorative Justice, is where members of the community (i.e., victims, offenders, family of the victims/offenders, interested stakeholders) meet together, with a neutral third party facilitator and talk about the conflict crisis and how to resolve the matter. |
| 7 | Collaborative Law | Not to be confused with Collaborative Justice, this is a form of ADR where attorneys, not the disputants in a conflict, work together in a non-litigation manner in order to come up with a mutually agreeable solution. |
| 8 | Negotiated Rulemaking | Similar to Community Conferencing, this is when a government entity seeks out the advice and input of the community, in a collaborative manner, in order to adopt new rules or adapt existing rules—some now say this is a function of Collaborative Justice while others argue that it is a form of Restorative Justice. |
| 9 | Peer Mediation | Student mediators take on the role of adult mediators under the supervision of a teacher or other qualified adult, to help other students in conflict resolve their situation. |

In the Unbroken Circles $^{SM}$ program, not all of these forms of Conflict Resolution and ADR are used. Rather, the program specifically endorses the use of Peer Mediation, Negotiated Rulemaking, Community Conferencing, and Mediation as being the core components of the Conflict Resolution element in this program matrix. Community Conferencing, in various forms, is used by this plan primarily for more onerous and serious violations of rights and policy. Negotiated Rulemaking, in regards to this program, should only be used for the development, oversight, and maintenance of the program. It is not a valid form of Conflict Resolution to use with the students. In addition, to a far lesser degree, Mediation, as a whole, is offered as an option only for special situations, those not typically covered or dealt with in the program. Peer Mediation is seen as a preferred, lower level methodology to use for most issues of student conflict.

## What is Restorative Justice?

So, what is this new-fangled "Restorative Justice" concept anyway? Surely, the idea of getting in a circle and talking about one's feelings or pairing up a victim and an offender together seems a bit odd and alarming to some. While the methods employed by Restorative Justice Practitioners may seem a bit hokey if not out-right dangerous, the results show, repeatedly, that Restorative Justice Practices produce desirable, and sometimes unimaginably positive, results.

Therefore, something else must be missing from plain sight that is working its "magic" on the offenders, victims, and other stakeholders. Moreover, the fact of the matter is that there is something "else" that should be strongly looked at and understood if Restorative Justice is to work.

Restorative Justice, and the Restorative Practices that comprise Restorative Justice, are not simply about the acts performed. Placing a bunch of children in a circle will not produce remarkable results. Rather, the processes, practices, plans, and modes of service employed by a Restorative Justice practitioner are just an enabling manifestation, or tool, of something deeper at play. That "something deeper" is the very philosophy and principles that guide, as well as define, Restorative Justice as a unique and separate conflict resolution and justice-dealing style.

Lorraine Stutzman Amstutz and Judy H. Mullet, in their book *The Little Book of Restorative Discipline for Schools*, utilize the following definition.

> Restorative Justice… focuses on harms and consequent needs (the victims', as well as the communities' and the offenders')… addresses obligations resulting from those harms (the offender's, but also the communities' and the society's)… uses inclusive, collaborative

processes... Involves those with a legitimate stake in the situation (victims, offenders, community members, society)... seeks to put right the wrongs... all of these principles must be rooted in respect for others.[2]

In regards to discipline methods rooted in Restorative Justice, what they called Restorative Discipline, the key hallmarks are that Restorative Discipline,

> Acknowledges that relationships are central to building community... builds systems that address misbehavior and harm in a way that strengthens relationships... focuses on the harm done rather than only on rule-breaking... gives voice to the person harmed... engages in collaborative problem-solving... empowers change and growth... Enhances responsibility.[3]

Belinda Hopkins, an accomplished author and CEO of the United Kingdom based group *Transforming Conflict National Centre for Restorative Approaches in Youth Settings*, mirrors Amstutz and Mullet's contentions. According to Hopkins, "Restorative Practices in school are inspired by the philosophy and practices of Restorative Justice, which puts repairing harm done to relationships and people over and above the need for assigning blame and dispensing punishment." Hopkins' Transforming Conflict website talks about how Restorative Approaches "provide an underpinning ethos and philosophy for making, maintaining, and repairing relationships and for fostering a sense of social responsibility and shared accountability." The Transforming Conflict website even goes on to show how Restorative Justice can be seen as a three-tiered pyramid with the foundation being rooted in philosophy, the next section being key skills, and the third actually being the practice employed.

Hopkins contends that Restorative Justice must have key values that "create an ethos of respect, inclusion, accountability and taking responsibility, commitment to relationships, impartiality, being non-judgmental, collaboration, empowerment and emotional articulacy." Of the key skills of Restorative Justice, Hopkins contends that Restorative Justice practitioners must exhibit skills that include, "active listening, facilitating dialogue and problem-solving, listening to and expressing emotion and empowering others to take ownership of problems."

Essentially, Hopkins argues that true Restorative Practices address four key questions, to wit:

1) What has happened?

2) Who has been affected?

3) How can everyone be involved who has been affected so that they can find a way forward?

4) How can everyone solve for future conflicts?[4]

In a recent revision of their site, Transforming Conflict has also added nine core needs that all people have. These needs are: respect, encouragement, consideration, recognition, appreciation, empathy, safety, belonging, and inclusion. According to the Transforming Conflict Group,

> When these needs go unmet, ignored, or violated, then people become sad, resentful, and hostile, and behave in negative ways toward others. This behaviour, in turn, has a knock-on effect on those around them—like ripples on a pond—a downward spiral of conflict and increasingly damaged relationships can impact the whole community. A range of restorative skills and processes adopted by everyone in a society can ensure that human needs are addressed and become the responsibility of that community.[5]

The key to both understanding and having an effective Restorative Justice program is to acknowledge that the philosophy and ethos of Restorative Justice is paramount to any tool or method deployed by a practitioner. Indeed, injustice is an intangible, nebulous, ethereally rooted problem that manifests itself from the lack of ethos of the offender into very tangible and physical harm. Therefore, one could further say that Restorative Justice responds in-kind to the nature of injustice by being rooted strongly in the intangible philosophy/ethos and ultimately manifesting itself with a very real and physically engaging program or tool of action when needed. This ability to attack all levels of injustice from intangible to tangible, from lack of values to values, from no power to ownership, is what truly sets Restorative Justice apart as a separate doctrine of Collaborative Justice.

## What is Collaborative Justice?

As of late, a number of practitioners have noticed that the fields of mediation-based Conflict Resolution and non-mediation based Restorative Justice are pushing and pulling on one another. A majority of practitioners now wish the two theories were considered distinct modalities. Conflict Resolution professionals, most of whom are mediators and arbitrators, claim that Restorative Justice Practitioners have abandoned core principles of Conflict Resolution such as confidentiality and impartiality (i.e., victim-oriented panels). They note that a core element of Restorative Justice is that the accused must admit guilt, or Restorative Justice cannot take place. Restorative Justice Practitioners claim that their practice is not about the resolution of the conflict but rather the ability to transform it. This is not a primary goal of Conflict Resolution. For this reason, some Restorative Justice Practitioners wish the practice to be called Conflict Transformation. However, despite all of this disagreement, the two fields are merging in many areas with mediation-based Conflict Resolution practices embracing what is known as "Transformative Mediation." Additionally, Restorative Justice Practitioners are embracing what is known as "Victim-Offender Mediation" or "VOMA," as well as the aforementioned "Community Conferencing" which is sometimes called "Community Mediation."

Ultimately, one must look at the core differences and similarities of the two. Mediation-based Conflict Resolution sees the field of Conflict Resolution as the same as ADR. For Conflict Resolution proponents, the primary objective is to reach a negotiated conclusion. In contrast, Restorative Justice Practitioners tend to see a conflict as a clear matter of perpetrator and victim. A growing number of extremists go so far as to claim that the process is solely for the benefit of the victim. Both beliefs are variants of the original practices.

In truth, early mediation practices were a way for parties to by-pass an onerous system of conventional justice—the same being true for how Restorative Justice was formed. Mediation is a way for parties to get outside help to settle their differences by openly discussing issues, engaging in fact-finding discussions, and collaboratively working together so both parties are made as whole as is possible, avoiding the need for court. Restorative Justice started in the courts as a way to resolve issues of crime and wrongdoing and taking the problem out of the courts. The victim and offender met with a neutral third party and interested stakeholders (i.e., family of victim/offenders, local church officials, local school officials, friends of victim/offender, counselors), openly and honestly discussing the nature of the crime, giving both victim and offender a voice in the matter. At this point, they come up with an agreed upon path to atonement, providing both victim and offender necessary support, and ultimately making all parties involved whole once more. Both methods work to make parties in catabolic conflict as complete as possible, yet they come from two drastically different places.

In fact, the early forms of Conflict Resolution and Restorative Justice were so identical that writers used to say that Restorative Justice was a form of mediation. It is like saying that a nail, a screw, and a bolt are all different, yet the same. While it is true that all three are different, they essentially do the same job, in almost the same manner, and yet they are used for different functions. Just as a nail, a bolt, and a screw are all called "fasteners", some professionals, such as myself, wish to classify mediation, negotiation, arbitration, Restorative Justice, conferencing, and panels under a broader umbrella. However, professionals in both ADR and Restorative Justice disagree with this, so a new term had to be created.

Collaborative Justice is the practice of using whatever forms of Conflict Resolution and Restorative Justice one needs in order to best serve the needs of the parties involved. In other words, if Circles works best for a given scenario, a Collaborative Justice professional is not going to use mediation. Moreover, the same can be said for not using a panel when mediation would work best. Ultimately, it is the original intent and spirit of both Conflict Resolution and Restorative Justice—with a different name so as not to offend those with a conflicting view. Therefore, it is the perfect pairing of the right tool with the right situation and need.

Sometimes I write that the program is a Conflict Resolution program. Sometimes I write that the program is a Restorative Justice program. In addition, other times I write that the program is based off Collaborative Justice. I am right in all three cases because of the understanding and definitions that I put forth. Everything that I do and teach, as a function of this program, is indeed Conflict Resolution. My understanding of Conflict Resolution is that it is same as Restorative Justice and that both are the same as Collaborative Justice. Moreover, most of the processes that I use are Restorative Justice-based. Even the few processes that are not typically associated with Restorative Justice are applied in a way fostered by Restorative Justice. Don't let the wording trip you up.

## About Santa Rosa County, Florida

In order to understand how all of this plays out, I thought it best to talk about where I come from and where I live. According to the oral history of my family, Santa Rosa County, as well as its County Seat of Milton, was founded by my ancestor, William Johnson. Before Santa Rosa was a county, it was a part of Escambia County, with Pensacola arguably boasting it was the oldest port town in America. Before Milton was named for the mills, it was called "Scratch Ankle" and "Hell Town." A centennial anniversary edition of the local paper, the *Santa Rosa Press Gazette,* posted a copy of an order from Escambia County, showing a man sentenced to spend two weeks in Hell Town as punishment for his crime. I should also mention that the same issue of the paper showed a picture of my father battling a historic fire in Milton that threatened the life and property of a large area of the town.

Back in family oral lore, William Johnson was reputed to be a Cherokee soldier of Andrew Jackson, who had to run for his life and lose his identity as a Cherokee man. Again, according to the oral lore of my family, Johnson owned multiple boats, ferries, and saw mills that employed numerous Native Americans on the run from an oppressive federal government system. The mill in Bagdad is where Milton is said to get its name. When Santa Rosa broke off from Escambia County, Johnson donated a parcel of land for the first courthouse. Even the name of the County is an emblem of who we were, and are, as a people since "Santa Rosa" is said to refer to the fondness of the "holy" or "sacred" pink roses that grew upon the banks of the Blackwater River of Santa Rosa County instead of a Catholic saint. The rose is an emblem denoting beauty, prosperity, endurance, and protection. Therefore, it should come as no surprise that issues of public service, the law, and social justice run deep in my family as multiple generations of Johnson's descendants have made their homes here with the other founding families.

Though the original parcel of the county was cut up into further formations of other counties, Santa Rosa is still a rather sizable tract of land. For those not familiar with the area, it is located in Northwest Florida. Poets have made numerous mentions of the ebony waters of the Blackwater River and the amber waters of the Yellow River being the heart of the county and its people. A local joke is that one cannot get more "Southern" in Santa Rosa or he would be up to his knees in water!

It is a magical place where one can travel thirty minutes in any direction and find a vast diversity of topography ranging from lush, untouched forests to pristine, white beaches or quaint, little towns to dynamic, city life. Cold, sweet creeks crisscross the northern end while brackish basins accent the middle like dark chocolate diamonds and the emerald green waters of the Gulf of Mexico kiss the southern beaches of the county. In the summer, one can go out to the beach on a moonlit night and see water aglow with the electric blue, phosphoric luminescence of micro-jellies while heat lightning dances overhead, contrasting the purple clouds with the lightning's orange glow.

Because of a huge impact by numerous military bases, it should come as to no surprise that economic growth is a bit muted. In fact, there are only three incorporated cities in Santa Rosa County: the Town of Jay, the City of Milton, and the City of Gulf Breeze. These three cities represent the three core sections, and economic bases, of the county. Jay is agrarian, Milton is commerce and military dependent, and Gulf Breeze is tourist and military dependent. Each city area has a major "suburb" area that is also culturally unique to the area in which the county was situated. However, for statistical purposes, only the unincorporated areas of Navarre (an area east of Gulf Breeze) and Pace (an area west of Milton) are usually looked at by government officials.

In 2005, there was an estimated 38,520 citizens (age 0-19) out of an estimated 141,750 total population. For the same year, the service industry hired more people than any other group with some 15,560 working typically low-paying service jobs. In 2002, the unemployment levels for Milton, Gulf Breeze, Jay, Navarre, and Pace were 6%, 2.5%, 3.1%, 4.3%, and 4.4% respectively. In 2006, some 36% of the wage earners in the Milton area, 23.9% for the county as a whole, made under $20,000 a year. Some 62% of the wage earners in the Milton area, 48.9% for the county as a whole, made well under $40,000 a year. The median household income in the Milton area was $29,833 while the median household income for the county as a whole was $41,164. The Cost of Living in Northwest Florida was roughly 1.1% higher than the national average—even higher than New York City's stated cost of living for that year. The five top employers in Santa Rosa County for 2005 were: Santa Rosa School District (3,000 employees), United States Government (1,999 employees), Wal-Mart (1,161 employees), Santa Rosa County Government (867 employees) and Baptist Health Systems (850 employees).[6] Since the recession of the Obama Administration, no conclusive data can be found as to such break downs. Santa Rosa County went from 8.5% to 8.7% unemployment in a single month according to a June 17, 2011 article in the *Northwest Florida Daily News*.[7] Figures would not have reflected those who were not counted because they were out of work too many months previously, therefore, not meeting counting criteria for the government as "usable unemployment data."

Despite what some would call a "bleak" economic/social landscape, Santa Rosa County's School District seems to be the "shining jewel" for the county. The Santa Rosa County School District has consistently been one of the state's top 10 school districts in the State. In 2005, based on the Florida Comprehensive Assessment Test (FCAT), Santa Rosa's School District was tied for first as the school district with the highest writing proficiency scores (89%). Reading and math proficiency scores on the FCAT placed them tied for second and third place as well with scores of 74% and 79% respectively.[8]

Suffice it to say, conflicts are bound to break out. Every year, the First Judicial Circuit of Florida's State Attorney Office, refers some forty juvenile cases for arbitration.[9] Additionally, there are some 100 misdemeanor/felony cases to mediation. This number does not delineate juveniles being tried as adults.[10] The Santa Rosa County "Teen Court" diversion program gets about 150-200 deferments a year.[11] Just one (unspecified) middle school in the southern portion of the county had 1,334 referrals with about 700 being low-level offenses (e.g., chewing gum, not completing work assignment). Moreover, there is no peer mediation or Restorative Justice-based conflict resolution program in place in any given school, or in the school district as a whole. The only program similar to peer mediation that the School District had was a voluntary program called the "Positive Behavior Support" (PBS) program. PBS was a school-wide program meant to teach children certain social skills such as active listening and following instructions.[12] There are 39 schools in the Santa Rosa County School District, seven of which are deemed "specialty schools" (i.e., online school, community school, vocational school).[13]

It is my hope that later you can look at the data in this section to compare how your school or district does before and after it has adopted the Restorative Justice approaches offered up in this book. This program was originally intended to address the harms that I saw in my own county. Much to my dismay, as I have said before, the district, as well as the surrounding school districts in the First Judicial Circuit, ignored Restorative Justice and peer mediation based programs. Therefore, I want you to understand better, how history, lack of resources, etc. may contribute to what school districts face.

Indeed, Santa Rosa is just another county—probably very much like one near where you live. Resources abound and there has been great success despite numerous instances of conflict outbreaks. As you think of Santa Rosa and how it relates to where you live, consider all of the souls harmed from referrals, suspensions, and trivial in-school offenses resulting in arrests by D.A.R.E. grant-funded law enforcement officers, and various programs. Remember from previous chapters that academics, as well as politicians, were calling for as much as 7% of all juveniles to be arrested and tried yearly for misdemeanor and felony level charges. Recall how they talked about the MacDonald Triad and the fact that juvenile offenders, once arrested, are evaluated to see if they might become future serial killers.

Are you a little bothered that over 1.3 thousand students a year in just a single, small county in Florida have to worry about such things as being cuffed, having a criminal record barring them from future gainful employment, and ultimately being evaluated as serial killers for trivial offenses? Are you a little concerned what something like that would do to a community, its economic base, and its competitiveness over the course of a decade? Has anyone thought of what it does to the "trouble makers" when drawing a simple picture lands them in jail on felony bomb threat charges or where taking a french-fry and saying "bang" lands one in the slammer with hardened criminals, on charges of using a "deadly firearm on school grounds?" What would a child think when his/her community is irrational and dead-set against his/her mere existence? Are you scared yet? It isn't the children who need fearing—it is the adults supporting a broken system that should be feared! That is what the Unbroken Circles [SM] program addresses. The goal is for communities to be made whole where hope and bright futures can be restored.

## Florida's Pop Tart Bill

Until recently, no state was taking the lead in dealing with issues of students being wrongly suspended and expelled. For decades now, schools have been suspending, expelling, and even filing criminal charges against students of all ages. For instance, in Washington, DC schools, Pre-K students receive suspension for offenses such as having bathroom accidents. Ultimately, students are punished for being children.

A seven-year old boy named, Josh Welch, recently made national news and changed how one state looks at certain wrongful actions. Josh's story takes in Baltimore, Maryland. In 2013, officials at Park Elementary School wanted to suspend the second grader for being in possession of a weapon. What was the weapon? School officials said it was a gun. However, this alleged gun was nothing more than a toaster pastry that the boy had nibbled on to look like a gun. Originally, he was trying to nibble the pastry into a mountain but he didn't like how it looked, and then it occurred to him that the treat looked more like a handgun.

After Park Elementary's attempt to suspend Josh, a number of states vowed to stop such tragedies from happening. So-called "Pop Tart" bills were filed in various states. For a while, it looked like legislation would be successful in Oklahoma. However, one-by-one, the bills died on the floor, were tabled, or languished away in committees.

All seemed lost until Florida took this situation seriously with House Bill 7029. In June of 2014, Governor Rick Scott signed into law the first-ever "Pop Tart" legislation. In the new law, which amends Florida §1006.07, it is illegal for school officials to suspend or expel a student for using their hands or food items as an imaginary weapon, using Lego-styled toys as toy guns, drawing a picture of a firearm, and other similar activities. It even exempts students from suspensions and expulsions for having toy guns two inches or less. Students can now wear shirts and clothes with guns on them or that have verbiage in support of the Second Amendment.

In response to this new law, I went on *The Francesco Abbruzzino Show*. As I told Francesco, this law is a great step forward. However, it still has a number of flaws to it. For instance, while a two-inch or less toy gun is allowable, a student still could be conceivably suspended or expelled for having a toy gun that was four inches long. Similarly, nothing in the new law prohibits law enforcement from arresting a child for similar activities. Therefore, a child can't be suspended for drawing a picture of a gun, but a School Resource Officer still has the right and authority to arrest the child on firearms charges.

This may seem illogical but you have to remember that Florida is a top arrester of children. The state takes into custody over 58,000 juveniles a year. This equates to about 7% of the juvenile population per year. Most of the charges stem from school-based arrests with many of the charges because of students drawing pictures, playing with toys, and other similar activities that are covered from suspension and expulsion by the new Pop Tart law.

A great first start, this groundbreaking new law is far from perfect. While acknowledging one issue, it seemingly ignores a whole host of similar, more egregious issues. Even with this promising new law, we cannot rest our faith on the government to bring sanity back to juvenile justice issues and student misconduct. Thus, the community must seek out new ways to handle wrongful actions.

# About Unbroken Circles[SM] – The Concept

Restorative Justice has several concepts that it utilizes. Two, out of the many characteristic traits inherent to all Restorative Practices, are the concepts of "Community of Care" and "Circles."

Modern society tends to see things only from the tangible side. For society, the term community often means a specific group of people tied to a specific geographical region (e.g., neighborhood, city block, region of a county, county, or region of the state,). For Restorative Justice, this idea of community is very problematic, if not useless, in a world that is quickly becoming more mobile, and where people are increasingly leaving behind most traditional trappings of community.

Before we go any further, let us stop here for a minute to evaluate this old understanding of community being tied to a geographic region. We need to understand why geographic location is no longer a valid trait of an active community. For this, I want you to do the "Tic-Tac-Toe Experiment." Roughly, draw out a large "tic-tac-toe" hash mark. Put your house in the center and then your surrounding neighbors in the corresponding spots on the hash mark. Finally, write down the names of your neighbors for each household. Do you notice neighbors that you don't know the names of? About nine of every ten people doing this experiment are unable to tell the names of all of the neighbors surrounding them in the hash mark diagram. This underlines why the concept of community cannot be tied to geography anymore.

Therefore, Restorative Justice Professionals have had to redefine what we see as a community in contemporary society. Many now utilize what they call a "Community of Care" (also known as a "Community of Concern", "Macrocommunities" and "Microcommunites"). What makes a Community of Care vastly different from a traditional concept of community is that it may lack a geographical or cultural definition or grouping type. Communities of Care may span vast distances, cut through an array of cultures, and may not use a quantitative number as a defining trait. A Community of Care may be a family, a group of friends, or a group of caring stakeholders.[14]

Circles are another intrinsic trait of most Restorative Justice Practices. From a group dynamics standpoint, circles make perfect sense as everyone faces each other and no one is over the other. Circles are used in various faiths and social gatherings to denote a sense of oneness. However, the connotation that circles take on, in the Unbroken Circles [SM] program, is more philosophical and intangible. Unbroken Circles [SM] gets its name because the program utilizes a vast number of Communities of Care that hold things in balance. Essentially, if you were to think of Unbroken Circles [SM] as several rubber bands in concentric rings, the Community of Care is the rubber band that keeps the offender from breaking through. Each level is more difficult for the offender to break through because the bands merge and lend greater strength. Therefore, a class member may also be a peer mediation volunteer, and a peer mediation volunteer may be a part of a conference or Circle Justice meeting. In other words, there is always a Community of Care, which never goes away.

Unbroken Circles $^{SM}$ is ultimately comprised of four primary components: Circles, Peer Mediation, Conferences, and Circle Justice. Each component of the program has a place and a purpose. No one portion is superior or inferior to the other. Rather, each component is a complement to the other on a continuum of Collaborative Justice.

The program components are:

- Chart 1        Program Scheme
- Chart 2        Program Deployment Plan
- Chart 3        Middle School Sample
- Chart 4        High School Sample

Though each component will be addressed later on in detail, it should be noted that all components adhere to strict Collaborative Justice philosophies, "respect for all concerned" being the ultimate guiding force followed by "volunteerism of all parties involved." Essentially, all parties must be willing to participate and be mutually respectful of each other, or the process will fail.

**Program Chart 1 – Program Scheme**

|  | Circles | Peer Mediation | Conferencing |
|---|---|---|---|
| **Grades K-4** | Daily morning; mid-day and end of day every other day | Training of principles but no mediations | -- |
| **Grades 5-8** | Daily morning; every other day for mid-day; daily end of day | Training and mediation | As needed |
| **Grades 9-12** | Daily morning; mid-day and evening once a week | Full blown mediations at various levels | Highly utilized |

This chart ultimately gives a better understanding of how the Unbroken Circles ᔆᴹ program is adaptive not only to schools but also to age groups and natural progressions commonly found in the American public and private education systems. For instance, Grades K-4 are given intensive work in circles but only training in the principles of peer mediation. This makes them aware of what peer mediation is while also building interest so they have something to strive for as volunteers once they are old enough. In contrast, Grades 5-8 receive not only the final training, but also, the opportunity to participate in the peer mediation program. Later, at what is commonly known as the high school age range, students are taught to use peer mediation extensively while circles are cut back to allow for additional educational and extracurricular activities. In addition, because higher-level offenses are more likely to occur at the high school level, other programs are employed to compensate as the proverbial "bands" are "stretched."

Naturally, this is only one example of how a school might use the program. Because the program is adaptive to schools it is up to the schools, stakeholders, participants, and a Conflict Resolution Specialist, who is certified in the Unbroken Circles [SM] program, to determine what programs will work best and how.

## Program Chart 2 – Development Plan

| YEAR 1 | Start Circles program in 1-3 middle schools, with at least 1 class participating per school; evaluate teacher input from surveys, make corrections and additions to the program as needed. |
|--------|--------------------------------------------------------------------------------------------|
| YEAR 2 | Have entire grade level for participating school(s) start Circles program; start peer mediation training and assembling a peer mediation corps; evaluate teacher input from surveys and make changes as needed. |
| YEAR 3 | Convert entire participating middle school(s) to the Unbroken Circles program; start up countywide conferencing program; evaluate teacher, administration, and other governmental authority input from surveys and make changes as needed. |
| YEAR 4 | Deploy pilot Unbroken Circles SM programs in elementary and high schools; develop Circle Justice Program; evaluate surveys and make changes as needed. |
| YEAR 5 | Convert entire school system over to Unbroken Circles SM program; create a Restorative Programs Office to oversee training and diversion programs; seek grants to study long-term success rate of program; hold community-visioning meetings to ascertain future long term Restorative Programs. |

This chart ultimately gives a better understanding of how the Unbroken Circles SM program can be employed over an entire school district. Using a slow and evidence-based approach, all stakeholders and participants will be aware of how the program is anticipated to develop over time, as well as what efforts will be made to ensure any concerns are addressed along the way.

For the sake of a starting place, a middle school base is picked since most complaints are usually found in middle and high schools. Virtually any school base can be a start, regardless of the age of the students. Conversely, a school district could very easily do a district-wide start. Naturally, this chart depiction is just a single suggestion. Again, only school district officials, stakeholders, participants, and a person who is skilled and certified in the Unbroken Circles SM program should collaborate and determine what is best for each individual school district.

## Program Chart 3 —Sample Circles Lesson Plan (Middle School)
TEXT: Mikaelsen, Ben (2001). *Touching Spirit Bear*. HarperCollins Publishers:New York, NY

| WEEK | LESSON PLAN |
|---|---|
| 1 | Discussion of Japanese Proverb and Ch. 1-4 <br> ☐   What do you think the proverb means? <br> ☐   What was your first impression of Cole? <br> ☐   What was your first impression of Garvey? <br> ☐   What did you think of Garvey's cake demonstration? <br> ☐   What is your impression of Peter? <br> ☐   What will it take to make Cole behave? |
| 2 | Discussion of Ch. 5-7 <br> ☐   Why was Cole scared to be alone (p. 43)? <br> ☐   Why did Cole not regret his actions? <br> ☐   What do you think of Cole's parents? <br> ☐   Can silence be hurtful (i.e., the mom's silence about Cole being abused)? <br> ☐   Is the spirit bear real? |
| 3 | Discussion of Ch. 8-11 <br> ☐   Why did Cole attack the spirit bear? <br> ☐   Why did Cole's attitude change towards the baby birds? <br> ☐   What do you think will happen to Cole? Why? |
| 4 | Discussion of Ch. 12-13 <br> ☐   Why did the spirit bear come back? <br> ☐   Why didn't the spirit bear attack Cole again? <br> ☐   Was Cole worth saving? Why? <br> ☐   Why did Cole throw away his proof—the hair of the spirit bear? <br> ☐   Would you have thrown away the hair? Why? <br> ☐   Is Cole a changed person? Why? <br> ☐   Have your impressions of Cole changed? Explain. |
| 5 | Discussion of Ch. 14-15 <br> ☐   Did Cole revert to his old self when he was safe from the bear? <br> ☐   Were the members of the Circle Justice right to question Cole so much? <br> ☐   What do you think of Edwin? <br> ☐   How has Cole changed from Chapter 1 of the book? <br> ☐   What is your impression of Cole now? Explain. |
| 6 | Discussion of Ch. 16-21 <br> ☐   What did you think of Edwin's lesson with the pool and the rock? <br> ☐   What is the importance of feasting? <br> ☐   What was the importance of Cole building his lodging? <br> ☐   Are the dances silly? Why do you feel this way? <br> ☐   What was the importance of the spark plug? <br> ☐   Had Cole known that the spark plug was back in, would he have left? Why? |
| 7 | Discussion of Ch. 22-24 <br> ☐   What is the significance of the totem pole? <br> ☐   What did Cole's dance of anger symbolize? <br> ☐   What do you think of Peter's actions? <br> ☐   Is Cole changed? |
| 8 | Discussion of Ch. 25-28 <br> ☐   What did you think of Peter's transformation? <br> ☐   What did you think of Cole not striking back at Peter? <br> ☐   Do you think that the boys are permanently changed? Why? <br> ☐   How did you feel about the book? <br> ☐   Has the book shown you an alternative way of handling problems? <br> ☐   Circle Justice is real. Do you think that it works? <br> ☐   Why do we meet in a circle to discuss this book? <br> ☐   Have you changed since you first read this book? How? |

While Circles are traditionally used to talk about whatever the group wishes, it is not uncommon for the Circle Keeper (i.e., teacher) to employ a study lesson as part of the circle to get the students to understand how core concepts work. In this case, the lesson talks about a book where circles are used to help a troubled boy and his victim make amends. The usage of weeks allows the Circle Keeper to involve the students not only in the discussions but also in the readings. Depending on the adopted schedule for Circle sessions, a Circle Keeper may have a schedule like the one above or go with a revolving schedule. The key is to make it engaging for all involved. Bored, disconnected students do not talk and ultimately will not learn as well. That is why it is critical for the Circle Keeper to look for compelling materials whenever it is necessary and beneficial to the Circle. Ask students to suggest books, movies, and even news articles. Sometimes what is compelling to an adult is not compelling to students. When students get to participate in the growth and development of their Circles, they undergo a sense of "buy-in" where they are now owners of the Circle. This makes for a stronger, more dynamic, and ultimately more effective Circle.

# Program Chart 4 —Sample Circles Lesson Plan (High School)

**MOVIE:** *Firelight* (2012). Hallmark Hall of Fame Productions

| DAY | LESSON PLAN |
|---|---|
| 1 | Discussion of the movie to the parable of the prisoners in the cave<br>☐ How does Caroline end up being arrested? Who sold her out and why?<br>☐ How many years did she get at the special facility? Is that a lot for the crime? Why?<br>☐ How do relationships affect our future? What relationships affected Caroline's future?<br>☐ Why was Caroline called "Butterfly" and what is it supposed to mean?<br>☐ Terry and DJ both warn Caroline about Pedra. Why does Caroline not listen?<br>☐ Explain the Voltaire comment and how it related to DJ's explanation of redemption and reality.<br>☐ What does DJ turn to in order to see things how they should be? Do you have such a thing?<br>☐ What is "The Cave" parable a metaphor of? Why did Terry tell the parable of "The Cave" to Caroline? |
| 2 | Discussion of the movie to just past the butterfly catching scene where Caroline is asked to consider Crew 9<br>☐ How did Nelson Mandela make it through 27 years of prison? What does his explanation mean?<br>☐ Why was DJ worried about the cigarette burns? Who does it remind DJ of?<br>☐ What is the importance of Crew 9?<br>☐ What is the importance of DJ teaching Caroline about "social graces?"<br>☐ What is the quote from Vince Lombardi and why is it important to Caroline? How do you value the quote?<br>☐ What does Caroline ask Terry as payment for the picture? Was it wrong for Caroline to charge Terry? Why?<br>☐ What did Terry do to save her friend? Why?<br>☐ What did the girls do for Terry? Why? Did Terry's character have anything to do with why the girls all were trying to help her?<br>☐ What is the importance of trying new things? How would it help Caroline? How about you? |
| 3 | Discussion of the movie to just after Keisha leaves the facility<br>☐ Who tells the prisoners in "The Cave" parable about the hoax? What is their reaction?<br>☐ How is "owning responsibility" different, or the same, for the girls at the parole hearing?<br>☐ How did the character of Terry's heart change between the March incident and the parole hearing?<br>☐ Terry was denied parole based off a perception. How hard is it to change perceptions? Why? How did a single perception change Terry's own self-perception?<br>☐ Why are goals important for Keisha? Why does DJ tell Keisha to remember Crew 9 when the detention center and all of the experts said to forget everything?<br>☐ What does Terry's comment to Keisha about "deserving" parole mean to you? Do we sometimes need to be made known that we deserve something? Do you do this? Has anyone ever told you this before? |
| 4 | Discussion of the movie to the end<br>☐ Why do people sometimes get mad at other people when they are trying to help them? What does it say about the person in need? What does it say about the person trying to help when they still want to help? Why do you think this interlay happens?<br>☐ Caroline refused to leave Protective Custody despite Terry offering her a way out. Why do you think she wanted to stay in a cage rather than enjoy the freedom that Crew 9 offered?<br>☐ What does it mean to be "part of the solution?"<br>☐ What was the importance of the "standoff" when Pedra and her crew with that of Crew 9?<br>☐ What does "owning one's self" mean and why is it important?<br>☐ For former offenders seeking atonement, how important is it for them to be able to distinguish between how they used to act from the person they are today?<br>☐ Punishment vs. Rehabilitation is a unique paradigm shift. What are the differences between the two? Can they look similar? How can the two fail? How can they succeed? What is your preference between the two and why?<br><br>Homework Assignment: Study the discussion topics (Day 5) and be ready to talk about them |
| 5 | Discussion questions<br>☐ In the 1990s, Professor John DiIulio, Jr. posited a concept called the "super-predator." Over the years, this concept was deemed a myth by multiple academics and government agencies. What is the "super-predator" myth and why is it dangerous for youth? How does it relate to Terry's first parole meeting? Do you still see it in play in your own life? If so, how?<br>☐ Researchers, in the State of Florida, found that, in most of the nation's schools, lower performing students are suspended longer than higher performing students. At present, about 857 students drop out from school each hour of each school day. What is the "Test-to-Prison Pipeline" theory and how valid do you think it is? How do you think this theory applies to juvenile delinquents and youthful offenders Do you see it in play in your own life? If so, how?<br>☐ What are problems that you see in your own school? Your own community?<br>☐ You know some of the problems that affects youth. What solutions do you propose? |

Books are not the only resource that can be used. As the high school circle lesson plan shows, a popular made for television movie was used to for a circle lesson discussion. However, practically anything can be used to convey basic core concepts and clarify understandings. Sometimes, for the sake of practicality, books and movies are used. There may be times when situations arise where news stories and shared incidences are windows of opportunity to introduce, integrate, and refresh concepts and understandings as needed while keeping student bonds and discussions strong and dynamic.

## Statement of Restorative Justice Principles

In the United States, Restorative Justice seems often times to be ill defined. However, in countries where Restorative Justice is legally mandated, there is little doubt about what it embodies. The most defining work so far on Restorative Justice Principles has come from the United Kingdom's Restorative Justice Consortium. As the Consortium aptly notes, there are seven topics governing Restorative Justice. They are:

1. Principles that relate to the interests of all participants

2. Principles that relate only to those who have sustained loss or harm

3. Principles that relate only to those who have caused loss or harm to others

4. Principles that relate to interests of the local community or society

5. Principles that relate specifically to agencies working alongside the judicial system

6. Principles that relate only to the judicial system

7. Principles that relate specifically to restorative justice agencies[15]

For all parties involved, participation must be voluntary and based on informed choice. There must not be any type of discrimination present, regardless of the circumstances of the case. Proper agencies must be available and accessible for help and advice to the participants. Access to various established methods of dispute resolution is required. The process must not compromise the legal rights of individuals. The meetings must be held with a great degree of confidentiality so the views expressed do not prejudice any party in subsequent proceedings. The process needs to insure the personal safety of all participants. Special considerations must be taken for exceptionally vulnerable participants. Moreover, the civil rights and dignity of all participants must be protected and upheld.[16]

For those victims who have sustained a loss or harm, the process must ensure that their personal experiences, needs, and feelings are respected. Acknowledgement of the loss or harm incurred must be acquiesced by all parties involved. Furthermore, there must be recognition of the claim for amends. If the offender is willing, there must be an opportunity for the victim to communicate with the offender. Most importantly, the process ensures that the primary beneficiary of any reparations is the victim.[17] In stark contrast to the conventional, retributive system—the victim has no government entity, acting as surrogate and taking away his/her/their voice(s). Instead, the victim is empowered rather than shut out. His/her voice now has standing and is a determining force in the process.

In regards to the offenders, the process affords them an opportunity to offer reparations, sometimes referred to as atonement, even before there is any formal requirement. The process must ensure that the recompense is appropriate to the harm done and within the capacity of the offender to fulfill the obligation. Lastly, and probably the hardest, the process ensures respect for the dignity of the person making amends.[18] Ultimately, the goal is for the offender to be allowed the opportunity to reassimilate into the community. This would be without, or with reduced, social stigma so that the offender and victim are made as whole as possible. Additionally, the community, too, may heal and be made whole.

The process must take on specific duties with the community so that communities may learn of restorative processes that are conducive to the reduction of crime or harm. The process promotes social harmony as well as respect for cultural diversity, civil rights, social responsibility, and the rule of law.[19] Most importantly, members of the community must be able to address their harms and losses. So often, we only see victim and offender through "black and white" issues. However, communities are dynamic and, therefore, do not exist in a pure "black and white" world. There can be the existence of secondary and tertiary victims in the community. Conversely, there can be contributing offenders to the offense at hand. Stakeholders may have endured harm, which, until discussed, may have gone unnoticed and unaccounted for. Ultimately, the community has a vested interest in the victim(s) and offender(s) as well as all those impacted by the offense.

Agencies working alongside the courts need the process to ensure that acceptable cases are not elevated needlessly to the courts. These agencies require the process to guarantee that legal rights are not compromised. The process also needs to make certain that there is a wide and flexible range of opportunities afforded to the offender to make amends.[20] Ultimately, the justice system has both a financial and moral obligation to require that their resources are used efficiently and effectively, even profoundly, to improve upon the general condition, standing, and safety of the public at large.

The courts require that the primary aim of the process be repair of harm caused and losses incurred. The courts need the process to be fair, appropriate, and workable. In the event that a victim refuses to participate, the courts need assurance that the process will provide opportunities for community reparation or reparations to others who have suffered harm or loss. In the event that the offender refuses to participate, the courts need assurances that community reparations will be enforced. Courts need the process to value cases when offenders voluntarily offer to repair harms or losses. Currently, offering to repair harm is often used against the offender. Importantly, due to legal constraints, the courts absolutely require that the process consider the contents of the meetings, aside from any written and binding agreement, to be privileged and subject to public interest qualifications.[21] Again, the offender's desire to atone for his/her crime should be valued just as much the voice of the victim and the needs of the community. In a dignity for all setting, the shackles of a retributive system can be cast aside so that healing is allowed and all parties have an opportunity to transcend the offense that brought them together. This should ultimately be, and historically was, the aim and duty of the courts.

Restorative Justice Agencies have special needs as well—though rarely talked about in public—let alone professional venues. Nevertheless, the needs, though oft unspoken, are still very much there. For the sake of the practice, they need all processes to embody a commitment to a needs-based practice. These agencies need all practices to safeguard legal human rights. Restorative Justice Practitioners need to be neutral and easily identifiable by the public as such. The actions of Restorative Justice Practitioners/Facilitators must be one of absolute impartiality. Restorative Justice Practitioners/Facilitators must play no other role in the case. It should be understood that the Restorative Justice agencies always keep meeting contents confidential. Restorative Justice Agencies need assurances that, as a practice, weaker parties are properly engaged to give them a fair voice. Respectful behavior should always be upheld. Practitioners must be able to dole out respect equally, regardless of the harm done. Practitioners must demonstrate impeccable ethics when engaging the public. Agencies must have in place a way to handle grievances effectively and fairly. Professionals and agencies will demonstrate a strong commitment for this program and its needs: a) Commitment to the accreditation of training, services, and practitioners. b) Commitment to improve the practices and guidelines of such.[22] c) Commitment to ethics and continual development. These three items, as well as maintaining a professional public impression, are vital to the livelihood, vitality, public support, and respect the program will need in order to continue as a paradigm-shifting alternative to our typically retributive system of governance.

## SNAPSHOT — *Taking a look at the facts*

Failed attempts at increasing school performance and budgets by penalizing low performers is ultimately killing America and placing us in an economic quagmire. The "test-to-prison pipeline" theory has become a reality for many youths all across the country. As these youths have become adults, we are just now feeling the effects of what this wrong-headed approach to education has done to our country. Here is a recap of some facts and figures:

➤ *Each day 7,000 students drop out of school. According to the National Center for Education Statistics' "Private School Universe Study," the length of the average American school year is about 180 days. That equates to about 1.26 million students dropping out each school year.*

➤ *The annual American dropout rate costs our nation $209,000 per dropout in healthcare, welfare, and criminal detention each year. Additionally, the American citizenry incurs $1.5 billion in future losses each school day.*

These figures, however, do not reflect the breakdown of students being affected by occurrence. The graph below shows the breakdown of California's high school dropouts by racial makeup and income.

**2009 California High School Dropouts**

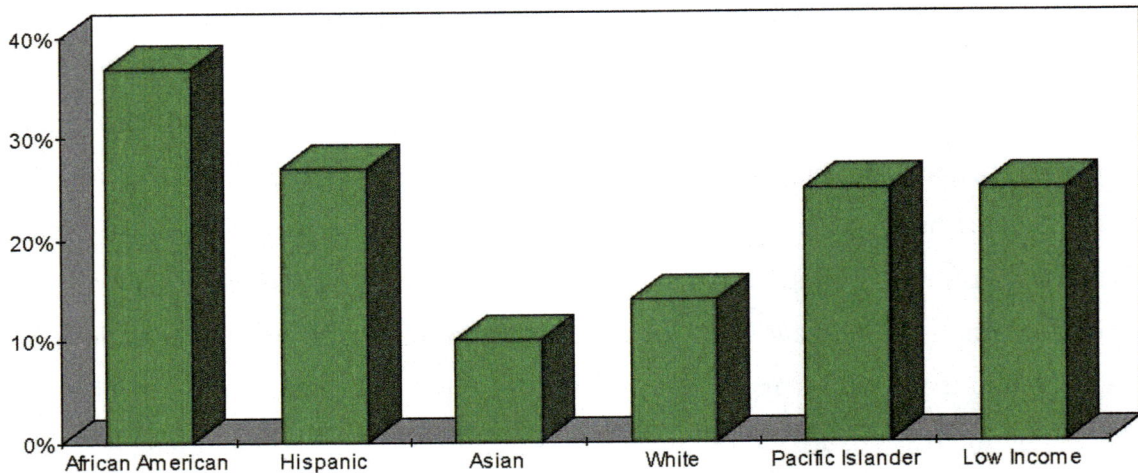

*Source:* **California Department of Education**

## The Dollars and Sense of it All

If armies march on their stomachs then schools teach based off their budgets. During this chapter, we have gone over the basics. However, going over the nuts and bolts of a concept is one thing while the cost is quite another. What proponents of Collaborative Justice efforts often fail to see is that cost savings and cost effectiveness can be an intrinsic component of a plan that merits serious review and analysis.

Many Americans who went to public school probably have a story or two to tell about outdated textbooks. When the USSR fell, it took some school districts nearly a decade to get the funds to replace textbooks, maps, and globes to cite that there was no longer a USSR. The schools simply were too financially strapped to equip every classroom with the basic fundamentals needed to learn about contemporary geography.

In some states, like Florida, funding for schools is directly tied to student performance. This tie is strong. It is common knowledge that Florida students are taught based on FCAT requirements. The livelihoods of the teachers, staff, and school programs are jeopardized each time a test is administered by the state. Not only do these professionals and programs have a stake, the students' futures are also in at risk. Simply put, an "A" student in Florida cannot progress to the next grade level if they have not passed the FCAT.

Ironically, as this issue has climaxed in public discussions, lawmakers in Florida have decided to abandon FCAT for Common Core. New standardized tests will be utilized by state officials. The long-term effects on school funding and students are yet to be seen.

It should not come as a surprise to anyone that public schools, historically, have embraced punitive programs, which either expel or incarcerate poorer performing students in order to clear up budgets and improve test scores. In the 1990s, the D.A.R.E. program and other pro-law enforcement based school, resource-officer programs allowed more juveniles to be incarcerated than all previous decades combined in US history. These programs taught the dangers of "super-predators" out of control. This was based on what is now known as the Super-Predator Myth first hypothesized by Professor John DiIulio, Jr. Ironically, while these programs primarily worked on fear and used made-up, faulty data as proof, true data collected on juvenile offenders found that the number of heinous crimes committed by juveniles was at a twenty-five year low. [23] This, however, did not stop the movement. In some meetings, it was conceived that fewer troublemakers in school would lead to more money and higher test scores. Soon, this idea became a national cry and mantra. After the programs were approved, very little effort was ever made to verify these claims.

Indeed, very little was thought about the well-being of the children. Children growing up in the public school system during the 1990s had impediments to their future, including a low chance of getting into the military or getting federal student aid. Moreover, what was the reason? Many had misdemeanor and felony convictions on their records for "crimes" that they committed as children. Some of the "zero tolerance" crimes were, drawing a picture at school that later resulted in a felony level bomb threat charge, pointing a tater tot at a teacher while saying "bang!" which then resulted in a felony firearms charge. The list goes on.[24]

"Every school day, 7,000 teenagers become high school dropouts," notes the Seattle, Washington-based Choices Education Group.

> With more than 26% of students failing to graduate on time each year in the U.S. we face a growing national crisis. Based on current reports from the National Center for Education Statistics the median income of high school dropouts is 40% lower than those who complete high school. Dropouts are more likely to be unemployed. They tend to be in worse health and they make up a disproportionately higher percent of the nation's prison and death row inmates. These outcomes affect not only them but also all of us when we consider the high social costs and our nation's loss of productivity and economic vitality.

To put things in a clearer light, Choices Education Group notes each dropout costs our nation $209,000 in healthcare, welfare, and criminal detention. Choices Education Group also notes that the American citizenry incurs an additional $1.5 billion in future losses each school day.[25]

New Orleans, Louisiana-based Rethink notes a similar finding stating, "In the United States 857 students drop out of school every hour of every school day. In the state of Florida, researchers proved that students with lower performance get suspended for a longer period of time than higher scoring students." Rethink calls the high dropout rate and the disparity in suspension times the "test-to-prison pipeline." Ultimately, this theory draws a correlation similar to the Choices Education Group findings; students are compelled to become a part of the Criminal Justice system if they are poor performers in school. Ironically, one of the ways that Rethink suggests stopping the "test-to-prison pipeline" is to refer at least five New Orleans area discipline cases each month to a Restorative Justice Circle session. This includes making Restorative Justice options a part of the New Orleans school discipline code, to include holding weekly community building circles and adopting community agreements where discipline and accountability is class specific.[26]

In addition to these issues, a nationally growing interest on the subject of "bullying" has revealed some interesting data. The National School Safety Center says that 90 percent of all students between fourth and eighth grade communicated having been bullied at school. It is estimated that each day some 160,000 students miss school due to fear of being bullied. Ten percent of high school dropouts claim that bullying was a major contributing factor.[27] The Carlsbad, California group, i-Safe, Inc., notes approximately 50 percent of all middle and high school students claim to have been bullied online.[28] The Center for Disease Control and Prevention states that 4,400 students commit suicide each year as a direct result of bullying—making bullying the third largest cause of death for young people in America. For every suicide committed as a result of bullying, it is estimated that another 100 attempts at suicide were made. Bully victims are two to nine times more likely to consider suicide than non-victims are. Nearly 7% of America's young people have attempted suicide with bullying being a primary motivator for many.[29] Bullying in America has become so out of hand that Fox News noted, in an August 3, 2012 news broadcast, how a non-profit was offering free plastic surgery, mostly to young girls, to help stop chronically, persistent bullying.

Restorative Justice-based programs tackle these issues head on. In fact, Restorative Justice Programs have been so successful at improving attendance, improving test scores, lowering disciplinary recidivism, lowering bullying, and more that the Republican National Committee put support of Restorative Justice Programs as a part of their 2012 national platform.

While still unknown in many areas of America, it appears that Restorative Justice Programs are gaining popularity based on a proven record of accomplishment. These programs have a direct effect on grades, attendance, and discipline. They also hit on other issues such as community and civic pride, patriotism, collaboration, team building, and a host of other beneficial elements espoused by academics, business professionals, politicians, teachers, and civic leaders as trademarks of a positive work ethic and sound life skills that lead to positive and productive citizens.

Billions in tax revenue is lost from low-income earning dropouts. Money is spent on failed punitive systems, and even more money goes to house dropouts who have found their way to prisons. It should be a "no-brainer" that school-based Restorative Justice Programs are indeed a socially economic response to bad behavior.

# References

1. Global Development Research Center (2012). *What is Conflict Resolution?* GDRC Programme on Urban Governance. Retrieved on 11/14/2012 from http://www.gdrc.org/u-gov/whatis-conflict-resolution.html

2. Amstutz, L. and Mullet, J. (2005). *The Little Book of Restorative Discipline for Schools: Teaching Responsibility; Creating Caring Climates.* : pp25-26 Intercourse, PA: Good Books

3. Hopkings, B. (2006, Revised 2012). *Restorative Approaches.* Transforming Conflict National Centre for Restorative Approaches in Youth Settings. First retrieved in 2006 and subsequently revision retrieved 8/19/2012 from http://www.transformingconflict.org/content/restorative-approaches-0

4. Hopkins, B. (2012). *Restorative Approaches in Educational Settings: Values-Based —Needs Led.* Transforming Conflict National Centre for Restorative Approaches in Youth Settings. Retrieved on 8/19/2012 from http://www.transformingconflict.org/content/restorative-approaches-educational-settings

5. TEAM Santa Rosa, Inc. (December, 2010). General information request, by author, as to the population and statistical data of Santa Rosa County. Milton, FL: Santa Rosa County Board of Commissioners

6. Ricketts, D. (17 June 2011). *Jobless Rates Continue to Decline in Okaloosa, Walton; Santa Rosa Sees Slight Increase. Northwest Florida Daily News.* Fort Walton Beach, FL:Halifax Media Group

7. TEAM Santa Rosa, Inc. (December 2010). General information request, by author, as to the population and statistical data of Santa Rosa County. Milton, FL: Santa Rosa County Board of Commissioners

8. Porter, C. (2006). Personal interview with Carmella Porter. Pensacola, FL: Mediations Plus

9. .Eddins, B. (2006). Personal interview with the Hon. Bill Eddins, State Attorney for the First Judicial Circuit of Florida. Pensacola, FL: State Attorney Office for First Judicial Circuit of Florida

10. Milstead, J. (2006). Personal interview with Jessica Milstead of Santa Rosa County's Teen Court program. Milton, FL: Teen Court

11. Crissy, D. (2006). Personal interview with David Crissey, Program Facilitator for the Santa Rosa County School Board's Exceptional Student Education program. Milton, FL: Santa Rosa School Board

12. Santa Rosa School Board (18 August 2012). *Santa Rosa County District Schools.* Retrieved on 8/18/2012 from https://www.santarosa.k12.fl.us/schools.html

13. Amstutz, L. and Mullet, J. (2005). *The Little Book of Restorative Discipline for Schools: Teaching Responsibility; Creating Caring Climates.* Good Books: Intercourse, PA

Bazemore, G. and Walgrave, L. Eds.(1999). *Restorative Juvenile Justice: Repairing the Harm of Youth Crime.* Criminal Justice Press: Monsey, NY

Bazemore, G. and Schiff, M. Eds. (2001). *Restorative Community Justice: Repairing Harm and Transforming Communities.* Anderson Publishing: Cincinnati, OH

Bazemore, G. and Schiff, M. (2005). *Juvenile Justice Reform and Restorative Justice: Building Theory and Policy From Practice.* Willan Publishing: Portland, OR

Crawford, A. and Newburn, T. (2003). *Youth Offending and Restorative Justice: Implementing Reform in Youth Justice.* Willan Publishing: Portland, OR

Hayden, A. (2001). *Restorative Conferencing Manual of Aotearoa New Zealand: He Taonga no a Tatou Kete (A Treasure From Our Basket).* District Courts of New Zealand: Wellington, NZ

Johnstone, G. Ed. (2003). *A Restorative Justice Reader: Texts, Sources, Context.* Willan Publishing:Portland, OR

McLaughlin, E., Gergusson, R., Hughes, G. and Westmarland, L. Eds. (2003). *Restorative Justice:Critical Issues.* Sage Publications: London, UK

Roche, D. (2003). *Accountability in Restorative Justice.* Oxford Press: Oxford, UK

Zehr, H. (1990). *Changing Lenses: A New Focus for Crime and Justice*. Herald Press: Scottdale,　PA

Zehr, H. (2002). *The Little Book of Restorative Justice*. Good Books: Intercourse, PA

14. Restorative Justice Consortium of the UK (March 2002). *Statement of Restorative Justice Principles.* Retrieved on 8/20/2012 from http://www.mediate.com/pfriendly.cfm?id=1025

15. Restorative Justice Consortium of the UK, March 2002, Principle 1

16. Restorative Justice Consortium of the UK, March 2002, Principle 2

17. Restorative Justice Consortium of the UK, March 2002, Principle 3

18. Restorative Justice Consortium of the UK, March 2002, Principle 4

19. Restorative Justice Consortium of the UK, March 2002, Principle 5

20. Restorative Justice Consortium of the UK, March 2002, Principle 6

21. Restorative Justice Consortium of the UK, March 2002, Principle 7

22. Schiraldi, V. (5 February 2001). *Will the Real John DiIulio Please Stand Up.* Washington, DC:Washington Post Newspaper

23. Johnson, Kenneth (2006 to 2012).　Personal Interviews and Research.

24. Choices Education Group (20 July 2014). Retrieved on 7/20/2014 from www.choices.org

25. Kids Rethink New Orleans Schools (20 July 2014). Retrieved on 7/20/2014 www.therethinkers.org

26. National School Safety Center (20 July 2014). Retrieved on 7/20/2014 www.schoolsafety.us

27. i-Safe, Inc. (20 July 2014). Retrieved on 7/20/2014 www.isafe.org

28. Bullying Statistics (20 July 2014). Retrieved on 7/20/2014 www.bullyingstatistics.org

# 1.4

## Core Challenges in Schools - Knowing the Enemy

While I would like to delve right into the program itself, it is important to actually know, and openly discuss, the multitude of problems that schools are presently facing. Already, we have covered a snippet of the problems that schools have to deal with. However, the true complexity of the challenges facing schools is something that no chapter, or even a book for that matter, could adequately address.

With that said, there are key areas of concern that schools spend vast resources dealing with. There are also items to address because we, as a society, spend copious amounts of money, time, and critical social services addressing them.

We are all in a partnership with one another; this includes the students. Yes, I said students. For far too long, they have been considered the enemy by society. In addition, as the popularity for performance-based school funding grows, a number of schools view certain demographic segments of the student population to be enemies. This, however, is not the case.

Every child has a right to a quality education without fear of social stigma, harassment, or the perception-laden judgments that morph into self-fulfilling prophecies. Children today are born into situations that are out of their control.

We expect them to know better, but sometimes the only structure and rationality that they get in life is that brief period when they are in the classroom. However, even the notion of a stable, five-hour class schedule is ludicrous. Think of it this way, each teacher usually has from 15-35 students per class. By the time students are seated, class roll is called, students are quieted down, disruptions are handled, individual questions are answered for students, students are made ready for going to the next class, lunch, actual teaching time is reduced. The average student might get as little as an hour to an hour and a half of actual structured instruction. This period isn't just for one class subject but for all subjects that the student was taught that day.

Nevertheless, getting a quality education is often the least of their worries. For far too many, getting a nutritious meal is a major daily concern. As a society, we have gone from a two parent married couple, to a divorced family with shared parenting, to absentee dads, to unknown dads, to absentee moms, to now having a grandmother or aunt or uncle or older sibling, hopefully, providing shelter for a thrown away generation. Children all over America have to come to school unbathed in tattered and unwashed clothing, wearing shoes that do not fit or have holes, dealing with untreated, medical ailments and the list goes on. In a world that is supposed to be run by responsible adults, no one is taking responsibility for their development. The present situation is enough to make any responsible, freethinking person sick to his/her stomach. This is the best country in the world. Surely, this terrible ordeal can be transmuted if we take our disdain for the situation and put it to good use. One way to do this is to reaffirm ownership of our community. We must not betray our most vulnerable citizens—our future!

Therefore, I am certain and specific when I say, the children are stakeholders in all of this. Similarly, so is everyone in the community. Yes, it appears that I think society is the enemy. In reality, society is the great hope because all societies, just or corrupt, are based on people working with notions and preconceptions. The "enemy" in all of this isn't the people, the students, or the institutions. Rather, the "enemy" is a wrong-headed approach and values system. Unbroken Circles[SM] works to fix this with collaborative practices that bring resolution, inclusion, and ultimately holistic transformation of the school community of care.

## The Status of Students in American Families

We have alluded to the problems students have. In previous chapters, we talked about theories suggesting that school systems in America may inappropriately handle these issues by suspending or expelling students rather than helping them. Today, what are students in America really dealing with? After all, knowing this will tell us what the schools ultimately need to do.

According to Columbia University's National Center for Children in Poverty (NCCP), the federal government considers poverty to be $23,021, or less, a year in income for a family of four to live off. Therefore, anyone living in such a situation is considered by the federal government to be impoverished. Presently, about 22% of our nation's children, which equates to about sixteen million children, meet the federal definition of living in poverty. However, as the NCCP notes, research has proven that families need twice this income level just to meet the basic needs of raising a child. Therefore, it is safer to say that 45% of our nation's children are low-income since their families are finding it difficult to meet the basic needs of raising a child. Research has indicated repeatedly that children raised in poverty or low-income homes have greater difficulty learning, which can contribute to social, emotional, and behavioral problems later on in life. This usually is exacerbated by the family's inability to meet physical and mental health demands the child may have. The younger a child is the more harmful and long lasting the effects of poverty can be on them. The three highest risk groups are American Indians, African Americans, and Latinos. To put this in perspective, in my home state of Florida, the NCCP reports that 45% of Florida's children are low income with 65% of all Florida's children having parents with nothing more than a high school diploma or GED. California does not do much better with 43% of their children living in low-income homes and a total of 62% of the parents having only a high school diploma or GED. Texas fairs a little better with 48% of their students in low-income families and 57% of their parents having only a high school diploma or GED.[1]

So, why use the states of Florida, California, and Texas? Ultimately, these three states determine the educational systems of America. While California and Florida rule the world of standardized testing procedures and performance-based education policies in America—Texas is the one state that determines which textbooks end up in our nation's schools. These "Big Three" states are considered the foundation of all present and future American educational policy, purchases, and operation. Thus, we look at these "Big Three" to see the state of our nation's educational system, and we focus on them to change things we see wrong with our educational system.

Another telling thing not mentioned is that the figures rarely tell other key data. This missing data can often be even more revealing. For instance, it is difficult to find data that accurately tells the level of education for parents of children in low-income families. While Florida has a 25% rate of the adult population with a bachelor's degree, a great deal of that percentage cannot find work or they are underemployed. According to the Economic Policy Institute, 8.7% of all workers with a bachelor's degree or higher, are underemployed. Roughly, 17% of all American workers, regardless of their education, are underemployed. If you are African American that rate jumps to a whopping 24.5% and Hispanics have a slightly less underemployment rate of 23.9%.[2] When you look at the NCCP data, their budget calculations are based on no debts. While the NCCP pushes for greater education in America, it fails to mention the enormous cost of student debt facing American households. The Center for American Progress notes that the cost of obtaining a degree in America has increased by 1,000% over the past 30 years. The average student loan debt for a bachelor's degree is $25,000, while one in ten has student loan debts higher than $54,000. Of these numbers, 81% of African American students are burdened with student loan debt while 67% of Latinos face a similar situation. Today, the student loan debt in America now exceeds $1 trillion.[3]

What does this mean? If a low-income family has a parent with a bachelor's degree or higher, the debt the family is saddled with makes the family worse off than families with no degree. In addition, according to the Federal Reserve Bank of New York, student loan debt is not the only cause for families to worry. The American public is presently shouldering over $730 billion in car loan debt and over $693 billion in credit card debt.[4] In particular, car loan debt is probably the hardest to fight since a car is so vital to the income of the home. Reliable transportation is not a want but rather a necessity. With the relative ease of unsecured debt to inexperienced borrowers, credit card debt can be the hardest debt for borrowers to understand and get a handle on. Moreover, these figures do not address payday loans and those of similar ilk which have super-inflated interest rates that bury the borrowers in insurmountable debt.

For this reason, many low-income and impoverished families are also homeless. According to the National Center on Family Homelessness, over 1.6 million children in America are homeless. These children are four times more likely than other children to be sick. Risks in this group for ear infections are twice as high. Homeless children are four times more likely to have respiratory infections and asthma. In addition, they are five times more likely to have gastrointestinal problems. Then again, they are also twice as likely to go hungry and, ironically, more likely to be obese due to nutritional deficiencies. Of course, there is also the issue of violence and developmental issues. Some 83% of homeless children become exposed to at least one serious act of violent crime by the age of twelve. Roughly one-quarter of all homeless children have witnessed serious family violence. These, and other reasons, increase the likelihood of homeless children experiencing emotional and behavioral problems by three times. Homeless children, in America, are four times more likely to show delayed development and twice as likely to have learning disabilities.[5]

Income, disposable income, and housing are all issues that affect children—this affects schools. However, nothing can have an impact on children, and therefore schools, like the makeup of a family unit. As Dr. John E. Desrochers noted in his National Association of School Psychologists article, *Divorce: A Parents' Guide for Supporting Children*, over one-half of all first time marriages end in divorce. Two-thirds of all divorces involve children. While 80% of these children will one day cope with the harms caused by the divorce, the other 20% will have life-long mental and behavioral health issues. According to Dr. Desrochers, "As adults these people are twice as likely to experience mental illness, substance abuse, and failed relationships. In children, warning signs of coping difficulties can include problems in sleeping or eating, increased anger or sadness, fears, or regression."[6] This is alarming since one-third of all people who divorced in 2008 remarried and went through a divorce again in 2010. Approximately one-third of all new marriages form stepfamilies in America, which can lead to future break-ups and other stepfamilies. Using national data, 60% of all second marriages end in divorce while 73% of all third marriages dissolve.

Studies have found that a stepfamily has three times the stress level than a first marriage family. A major source of stress is how the new marriage affects the children.[7] This is one reason about 26.3% of

America's children are being raised by a single parent.[8] The average American child is, at some point in his/her life, going to be subject to a divorcing family unit. For most of this transition time, as national data suggests, the children are not given a stable male role model. Psychologists now suggest this is a key issue in childhood development and social adaptation in adversity. An article in the *Journal of Research on Adolescence (2004)* said that males raised in a fatherless home, and without a positive male influence in their lives, are twice as likely to go to jail or prison. According to the US Department of Health and Human Services, approximately 63% of youth suicides in America relate to the lack of a positive male influence in the life of a child from a broken home. The Center for Disease Control says 85% of all behavioral disorder cases in children come from broken homes. The National Principals Association did a study on the state of America's high schools and found that 71% of all high school dropouts came from a fatherless home that lacked a positive male influence. The *American Sociological Review (1991)* published an article noting children from fatherless homes, and without a positive male influence, had lower academic desires and reported lower academic expectations from their parents. Indeed, one finds sexual identity confusion, aggression, poverty, and a host of other profound issues that are destroying our society and culture are directly attributed to one thing—the lack of a positive male influence in the life of a child.[9] This, by default, translates into issues that the school systems of America have to deal with.

One of the greatest and most underreported phenomenon that affects children in America today is molestation. Up to 16% of our nation's youth are abused, molested, or mal-treated each year. Approximately 15% of our children are neglected while 10% of our girls and 5% of our boys suffer from severe sexual abuse. Only 1 in 10 cases are reported to, and/or verified by, child abuse reporting authorities.[10] This translates to 3.3 million reports of child abuse, involving over 6 million children, reported to authorities. That is one report of abuse every 10 seconds! In America, five children die every day due to abuse. As much as 60% of those deaths are never reported as such on their death certificates. More than 90% of children who are sexually abused know the sexual predator, and roughly 30% of abused children ultimately grow up to abuse their own children. Some 80% of 21 year olds, who were abused or neglected as children, have at least one psychological disorder. Abused children have a 25% chance of an unwanted teen pregnancy. As many as two-thirds of adults in treatment for substance abuse claim to have been abused as children. Prison data reports that 14% of male inmates and 36% of female inmates claim abuse as children. Further investigation into criminal justice reports find that 59% of juveniles arrested in America were victims of child abuse and molestation themselves. These same juvenile offenders are 28% more likely to be arrested as adult offenders and 30% more likely to commit future, more violent crimes as an adult. The cost of abuse and neglect in America related to this was $124 billion for the fiscal year 2008 alone.[11]

To put things in perspective, regardless of income or mal-treatment, there were over 1.9 million juveniles arrested in America in 2009 alone. From 2005 to 2009, over 10.84 million juveniles were arrested in America.[12] In 2008, nearly 7% of all girls between 15 and 19 became pregnant. In Mississippi, where teen pregnancy rates are the highest, some counties report rates as high as 111 teen pregnancies per year for every 1,000 girls. Studies suggest that teen births beget future teen births in their offspring—therefore, a dangerous cycle is set into action with each teen pregnancy.[13] Concerning substance abuse, a 2007 survey of juveniles aged twelve and older revealed that 19.9 million were users of illicit drugs, 28.6% reported using tobacco, and 14.4 million reported using marijuana. In 2008, another survey revealed that 15.4% used Vicodin.[14]

These findings not only show how much we have ignored our children, but they also show a snippet of what the state of student health is in the U.S. Our children are more vulnerable now than possibly at any point in American history. Nearly half come from families that financially are having difficulties meeting basic needs. Up to a quarter of the juvenile population comes from unplanned teen pregnancies. Over half of America's juvenile population presently has to deal with broken home situations with no stable family unit in place. Some school classes report having nearly all of their class as victims of child abuse and sexual molestation—linked to both low income situations as well as broken home situations. This has led to a vast majority developing mental health, behavioral health, and sociological development and coping issues. The consumer market and need for physical needs to be met has also led many to develop issues of low-impulse gratification, which only leads to the development of poor life skills development. These vulnerable students are using sex, alcohol, drugs, and whatever else they can to cope with the life they have been dealt. Moreover, for better or worse, it is what our education system now must deal with.

## Bullying

When writing this book, I did not want to display the "already known." Instead, I wanted to highlight what is in plain sight and showcase modes of thought. We know that tardiness, absenteeism, class disruption referrals, fighting, insubordination, and low student performance are issues in schools. Bombarding you with statistics on such things would be pointless, nothing more than a book filler. Instead, I wanted to shed light on why this may be happening and unveil ways of approaching the matter. In regards to contemporary school reform writings, it appears that the experts wish to talk about "bullying." The problem, however, is few authors are appropriately framing the issue with usable data. After all, I remember growing up, like most Americans, having to deal with bullies. They were never fun, but they were viewed as a part of childhood development. Many of us were taught to confront them, "Give them a good slug between the eyes," ignore them, and a host of suggestions that may not necessarily be applicable to contemporary bullying situations.

There are multiple definitions out there attempting to explain bullying. The federal government says that bullying is an aggressive behavior that involves a real or perceived power imbalance. It is a repeated pattern or has the potential to be a repeated pattern, and it can cause serious lasting problems. It can be verbal, social, or physical. It is typified by making threats, defamation of character through the spread of rumors, and even exclusion of the victim from social groups and gatherings.[15] While this is surely a more comprehensive understanding of bullying, one definition, which I tend to favor, simply defines bullying as the theft of another person's power and control over their own self-determination. Wow! Although it is not as specific as the federal definition, the latter definition is very telling when applied to the state of students in the United States. Over half of America's juvenile population is already having issues concerning self-determination, and then a bully steps in and wants to make matters worse. How harmful is bullying, really?

According to the federal government, bullying affects the victims, the offenders, and the bystanders. Victims of bullying can have issues of depression, anxiety, problems sleeping, increased feelings of loneliness or sadness, changes in appetite, loss of interest in past time activities, health complaints, decreased academic performance, and an unwillingness to attend school that may lead to dropping out altogether. The mental health, behavioral, and social development issues caused by bullying may carry over into adulthood. For a small percentage, the victim may resort to using drastic physical force. School shooting perpetrators have typically been linked with having been previously bullied themselves. Bullies, on the contrary, are profiled by the federal government as typically having:

a) substance abuse issues,

b) anger management issues leading to fights and vandalizing property,

c) attendance issues in school that may one day lead to dropping out of school,

d) engagement in sexual activity at an early age,

e) possible criminal past or present/future traffic citations, and

f) abusive to romantic partners, family, and children.

Bystanders, whom most officials usually discredit as being valid parties in such issues, are affected as well. According to the federal government's profile of bystanders, they are typified as developing an increased use of substances (i.e., tobacco, alcohol, drugs) after witnessing a bullying event, mental health issues that may also result in depression or anxiety, and bouts of tardiness/absenteeism that occur for no apparent reason. Ironically, the federal government is quick to point out that any link between bullying and suicide developed due to the media's coverage of the subject. Instead, they note that there can be a host of issues causing juveniles to commit suicide. They also note this when reporting the at-risk groups for suicide. These special at-risk groups are children who are depressed, victims of child abuse/molestation, juveniles with no sound family structure in place, those with a sexual orientation other than heterosexual, and minorities.[16]

The "at-risk" groups the government speaks of typify about 40% to 60% of the juvenile population at any given time for four out of the five at-risk categories. Ultimately, the federal government may be correct when stating that bullying, in and of itself, does not cause a juvenile to want to commit suicide. However, officials are neglectful, at best, by not at least inferring that bullying is a potential catalyst that can lead an already troubled, and quite sizeable percentage of the, juvenile population to follow through with pending thoughts of suicide.

To exemplify what we are talking about here, let's look at a Center for Disease Control study of 15,000 high school kids. This study gives a "best case scenario" since government studies have typically under-reported and understated findings that academics usually report with larger and more diversified samplings. As Meghan Neal of the *New York Daily News*, reported in her piece on teen suicides, "Nearly 1 in 6 high school students has seriously considered suicide, and 1 in 12 has attempted it." Ms. Neal goes on to report,

> More female teens than males have attempted or considered suicide, the survey found. The rate was highest among Hispanic females as 13.5% and lowest among white males at 4.6%. Students struggled with suicide more during the first two years of high school—roughly ages 14-16. Rates dropped off slightly when students reached junior and senior year.

Ms. Neal also noted that the rates have been climbing steadily, "from 6.3% in 2009 to 7.8% in 2011, numbers which reflects the trend gaining national attention as more teen suicides are reported as a result of bullying."[17] What the CDC, nor Ms. Neal, failed to note is that most states do not allow juveniles to drop out of school until they have reached the age of sixteen. Therefore, comparing and correlating national high school dropout rates with the drop in interest of suicide by juniors and seniors who were aged sixteen and over is a bit misleading and deceptive since a substantial portion of the sampled cannot legally drop out of school. Along these same lines, when gender is concerned, there tends to be a general misrepresentation of the facts concerning vocalized thoughts and attempts versus those of actual suicides. Often, nothing is said about the percentage who successfully commit suicide—which overwhelmingly is male.

To put things in a different light, according to the Youth Suicide Prevention Program (YSPP), based out of the State of Washington, suicide rates are the highest in the gay, lesbian, bisexual, and transgendered communities. Here, 30% per year report at least one suicide attempt, and more than 50% of the transgendered community reported trying to commit suicide by their 20th birthday. Just in the state of Washington, approximately two youths kill themselves each week. Nearly one-quarter of Washington's 10th grade population, and over one-half of the 12th grade population, report being bullied and feelings of hopelessness, almost every day for two weeks in a row.[18] The YSPP notes what one would expect from the CDC survey. Looking at high school dropout rates, suicidal thoughts, as well as bullying, one sees it progresses through high school rather than regressing as the CDC survey indicates.

The federal government attacks the issue of bullying from a legalistic standpoint—much like what we talked about in previous chapters with the 1990s assault of juveniles and the DiIulio Super-predator Myth. On October 26, 2010, CNN reported that the federal government was speaking out against bullying and specifically noting how bullying attacks federally protected civil rights. The federal government even threatened school administrators indicating they would cut federal funding for failing to report bullying properly based on gender and race. As President Barack Obama noted, the nation must "dispel the myth that bullying is just a normal rite of passage or an inevitable part of growing up."[19] Sadly, for all of President Obama's wise vision casting for the issue, he is a poor student of history. His administration has started pursuing this issue using the same wrong concepts and programs, that his predecessor, President George W. Bush, used in the 1990s with faith based programs and the DiIulio Super-Predator Myth.

If the President, as well as other officials, would look at the data, they would find that it is very clear. The same set of situations makes a bully and a victim. It is the old axiom of "fight or flight" revisited and actualized in our juvenile community. Given the same set of circumstances of unmet needs, neglect, abuse/molestation, and mental/emotional health issues, some segments of the population become aggressively extroverted and regressively introverted as a part of the human coping mechanism. Therefore, the problem is not an issue of further demonizing, further victimizing a neglected segment of the community. Rather, confront offenders with their wrong doings and afford them the dignity to speak on their own behalf, giving them an opportunity to address their issues. This offers the chance to understand the offense itself, the harm caused to the victim, the community structure, the needs of the offenders, and a path to reintegration in the community structure. It provides reintegration as a whole person without social stigmas attached to the former offender.

A community-style collaborative approach is viewed as the correct path to go. This means all parties involved must be properly trained, educated, and sensitive to the contemporary issues at hand involving bullies. One topic that most bullying resources fail to address is adult bullying of students. In 2005, Drs. Stewart W. Twemlow and Peter Fonagy wrote a groundbreaking but under publicized article about teacher-based bullying. In their research, they found teachers who reported a high degree of bullying students had a childhood history of being bullied. The bullying by teachers, and their pro-bullying attitudes and perceptions, was found to foster problems in psychologically and behaviorally, troubled students that promoted bullying traits in students and helped to create a high degree of bullying in schools with an already high level of behavioral problems. The researchers also noted that teachers who reported they bullied students were found in schools who reported high levels of bullying. Thus, a correlation was made that part of a school's bullying levels was inherent to the childhood past, and, therefore, pro-bullying beliefs, of the instructional staff.[20]

## Generational Cycle of Violence

One of the greatest problems when tackling issues in our educational system is most school districts are insensitive to the concept of the Generational Cycle of Abuse. The Generational Cycle of Abuse is a well-accepted and understood concept about child abuse, which simply notes that children who grow up abused will most likely become abusers themselves.

Crisis Connection, Inc., the Indiana-based non-profit on abuse and domestic violence, notes that the home is actually the least safe place for children to be when it comes to witnessing and being a part of a violent act. Using data from the National Coalition Against Domestic Violence, Crisis Connection notes that, "In homes where one parent perpetrates violence against the other parent, the children are abused at a rate 1500% higher than the national average." According to US Senate testimony data pulled by Crisis Connection, "Little boys who grow up in homes where domestic violence is occurring are 100 times more likely to become abusers than boys in violence-free homes." This is telling when one realizes "81% of men who batter had fathers who abused their mother." Additionally, "as violence against the woman becomes more severe and more frequent in a home, the children experience a 300% increase in physical abuse by the adult male abuser." For this reason, according to Crisis Connection's own research,

63% of young men 11-20 years of age who are serving time for homicide have killed their mother's abuser" which means "a history of child abuse increases a person's likelihood of being arrested by 53%." Crisis Connection also notes that, "A child's exposure to the father abusing the mother is the strongest risk factor of transmitting violent behavior from one generation to the next." They are careful to also note that, "Children who experience violence at home often turn this violence out on the community. A high percentage of juvenile delinquents are battered children. 80% of men in prisons grew up in violent homes." Because of this, " teenagers from violent homes turn to drugs and/or alcohol for release and comfort. Many escape into early and poor marriages and/or pregnancies.

This further carries out the cycle of abuse.[21]

It is important to note that the Cycle of Generational Abuse is different from the understanding of conflict posited to you in Chapter 1.2. Whereas Chapter 1.2 gave a history of conflict and explained the reasons why people may hold certain positions, the Cycle of Generational Abuse has no justifiable rationale behind it. Returning to the Lohman Cabbage Conflict Model, note that the "core" of unresolved conflict could grow "seed" to spread to others. The Cycle of Generational Abuse is this understanding of the Lohman model in its most heinous form—children witnessing, and/or suffering from, abuse only to later grow up to be abusers themselves.

This adds another layer to the issues that schools must face. Moreover, it colors the understanding of what and who a victim is versus an offender. It blurs lines and complicates matter. For this reason, if all parties are to be made as whole as is possible—what the ancient Hebrews called a state of shalom or all-rightness—these underlying issues must be addressed in addition to any contemporary wrong doings that are being dealt with currently.

## Discussion

When looking at implementing a pro-Restorative Justice style program, using Collaborative Justice tactics, one has to re-evaluate methodologies and perceptions. Collaborative Justice Programs, like the Unbroken Circles [SM] program, tend to view problems from a holistic perspective. It is not just a matter of wrong versus right or offender versus victim. The point of view that such programs take, in the case of a harm done, is that everyone is harmed. Additionally, everyone has needs. Only by addressing the harms and needs, in a collaborative and inclusive environment, can the situation be transcended.

It has been said that there are more psychology students in college today than there are jobs waiting for them when they graduate. However, the US Department of Labor projects that school psychologists will grow by 22% between 2013 and 2020. With only a 1.4% unemployment rate, and a critical shortage, this field was listed as the #1 Social Services job for 2013 in the *US News & World Report* Best Jobs of 2013.[22]

The world of education has changed drastically in the past twenty years. We see mass shootings, suicide rates that exceed homicide rates in teens, and an essential change in the makeup of the historical family structure paradigm. We see a population that is facing socio-economic issues like those that this country has never seen before. It is not enough to focus just on grades, tardiness, absenteeism, skipping classes, etc. There are deep-rooted issues that intertwine with other deep-rooted issues. Therefore, it should be understood that no school should even start such a Collaborative Justice program without consulting with a school psychologist or mental health professional.

Ideally, a school psychologist or mental health specialist is fully involved with the final program. Just as you will read in the next chapter about creating a peer mediation board, it is strongly suggested that the school establish a peer counseling team as well. When I was in high school, peer counseling was still in its infancy. I co-founded a peer-counseling club called Students Against Violence in Education (SAVE). Through SAVE, at-risk teens could talk with a contracted mental health counselor or choose to talk with specially trained peer counselors. Peer counselors reported to me that students confided profound issues they were able to assist in resolving. I personally attest that I served as a counselor during a major period of grief for the school, helping teens with substance abuse issues and helping students victimized by family members. I also handled complex cases of suicide attempts in troubled teens—with the assistance of a qualified mental health counselor.

It has been said that the contemporary culture of America is one of a victimized society where everyone seemingly is a victim. The belief is, if a teen does not get a brand new car, and his/her other friends do, then the teen has been victimized by his/her parents. This is not what I am supporting or proposing in this chapter. There is a distinct line between true victimization and vulnerability and just being spoiled and whiney. Complaining about not getting a new car and having to ride the bus to school is nothing more than the actions of someone that is spoiled. Riding the bus does not hurt a person. Living out of a bus or car where your only meal may be what one gets from school is different. That has the hallmark of someone who might end up as a victim or troubled person later on in life. We must be able to see the differences and understand perceived harm versus real harm.

For that reason, peer counselors are an ancillary tie-in service that not only assist the program but also assist students desperately in need. The service allows students, who may not have any frame of reference, to gain understanding and support in times of need. The peer-counseling program is for the students. The school psychologist, in relation to the program, is for the health of the educational structure and ensures that the program is appropriately handling issues in a healthy manner. Ultimately, in an ideal world, the school psychologist is an intimate part the program so that both victims and offenders are evaluated and counseled in an on-going manner until the matter is resolved. The school psychologist also routinely evaluates staff, teachers, and administrators to make sure that attitudes and activities are conducive to the environment that the program strives to foster.

## SNAPSHOT   *Taking a look at the facts*

### *What is Bullying?*

Bullying is typified as an aggressive and intentional action to do harm. It is done repeatedly and can cover long periods of time. It is most characterized as an imbalance of power within an interpersonal relationship. Bullying comes in two forms: Direct and Indirect. Direct Bullying is typified as physical (i.e., hitting, kicking, choking, pushing) and/or verbal (i.e., name calling, taunting, threatening, slandering) in nature. Meanwhile, Indirect Bullying is typified as being a subtle manifestation of power imbalance where face making, manipulating relationships with others, social isolation, and other such actions are taken to victimize the target. Lately, a new trend in Indirect Bullying has taken place called Cyber Bullying where technology has been used in the form of cell phones, tablets, computers, social media sites, etc. The difference between historical bullying (Direct and Indirect) versus that of Cyber Bullying is that the bully can attack the victim 24/7 and postings are generally easy to disseminate while extremely difficult for victims to have deleted.

### *Where Does Bullying Happen?*

Historically, bullying has taken place in classrooms, on playgrounds, in gyms, in locker rooms, in hallways, and in bathrooms. Historically, such occurrences have been up to three times more likely to happen at school than traveling to and from school. However, Cyber Bullying has been on the rise, with as many as 16% of high school students (grades 9-12) reporting in 2011 that they were bullied electronically within the past year.

### *What are the Harms Caused by Bullying?*

The initial harms reported are usually victim-centric and generally include reports of the victim abusing substances, skipping school, unwillingness to attend school, poor academic performance, reports of health problems, and depression/self-esteem issues. However, the harm caused by bullying is far more dynamic. Researchers are now showing both short and long-term issues for the victims, long-term issues for the bullies, and even harm caused to on-lookers and the local community structure.

For the victims of bullying, there are certain distinct effects that can be actualized and manifested because of the bullying event(s). From a short-term perspective, the victim may feel emotional pain and confusion. Feelings of anxiousness and loss of security may later develop; this may further decay into issues of severe negative viewing of one's self and potential. This may include psychosomatic symptoms involving stomach aches and other health issues. Finally, this may lead to depressive thoughts and even suicide. From a long-term perspective, the victim, as an adult, may have issues of lowered self-worth, self-esteem, and depression at higher rates than their non-victimized counterparts.

Bullies are not immune to the harms of bullying. Especially male bullies are prone to antisocial and delinquent behaviors that only grow into adulthood. Physical bullies during childhood run a moderate risk of committing serious violence between the ages of 15 and 25. By the age of 24, people who were bullies as children have a four times greater chance of crime conviction than non-bullies.

Communities are also affected. Schools, where bullying is heightened, report that students are less willing to attend school and participate in activities. If bullying is not addressed early on, schools may experience heightened bullying activity as students learn to see it as acceptable behavior.

99

*Sources:*

Center for the Study and Prevention of Violence (2001). *Safe Communities —Safe Schools: Fact Sheet.* Institute of Behavioral Science. Publication FS-SC07. University of Colorado:Boulder, CO

Stopbullying.gov (2013). *What is Cyber Bullying.* Retrieved on 1/18/2013 from http://www.stopbullying.gov/cyberbullying/what-is-it/index.html

# References

1.  The National Center for Children in Poverty (12 January 2013). *National Center for Children in Poverty*. Columbia University's Mailman School of Public Health. Retrieved on 2/1/2013 from www.nccp.org

2.  *Economic Policy Institute (15 February 2012). Economy Track. Retrieved on 2/15/2013 from www.economytrack.org*

3.  *Johnson, A.; Van Ostern, T. and White, A. (25 October 2012). The Student Debt Crisis. Center for American Progress.* Retrieved on 1/13/2013 from http://www.americanprogress.org/issues/higher-education/report/2012/10/25/42905/the-student-debt-crisis/

4   Brown, M.; Haughwout, A.; Donghoon, L.; Mabutas, M. and van der Klaauw, W. (5 March 2012). *Grading Student Loans*. Federal Reserve Bank of New York. Retrieved on 1/13/2013 from http://libertystreeteconomics.newyorkfed.org/2012/03/grading-student-loans.html

5   National Center on Family Homelessness (13 January 2013). *National Center on Family Homelessness*. Retrieved on 1/13/2013 fromwww.familyhomelessness.org.

6   Desrochers, J. (2004). *Divorce: A Parents' Guide for Supporting Children*. Excerpt from *Helping Children at Home and School II: Handouts for Families and Educators.*National Association of School Psychologists: Bethesda, MD

7   Smart Stepfamilies™ (13 January 2013). *Smart Stepfamilies*. Retrieved on 1/13/2013 fromwww.smartstepfamilies.com

8   Grall, T. (November 2009). *Custodial Mothers and Fathers and Their Child Support: 2007*. Publication No. P60-237. U.S. Department of Commerce: Washington, D.C.

9   Johnson, K. (May 2011). *Importance of a Positive Male Role Model in the Lives of Developing Children*. Public Speech. Milton First Assembly:Milton, FL

10  Sharples, T. (2 December 2008). *Study: Most Child Abuse Goes Unreported. Time* Magazine. Time Warner: New York, NY

11  Childhelp® (23 July 2014). *Childhelp*. Retrieved on 7/23/2014 fromwww.childhelp.org

12  Office of Juvenile Justice and Delinquency Prevention (19 April 2012). *Office of Juvenile Justice and Delinquency Prevention*. Retrieved on 4/19/2012 from http://www.ojjdp.gov

13  National Public Radio (19 April 2012). *Teen Pregnancy Declines, But U.S. Still Lags. All Things Considered* Radio Program. National Public Radio: Washington, D.C.

14  National Institute on Drug Abuse (19 April 2012). *National Institute on Drug Abuse*. Retrieved on 4/19/2012 from www.drugabuse.gov

15  Stopbullying.gov (22 August 2012). *Stop Bullying*. Retrieved on 8/22/2012 from www.stopbullying.gov

16  Stopbullying.gov (22 August 2012). *Effects of Bullying*. Retrieved on 8/22/2012 from http://www.stopbullying.gov/at-risk/effects/index.html

17  Neal, M. (9 June 2012). *1 in 12 Teens Have Attempted Suicide: Report CDC Finds Suicide Among High School Students on the Rise*. New York Daily News: New York, NY

18  Youth Suicide Prevention Program (22 August 2012). *Youth Suicide Prevention Program*. Retrieved on 8/22/2012 from www.yspp.org

19      Cohen, T. (26 October 2010). *Government Warns Schools that Bullying Can Violate Civil Rights Laws.* CNN Cable News Network:Atlanta, GA

20      Twemlow, S. & Fonagy, P. (2005).*The Prevalence of Teachers Who Bully Students in Schools With Differing Levels of Behavioral Problems. American Journal of Psychiatry.* 2005; 162:2387-2389

21      Crisis Connection, Inc. (21 January 2013). *The Generational Cycle of Abuse.* Retrieved on 1/21/2013 from http://www.crisisconnectioninc.org/justformen/generational_cycle_of_violence.htm

22      US News & World Report (2013). *Best Jobs of 2013.* US News & World Report

# 1.5

## Review

Before we start, I want to go back to the Introduction of this book and review how I developed the Unbroken Circles $^{SM}$ program. If you will remember, I noted how I became obsessed with rubber bands. I also detailed observing that some rubber bands were small and could not take a lot of force when stretched beyond its limits. Others allowed for more give but they also allowed for so much slack that sufficient force could build up from the inside and burst through the band. In essence, by playing with the rubber bands, I decided how I could maximize their benefits by playing off their limitations.

I brought this up because Unbroken Circles $^{SM}$ is based on understanding core concepts and pairing programs and strategies to give maximum impact. An elementary school in Rhode Island may not need the same services of an inner-city elementary school in Illinois. The same can be said for the services and strategies that the inherent set up of a high school would have over that of an elementary or middle school. It is a balancing act of understanding needs. Just as I learned which programs could best work with other programs—schools need to know what programs are needed and how best to implement them. Remember, the program itself is just a suggestion. The school needs to determine and produce a needs-centric course of action.

This text includes a wealth of knowledge about how society handles issues of catabolic (destructive) conflict, critical problems with established educational and juvenile justice systems, harm caused from these problems, and the history of how society has dealt with these problems. It has been relayed that there is a better system out there, seeking to repair harm and bring healing. We have reviewed the severe problems that schools face today as well as the single-biggest catalyst for juvenile suicide. Until now, everything discussed was just an overview. If we talk on academic terms, the first couple of chapters were introductory courses. Then you had an intermediate level exposure to the concepts of the program as well as the program itself. Following this were lessons on why students may act the way they do, the scope of the situation, and a logical continuum of thought as to how this may play out in the future if left unresolved and untransformed. All previous chapters in Section 1 of this book have expressly talked about the key elements used in the program in some form or another. Chapter 1.2 was the most important chapter at building a foundational vantage point to understand Conflict Resolution. Chapters 1.3 and 1.4 are essential for the practitioner in establishing his/her practice and establishing effective programs. Finally, after all this time, we get to the meat of the subject and actually talk about the program itself!

## Communities of Care

In Chapter 1.3, we familiarized ourselves with the notion of Communities of Care. As was noted in that chapter, contemporary society tends to see things from the tangible side. Historically, the term community meant a specific group of people tied to a specific geographical region (e.g., neighborhood, street, block, city, county, state, region of the nation, etc.). For Restorative Justice Professionals, the idea of community is problematic, if not useless. This world is quickly becoming more nomadic, and society is leaving behind most traditional trappings of community.

Back in Chapter 1.3, I asked you to conduct an experiment in order to gain a better understanding of how the old paradigm understanding of community works when tied to a geographic region. This illustrated why it is no longer a valid trait of an active community. The experiment I refer to is the Tic-Tac-Toe Experiment. It is probably the simplest Social Sciences experiment in existence.

# Tic-Tac-Toe Experiment
## A Social Science Experiment on Community Awareness

MY HOME

Your house has been placed in the center of a large "tic-tac-toe" hash mark. Keeping in mind the placement of your house in the center, write down the names of your surrounding neighbors in the corresponding spots on the hash mark. Be sure to note the names of everyone in the household and even the names of their pets.

After doing the experiment, did you notice many neighbors whose names you don't know? About nine out of every ten people doing this experiment are unable to tell the family surnames of all of the neighbors surrounding them in the hash mark diagram. A smaller percentage is actually able to give all of the accurate names of their neighbors and their pets. Ironically, about thirty to forty-five days after the experiment, the test results stay the same when people retest using this same experiment and knowing the exact same parameters upon which they will be tested. So, if you made the same score that you did in Chapter 1.3, and you were unable to give just the surnames of your neighbors, do not be alarmed since that is the anticipated result. What this experiment does is underscore why the historical concept of community and geography are no longer related.

Restorative Justice Professionals have had to redefine what we see as a community in contemporary society. As you have learned, many now utilize what they call a Community of Care (also known as a Community of Concern, Macrocommunities, and Microcommunites). You now know that Communities of Care may lack a geographical or cultural definition or grouping type. They can span vast distances, they can cut through an array of cultures, and they may not use a quantitative number as a defining trait. A Community of Care may ultimately be a family, a group of friends, a group of caring stakeholders, etc.[1]

## Generational Cycle of Violence

As was discussed in Chapter 1.4, one of the great problems plaguing our society today is rampant victimization of our youth. While there are still a large number of children raised by loving and caring families who never have to worry about such matters—such a situation is quickly becoming the exception rather than the rule.

# SNAPSHOT   *Taking a look at the facts*

## *Common Forms of Child Abuse/Neglect in 2010 Reported Cases*

(**Note:** Totals add up to more than 100% due to multiple types of abuse happening in single reports)

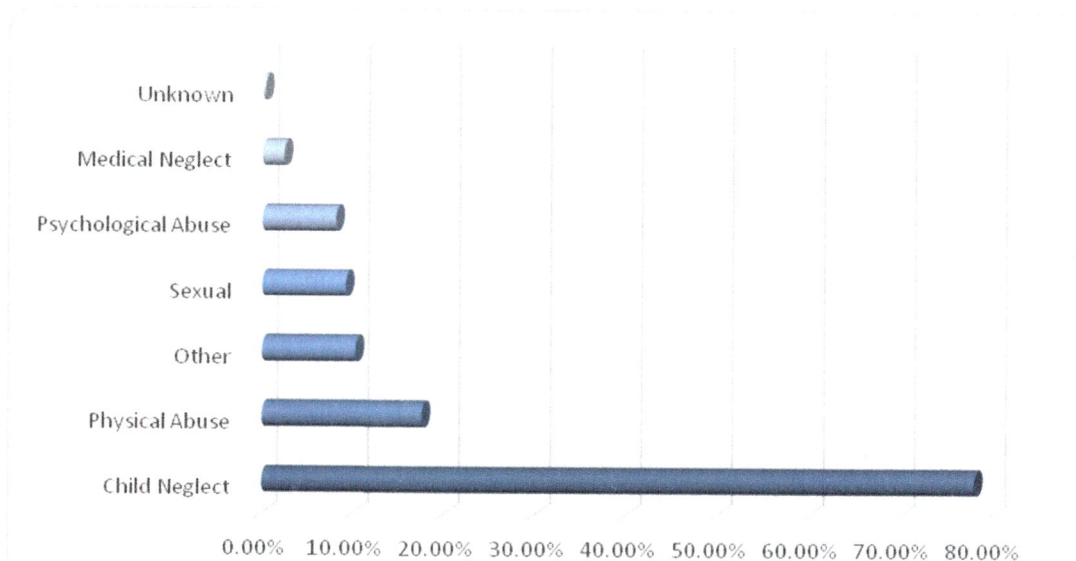

*Source:* **Children's Bureau (2011).** *Child Maltreatment 2010.* **Available from**
**http://www.acf.hhs.gov/programs/cb/stats_research/index.htmcan**

## *Impact of the Generational Cycle of Violence on Children*

➢   63% of young men, 11-20 years old, serving time for homicide killed their mother's abuser.

➢   81% of men who batter their partners had fathers who abused their mothers.

➢   Over 3 million children witness acts of domestic violence every year in their home.

➢   Children are abused at a rate 1,500% higher than the national average in homes where domestic violence takes place.

➢   In homes where the mother was abused, the children experience a 300% increase in physical abuse by the abuser.

➢   80% of men in prisons grew up in violent homes.

*Source:* **Crisis Connection, Inc. (2013).** *The Generational Cycle of Abuse.* **Retrieved on 1/21/2013 from**
**http://www.crisisconnectioninc.org/justformen/generational_cycle_of_violence.htm**

Sadly, for a majority of our youthful population, life is anything but "child's play" as children sometimes go to school just for a meal. Broken homes are rampant with the average American child not having parents who will stay together more than six years before divorcing. Going through two, three, four, and more stepparents is becoming a way of life for children as divorce rates go unmitigated. Many of these relationships often end in loud and violent confrontations that the children are subjected to, relationship after ended relationship.

In all too many circumstances, victimized children have absentee parents who favor drugs, alcohol, sex, money, and their own happiness over that of the children they sired. Rather than trying to marry and create a stable family unit, these people either pawn their children off on relatives, (if the child is lucky) or the children are exposed to a barrage of "special friends," live-in lovers, and party-going friends. This constant bombardment of party-going friends, live-in lovers, special friends, and drug dealers in the life of a child creates a host of behavioral, mental health, and sociological development issues. These issues may exist because his/her parents were abused or neglected. Now, if left unmitigated, research suggests that the children will one-day participate in abusive/neglectful behaviors that will lead to possible incarceration, as well as increasing the risk of future issues of domestic violence and/or abuse/neglect of children.

## Reintegrative Shaming

An America Journalist, Mignon McLaughlin (1913-1983) once said that, "True remorse is never just regret over consequence; it is regret over motive." In other words, true justice means that the punishment must fit the motive rather than just the crime. However, such beliefs, for well over 200 years of American history, have been lost on lawmakers and criminal justice officials. The belief of social retribution is the prominent paradigm of choice. Social retribution occurs when offenders are punished for being deviants, miscreants, and other terms used to socially stigmatize offenders.

In the Restorative Justice community, the topic of Reintegrative Shaming is one that has been hotly debated since its inception. First developed in 1989 by John Braithwaite, an Australian criminologist, the theory repositions the focus of shame from the offender to the wrongful actions of the offender. Thus, the offender can atone for his/her wrongful actions and reassimilate into the community.

According to Steven Dellaportas, a writer and lecturer on white-collar crimes, recidivism is one indicator of the failure of a system to meet demands. Dellaportas notes in his research that, "Overall, shaming theory posits that restorative practices rather than retributive practices are more effective in inducing remorse that constitutes the type of shame that prevents future crime." This is further explained by Dellaportas as such;

"Shaming is partitioned into two forms of disapproval (reintegrative and stigmatic shaming) that sit at opposite ends of a continuum. Reintegrative shaming involves disapproval while sustaining a relationship of respect, whereas stigmatic shaming involves disrespectful humiliation of the offender and disapproval of their deeds." Dellaportas also properly notes "Reintegrative shaming occurs when the disapproval is focused on the deed, and not the individual, so the offender may accept responsibility and reflect on their behavior. By shaming the deed, the offender is less likely to be labelled an evil outcast who is stigmatized and separated from mainstream society."[2]

While Dellaportas is an expert on white-collar crimes, his findings and assertions actually pair well with that of juvenile offender reform. After all, as Dellaportas would most assuredly attest, white-collar criminals have a history of previous crimes and recidivism. White-collar criminals are also prone to benefitting from Reintegrative Shaming. It eliminates the stigmas that could cause future harm to the offenders and lead them to reoffend for a perceived lack of options. Juvenile offenders also usually have a history of past offenses as well as recidivism. The skyrocketing recidivism rate of our era indicates that the present system is faulty and failing to meet the rehabilitation demands of society. In addition, like white-collar criminals, juvenile offenders cannot afford to have a social stigma tied to them because future earnings, education, etc. are also on the line.

One example of how Reintegrative Shaming is used can be found with the Anoka, Minnesota Police Department's Police Accountability Conferencing program. Here, the police call Reintegrative Shaming, "shaming with compassion." The program, which mirrors New Zealand and Australian panels and conferencing practices, allows a juvenile offender to participate in a conference within two weeks of admitting guilt to the police and getting parental approval to participate. The program was started due to a high rate of juvenile-based offenses. One reason the City of Anoka took up this style of justice was the high success rate. Since its use in Australia, beginning in 1991, approximately 95% of juvenile offenders do not reoffend after participating in a conference. In addition, while many in contemporary society fear the stigma of shame in its traditional understanding, Reintegrative Shaming is far different. As proponents of the practice note, shame is critical to social behavior. Its impact on us is two-fold. There is an internal and an external component where the internal is our own conscience and the external is society's disapproval of a given action. Since social shame is more harmful and impactful than the conscience, people are actually more prone to go by what society thinks best than what their own conscience believes to be best. Official shame, or punishment, is considered less impactful, being that it often has no bearing on social shame or societal values. Reintegrative Shaming takes all of this into account to place internal, external, and official regulators in line with each other. The youthful offender understands the impact of the harm caused, and a path is offered so the offender can repent for his/her offenses, atone for his/her actions, and seek healing reassimilation without social stigmatization. This understanding of human behavior is why the City of Anoka found in a year and a half time span, only one juvenile reoffended in the over seventy case conferences that they held. The police force also noted that beat officers, whom had grown tired and weary of ineffective juvenile courts, became staunch supporters of the conferencing program and Reintegrative Shaming.[3]

Reintegrative Shaming is a very delicate issue. It takes time to learn and apply it properly. A professional trained in Reintegrative Shaming should be consulted before any such practice is carried out in a real life situation. Part of this consulting and training should also involve numerous role-playing situations with various cases and various levels of unknown factors. The following is a role-playing scenario that might be used at the very end of a training program on Reintegrative Shaming.

## Reintegrative Shaming Training Exercise

*Below is a tentative group training exercise to help program participants better understand the usage of Reintegrative Shaming (RS). Such exercises are used by many training and certification programs in order to give participants an appreciation of subject matter contents in a near "real world" mock up environment. The following is portraying RS in a conference styled setting. The story is typical of what one might find in a school district in any part of the country. Copies of the players list should be cut and doled out to participants so that they are unaware of what the other players know. Later, a discussion should be conducted to let all parties know what information each player had and to afford participants opportunities to reflect upon where they could improve, as well as what they were feeling during the process.*

### The Case:

Three weeks ago, a local high school had its alarm tripped in the middle of the night. Sgt. Jones pulled up on the scene to find a side door to the school standing open. Inside, Sgt. Jones found the halls strewn and graffiti ridden with multiple lockers and rooms desecrated. In a Science classroom, Zachary Wayland "Zach" Johansen was passed out with beer bottles all about him. He was taken to the hospital and treated for alcohol poisoning. Shortly thereafter, he was arrested on multiple misdemeanor and felony level charges. Zach, with his parent's approval, petitioned the court to allow Zach to participate in a special diversionary program based on the foundational principles of ***Unbroken Circles SM for Schools: Restoring Schools One Conflict at a Time***, which the local School Board developed. By order of Judge Ryan, the case was sent to the school diversionary program. Dale Peters, a trained and certified Collaborative Justice professional with the school district was assigned to this case. After interviewing the principle parties, a notice of conference was issued to the press inviting interested parties to attend.

### The Players:

### Dale

The Collaborative Justice professional, he is in charge of maintaining order during the conference. Dale's main job is to ensure that only one person speaks at a time. At times, Dale will be required to ask probing questions such as the legal ramifications of Zach's actions, how Zach plans to pay for the damages, etc. The order of this meeting will be Dale going first. He will tell what the meeting is about, that the keeper of the conference (Dale) will only allow one person to speak at a time, and that speakers are urged only to speak openly and honestly without condemning Zach personally. From there, Zach will be given a chance to speak. Sgt. Jones will follow to tell what he found, the nature of the charges, and consequences. Mrs. Juarez (Zach's mother) will follow to talk about her feelings. Mr. Johansen (Zach's father) will follow. Pastor Babbins will follow Zach's parents. Principal Wilhoit will follow to talk about the harm caused to the school. Janitor Mason will talk after the principal about how hard it was to repair the harm caused. It should be noted that, about a week before, in preparation for the conference, you (Dale) met with the principle stakeholders and interviewed them individually.

Zach was adamant that he did not cause the damage and that he was with guys from a party that he'd never seen before. Zach contends that he went to a party and started drinking hard and heavy. After agreeing to break into the school, he went into a classroom and passed out from alcohol poisoning. He woke up in the hospital. Zach sees himself as being like his father—what he deems as a "loser." Despite Zach's low opinion of himself, he tested out as a genius according to school records, with numerous awards and honors. As for Sgt. Jones, he was adamant about Zach's guilt, and he has no faith in the process. He notes he also has a child. He feels society is getting so out of control that his own child may turn out like Zach unless something is done. Zach's mother and father also revealed to you, individually, how Zach's dad was tried and convicted on drugs. The drugs were Mrs. Juarez's, but the court held Mr. Johansen responsible since he was the only one in the car. Both agreed that Mr. Johansen has never done drugs, and he only drank when the arguments in the home got too much to bear. One time, neighbors called the police because of shouting in the house. Law enforcement officers tazed Mr. Johansen multiple times, with 50,000 volts, in front of Zachary. Zach's parents have never told him about the drug conviction past or his mom's use of drugs. In the divorce, the drug conviction was used against Mr. Johansen, but Mrs. Juarez adamantly claims it was something that her attorney did at the last minute without her permission. Because of the drug conviction, Mr. Johansen could not go to college or get a stable job. He was often paid late, which has made him late on child support or away for times when he was supposed to have custody of Zachary. Both note, he has not been there for Zachary as he should. Mrs. Juarez thought that it would help for her husband, Tony, to adopt Zachary—which Mr. Johansen saw as an assault against him. Pastor Babbins confided that he thinks that Zach's parents overlook his advice and have both neglected Zachary. Pastor Babbins also noted that Zach's great grandfather helped the Pastor out in a similar situation. Pastor Babbins praises Zach for fixing the unfixable, coming up with plans to build drones to help the military, and being a sort of big brother to the children of the church.

In your talks with the principal and janitor, they both spoke highly of Zach and were shocked that he did what the sergeant claimed. They cannot believe that Zach did all of that. After everyone has had a chance to talk, questions need to be asked to try to get helpful data out of people who would change Zach's understanding, the community's understanding, and put Zach on a path to take ownership of what he did. There will come a time that a path for repentance, atonement, and reassimilation be called for between the parties (they make a plan for Zach to follow). The plan should involve some way for Zach to pay restitution. Possibly he could work off his damages to the rest of the community, maybe speak or write about the issue and have it showcased in a public way. You are to try to alleviate contributing issues that caused Zach to get to the state he was found in at the high school, and work on a way to get Zach back on track. The goal is for everyone to forgive him for his actions and see him as a whole person who has paid back his debt. Be sure to ask everyone in the audience for their help. He may need a job. He may need a mentor. He may need someone whom he can talk with in times of need. He needs people to hold him accountable and who will check in on him to make sure he is doing what he is supposed to do. All of this will need to be jotted down as an agreement that Zach and his parents will sign off on. Dale will also sign off on behalf of the Community of Care. At the end, the conference will be closed with a promise to meet again in 2 months to evaluate the progress.

## Zach

Zachary, as he is called by his parents and church pastor, is a junior in high school who broke into the school after hours and wrecked the halls and multiple classrooms with graffiti. He was found passed out from drinking by the authorities when he tripped an alarm. His parents got a divorce the summer that Zach was going into high school, after years of fighting that even had the authorities called-out from time to time. The church has worked to help both parents. Little effort has been spent on Zach as his parents have both remarried; his dad has a new child on the way with his new wife. Zach's mother married a man with three young girls.

You have been tested as a genius, and you are particularly interested in electrical engineering. This offense will bar you from being admitted into a well-known university to study robotics and electrical engineering. You have spent the last three weeks being evaluated by Adoptive Services child psychologists in preparation for a proposed adoption by your mom and her new husband, Tony. Your dad has contested the adoption only to drop a bombshell on you that his new wife, Tina, is pregnant. The day of the crime, a teacher made a comment about history repeating itself. A flood of feelings washed over you, fear that you were going to be like your father and mess up everything somehow. You saw your future self in a divorce with a messed up and forgotten child. You see adults as superficial. That night was supposed to be your night to "let loose."

You went to a party held at a student's house while his parents were away. By the end of the night, you had downed several shots and other drinks, meeting up with some guys who were from another school the next county over. They were the ones that suggested, "pranking" the school. On the way to the school, you downed what was left of a bottle of vodka and a bottle of beer. You entered the school but quickly went to the Science wing where you had a few beers and passed out. Now, after being hospitalized and arrested, you realize that history is repeating itself. You told the cops that you were not alone, but they could care less since you did not know the names of the guys you were with. Looking around, the only person that you see that bothers you is Pastor Babbins. If you have let anyone down—Pastor Babbins is it!

### Sgt. Jones

The police officer who pulled on the scene when the alarm to the school was tripped. The halls and a few classrooms were desecrated with graffiti. Zach was found passed out in the Science room with beer bottles strewn about him. Sgt. Jones does not believe in these sorts of meetings—though this is, admittedly, his first one. Too many juveniles end up in the courts only to be let back out and reoffend. You notice that Zach's parents fit what you see every day. Troublemakers coming from parents who care more about themselves than the kids. You see an endless cycle and secretly want this to work since you have a young boy.

### Mrs. Juarez

You are Zach's mom…though you call him Zachary. Zachary was your rock during the horrible fights between you and your ex-husband. You thought that Tony, your present husband, would give Zachary all of the things that he didn't have growing up—a loving family, a stable income, and a father figure in the home. You feel guilty that Zachary is rebelling. You blame his father because he fought proceedings to grant you sole custody of Zachary. Mr. Johansen, Zachary's father, has been late with his child support payments. Until recently, he seldom had time to spend with his son during his court-appointed days. To compound matters, Zachary's dad has recently remarried and has a child on the way. You feel that he is trying to start a new life when he has neglected his son and his old family. In a weird way, you feel at fault for most of this since your drugs were found in the car of Zachary's dad when you both were teens. Mr. Johansen was arrested when an officer pulled him over for speeding. He saw the drugs in the glove box when Mr. Johansen went to get the registration. This event still bars Mr. Johansen from gainful employment and stops him from going to college. However, in the divorce, your over-zealous attorney used Mr. Johansen's past drug conviction, trying to sway the judge to give sole custody of Zachary to you. Both you and Mr. Johansen have never told Zachary about any of this.

### Mr. Johansen

You are Zach's dad… though you call him Zachary in remembrance of your grandfather who was like a father to you. A past drug offense, when you were 18, left you with a record that bars you from employment in most places. The judge did not care that your girlfriend, Zachary's mom, had left the drugs in your car without your knowledge. You have never told Zachary this or the fact that this offense barred you from going to college or getting a decent job locally. You have had to work as a traveling construction worker building bridges and such to put food on the table and clothes on everyone's backs. Sometimes you are not paid on time, or you have work that does not allow you to see Zachary, as you would like. This is your eleventh job in six years. Financial hardships caused the last few years of your failed marriage with Zachary's mom to get more heated than you would have liked. You started drinking, which only made things worse. The cops were called out once, and you were tazed in front of Zachary. To compound matters, during the divorce proceedings, your ex even tried using your previous drug conviction to get sole custody of Zachary.

You have tried to comply with court orders, but it has been hard. Your new wife has tried to pick up the slack where she could. She spurred you on to seek a position with a local company that is hiring people looking for a fresh start. Getting a new start has been crucial because you know that Zachary desperately needs his father. You and your wife did not really want a child right now; specifically because you know that, your time with Zachary is falling short. When Zachary found out about Tina, your new wife, being pregnant, he was livid and left the house. Recent court battles to take Zachary away from you have only made things harder on you. You have tried to fight for Zachary's future, as well as the future of your new wife and unborn child. You think that Zachary sees you as a failure and that you are mostly to blame for his arrest.

## Pastor Babbins

Pastor Babbins has counseled both of Zachary's parents. You call Zach "Zachary" because you knew his great-grandfather of the same name. He was the one who took you out of a bad situation when you were young and led you to your path as a minister and counselor. When Zachary's parents were acting as children in their divorce, Zachary took ownership of the situation and tried to play the part of the adult. With so many laws now stopping religious free speech, you did not press too hard for Zachary's parents to put Zachary in counseling with the church. When you asked them to go to a family counselor, for the benefit of Zachary, they fought too hard against each other to listen to anything you had to say. Now things have come full circle. You know Mr. Johansen's history, though Zachary does not. You know it was Zachary's mom who hid drugs in the car of her boyfriend, Zachary's dad. When Mr. Johansen was caught and charged with the crime, it was Zachary's great-grandfather who took care of Zachary's mom when she was pregnant with Zachary.

You have been counseling both parents off and on. Their shame and guilt has blinded them and turned into blame. They cannot see that their fighting not only hurts the other but Zachary as well. Sometimes you feel that they ignore you. Somehow, you feel that something great is about to happen with Zachary. He is a wonderful brother and has been a tremendous son. Until his parents' recent marriages and subsequent court battles, the youth in the church looked up to Zachary as a big brother. His work with electronics is astonishing. He can fix things that people say are unfixable. He even helped to rewire the nursery of the church. You have seen drawings of unmanned drones that he has designed to help troops overseas avoid traps and hazardous situations. Now, as you look at Zachary, feelings of remorse hit you for not fighting harder for Zachary. You feel that you have let him down. Having a conviction would only put Zachary where his father is. Now is the time for you to stop this circle of harm. Besides the feelings of guilt and shame, you are here in memory of Zachary's great-grandfather, to help his namesake in his time of need.

## Principal Wilhoit

You are the principal of the high school. The call came in the middle of the night. The school was a mess! It took a professional cleaning crew to clean the graffiti. School maintenance workers had to work days fixing locks and windows. Bills are still piling in from window companies, locksmiths, etc. Already, the bill is well up into the thousands. You are feeling a lot of heat. This is an election year. You are naturally feeling the heat from School Board members who want Zach to pay for this. This sentiment seems to be prevalent with taxpayers and the media. Even Sgt. Jones' has publicly noted Zach's guilt. Despite Sgt. Jones' insistence that Zach was alone and the culprit, you know Zach well. Things just did not add up to you when you saw the devastation of that night. Zach has had a rough time lately, and you would expect some sort of rebellion—this just isn't the rebellion you'd expect from someone like Zach.

## Janitor Mason

There were three large windows broken, over a hundred lockers were defaced and their locks jimmied, the walls and carpets were covered in spray paint graffiti in the main hall and in several classrooms, light fixtures were smashed, and the side door had the lock busted. Repairs are still going on. A locksmith was called in as well as an electrician. The school also had to call in a flooring company, paint crew, and a professional cleaning company. Just looking at the cost of the invoices you have signed off on, the damages are more than what you make in a year. The whole event has been surreal for you. You see hoards of teens every day. Most laugh and make jokes about you. They make messes for you to clean up. Yet Zach has always been courteous to you. He picks up trash left behind by others. You know that the community is out for blood and wants Zach to pay dearly for all of this, but you just know that Zach is incapable of such damage.

## James Williams

You are a local electrician who happened to hear about this case and wanted to attend to see what this Collaborative Justice program is all about. Your son is presently studying electrical engineering at the university that Zach wants to attend. You are a ham radio operator who loves ultralight aircraft and remote controlled aircraft. Some college buddies of yours host a number of robotics competitions that really helped your son to apply his skills. When fixing some wiring at the school one time you remember Zach asking you a host of detailed questions about AC and DC current, polarity, grounding, electromagnetic insulation, etc. Lately, business has been doing well for you, and you have needed to hire someone that you, in time, could train to do electrical work. For now, you need someone who could inventory the equipment, clean up the warehouse, and set appointments. As time passes, you will begin teaching this person the basics of electrical work.

## Eugenia "Genie" Westmoreland

You came because you are a mental health counselor and are interested in this new Collaborative Justice process. On occasion, you will take a case pro bono (free) because you are moved by a situation and want to help. You have petitioned the School Board for in-school mental health professionals to be provided, but the Board said that they did not have money. Your primary specialty is working with juveniles in troubled situations. Your practice has a group of like-minded professionals who deal with addiction, family counseling, etc. Before the conference, you had already called a meeting, and the principle owners of the practice said that they would support any pro bono work that you committed the practice to if you thought it would help out this situation.

## What to Do:

Each player has a slip that tells about his or her character. The players should be given a few minutes to understand their character's point of view and understanding. They will also be given a note pad to write down notes about their character as well as the conference in which they will be role-playing. It is important for the role players to know that in a real world situation, someone like Dale would interview key parties in a case, such as Zach, his mom, his dad, school officials, law enforcement, etc. In addition, stakeholders and interested parties would be called in to give a sense of community—what we know today as a Community of Care. A neutral professional, trained in such issues, usually leads the group and assists the process along so that pertinent data can be revealed, and healing can take place. Think of such a professional as a conductor of an orchestra—(s)he can guide things along, but it is the duty of each participant to give his/her full effort, or the result will be lacking.

The player portraying Zach will sit down with Dale off to one side. Arched in front of Zach will be Sgt. Jones, Mrs. Juarez, Mr. Johansen, Pastor Babbins, Principal Wilhoit, and Janitor Mason. Behind this group will be other interested parties. It is important for all primary parties to be able to see each other and that Zach see the whole Community of Care.

When role players speak, they need to remember that they have data others may not know about. It is up to the skills of the professional and the process to reveal hidden information. Data revealed, as in real life, normally is only done if the person feels it would be beneficial. The character of Dale has the driving force since data should have been revealed in the interviews; this would allow Dale's character to pull useful data, very tactfully, out of people. Nothing should be said to condemn or stigmatize Zach. By the same token, the participants in the Community of Care should not be condemned or stigmatized if they have data that contributed to the problem. The goal is to show disapproval of what he did and hold him accountable for his actions in a way that allows him to seek repentance and atonement for his crimes. In the process, there may be times when other contributing issues are at play. Here, the conference would seek to help as best it can so any contributing pressures to aberrant behavior are wiped away or diminished significantly.

After the role playing session is over, have everyone gather in a circle and talk about his or her feelings. Was the set up a little odd? It is normal to feel a little weird at first about such situations, but it allows for significant mental and emotional impact on both accusers and the accused. Going into this matter, how did the individual people see this issue? Did it change at all? How true to life do you think this situational scenario was? It should be noted that the scenario was created by meshing up a host of common traits found in juvenile cases across the country. What did everyone think of the secrets and hidden thoughts? Do secrets and hidden motivations, or just an unclear perception for that matter, color how we act and behave around people? Is Zach really a criminal? Did anyone have any knowledge that he or she did not reveal? What would it have taken to reveal the hidden data? Do you think that the hidden data would have helped any? Roughly, half of the major stakeholders in this case have some sort of guilt or shame that they were harboring. What could have been done better by the participants? How could something like a conference help a Community of Care? It should be noted that, over time, research has shown Communities of Care to grow stronger and more cohesive. Usually, the strongest supporters of Communities of Care and Reintegrative Shaming are former offenders who have been through the program and are now adults with professions and skills beneficial to helping others in need. The idea of paying back the community seems to stick with them, and they see these events as a way to offer offenders support that they needed as juveniles.

In all fairness, it should be noted that a great number of criminologists and Restorative Justice researchers have hotly debated and investigated Reintegrative Shaming. Though the concept, in its present understanding, is over two decades old, it is hard to find consensus about whether or not it is a valid practice to use. The field of Restorative Justice is torn in half with both sides making passionate declarations either in support or in rejection of the practice. The polarization of the arguments has caused outlandish claims by zealots on both sides of the continuum.

With that said, the practice, when used, has proven successful. The developer of this concept, John Braithwaite, consistently maintained that practitioners be careful, ensuring feelings of remorse are fostered while avoiding harmful stigmatic shaming. This means that one has to understand what "shame" is. For many, stigmatic shame is the only understanding of shame. Some professionals refuse to accept Braithwaite's understanding of shame and instead purport that Braithwaite, and any supporters of his Reintegrative Shaming Theory, refuse the term "shame" altogether. Instead they suggest that restorative practices should embrace the idea that offenders gain "empathy or understanding" for the effects that the offense had on victims. In studies involving recidivating versus non-recidivating juveniles, stigmatic shame caused juveniles to recidivate, while non-recidivating juveniles noted that they appreciated not being stigmatized. A closer look at the families of polled juveniles found that in recidivating juveniles, the families felt that they as a family and the children were stigmatized by the event. Conversely, of non-recidivating juveniles, the families said that being non-stigmatized allowed them to fix problems and allowed the family to grow closer. For this reason, opponents of Reintegrative Shaming Theory suggest that misunderstandings and misconceptions of what shame is causes more harm than help, and that shame should be taken out of the equation altogether.[4]

Naturally, since this theory is used in the Unbroken Circles [SM] program, I totally disagree with the critics that the theory is pointless, or that it should be altered from what John Braithwaite is proposing. It has been my personal experience that opponents of Reintegrative Shaming Theory favor a victim-centric approach. In these, the offender(s) and their family(ies) play a part in feeling remorse and seeking to make reparations, but no atonement or attention is given to rehabilitate the offender. Rarely have opponents of Reintegrative Shaming shown paths or tactics that heal a whole Community of Care (i.e., offender, victim(s), and other stakeholders). With that said, the truth is a three-edged sword most times and neither side of an argument is ever truly right. Some supporters of the theory do not understand Braithwaite's contentions and definitions of shame. For this reason, I do agree with opponents in that it is the definitions, and subsequent understanding of what shame is, as well as what it can be, that is the crux of the debate. What John Braithwaite proposed is an entirely new field of study. Here, shame can have multiple facets and functionalities that run a continuum with destruction on one end and total transformation on the other. For far too long, society has used only one understanding of shame—stigmatic shame that tears down and destroys a person. Reintegrative Shaming is essentially a paradigm shift in understanding where positive, holistic transformation of potentially negative situations is placed in the forefront. That is why it cannot be overstated that a professional trained in Reintegrative Shaming should be used before ever including this concept into a Collaborative Justice Program aimed at transforming and repairing harm done by an offender.

## Repentance and Atonement: The Paradigm Shift from Retribution

The Reintegrative Shaming role-playing session embodies many concepts. In addition, while it is used to highlight Reintegrative Shame Theory in practice, the elements of the role-playing session laid many concepts that I will refer back to in this chapter. One of the reasons such conferences work is they deal with repentance and atonement rather than retribution.

The word retribution is an old term not often used in contemporary society. Instead, the usage of this word relates to theological writings. However, the modern secular understanding of the word is the foundation upon which our present Juvenile Justice System formed. One definition is, "requital according to merits or desserts, especially for evil." The word is Latin based, and the original definition hails from "retribuere," which means, "to restore."[5] The former, rather than the latter, definition is the secular definition most often used today. Offenders suffer punishments based upon the merits and gravity of the crime committed as a result. This is why criminal courts have historically required the "actus reus" (guilty action) and "mens rea" (guilty mind/heart) components that we alluded to in Chapter 1.2 of this book. The two are used in conjunction to determine the gravity and nature of the crime in order to equalize the punishment with the offense and restore the community under the "retribuere" understanding of the word retribution. Sadly, in today's society, laws no longer require a "mens rea" component, so retribution has simply embodied punishment with no governor or gauge to determine the heinousness of the crime. Restoration, as a goal, is abandoned, as an objective of criminal law and justice dealings in today's system.

In order to shift the paradigm to that of restoration, it seems logical that the offender's heart and mind be placed back in the equation related to the offense committed. The Unbroken Circles [SM] program, as highlighted in the role playing exercise, supports including the notions of repentance and atonement. While both words, to the uninitiated, seem synonymous with one another—the two are at opposite ends of a timeline on the pathway to restoration.

Repentance is an old English word with deep roots in the Anglo-Saxon culture. Specifically, it, like retribution, has a history of being attributed to theological understandings rather than secular ones. Definitions usually affix this word to acts of "sin." For instance, a very good definition of the word says that repentance is, "deep sorrow, compunction, or contrition for a past sin, wrongdoing, or the like." In other words, it is the "regret for any past action."[6] However, replace the word "sin" with either "offense" or "transgression," which are both original understandings of sin, to define repentance. A very workable secular definition can be appreciated. Repentance is the beginning to a path of restoration. It involves remorse through empathy for those harmed. It is a catalyst to fuel the desire to make right the wrongs, which the offender has caused.

Over time, after an offender has done all that (s)he can to restore the victims, a point of transformation is reached. At this moment, the person is no longer an offender, rather they are a whole person with full ethical and moral rights to be seen as such within the community. This point in time is called atonement. This is a point of "satisfaction or reparation for a wrong or injury, amends." The Medieval Latin base of the word "atonement" is "adūnāmentum," meaning "at one in harmony." This is comparable to the Middle English word "onement" which means "unity."[7] While the word, "atonement" is tied historically to Christianity, the actual contemporary and historical definitions of the word are applicable in a secular setting. When justice is actualized, both the victim and the offender must be transformed and made whole. Atonement is the offender being transformed and made whole and implies, but does not necessarily mean, that the victim is whole or at a point that he/she should be whole.

## Forgiveness and Shalom

There is a field of study within criminology called "victimology." In the actual study of Restorative Justice, many proponents support a victim-centric approach over a holistic one. At the forefront of this approach are multitudes of victimologists, who support the action of forgiveness as a path to restoration. There are institutes and degree programs, teaching forgiveness studies. In such teachings, the victimologists frequently suggest that victims of crimes and offenses forgive themselves and their offenders. I disagree that restoration can be made with a totally victim-centric approach; however, the notion of forgiveness, as a critical tool in restoration of harm done, is totally merited and something I support.

The problem is that like Reintegrative Shaming Theory, there is a misunderstanding of what "forgiveness" actually means. Indeed, the root word, "forgive" is multi-faceted in use and application as well as the vantage point from which it is used. It appears that the understanding of forgiveness is in need of clarification so it can be used properly to restore harmony.

Unbroken Circles <sup>SM</sup> divides the stakeholders in an offense into three segments: victim(s), offender(s), and the community. The nature of forgiveness embodies these three perspectives as well. To forgive can mean, "to grant pardon for or remission of (an offense, debt, etc.); absolve" or "to cease to feel resentment against: to forgive one's enemies" or "to give up all claim on account of; remit (a debt, obligation, etc.)."[8]

The first definition is consistent with what one would expect from the community, or a Community of Care, in regards to an offender who has atoned for his/her actions. When offenders meet the requirements of their penitence, they are pardoned/absolved/remitted of their offense by the community and, henceforth, are viewed as a whole, unblemished person in the community.

The second definition is victim-centric and more complicated due to the intrinsic nature of what it means to be a victim of a crime or offense. Victims, due to their unique status in the community, have the power to forgive their offenders at any point in the process. However, as many victimologists aptly note, victims cannot move forward to an unblemished state of mind until they have forgiven not only the offender but also themselves. You see, holding the title of "victim" is a power that the titleholder allows the offender to willingly, or unwillingly, lord over the injured party. Therefore, victims of crimes often have feelings of resentment, not only towards the offender, but also inwardly toward themselves. The victim has feelings of guilt, seeing him/herself as a partial offender for lack of care or negligent actions, which led the offender to violate them in some way. This is frequently noted in people who have experienced a significant injury and sought medical treatment but refused to go through physical therapy. Over time, the failure to undertake physical therapy leaves the patient at a worse state than what he/she was in before medical treatment was rendered. He/she is, in essence, an "injured bird" whose "wings" are no longer able to allow him/her to "fly." The patient feels resentment at not only him/herself but at the world and everyone around him/her. He/she fails to see the path that would set him/her free and dwells on the path that took him/her to the injury—thus, he/she always stays in a perpetual fixed state. In relation to forgiveness, victims can grow bitter at themselves and the world. Others retreat and become sorrowful. Over time, many express guilt because they feel they have contributed to their victimization, and it is their fault.

In all of these stages of victimization, the persons victimized fail to see a way out of their victimhood. It soon becomes a mantle worn and a state of existence they identify with. Therefore, the absolving harm from the offense requires the victim to pardon the offender for the wrongful action and himself or herself for holding on to that injured state. Depending upon the severity and nature of an offense, victims may forgive themselves well before or well after they actually forgive the offender. In some cases, the offender may reach atonement months or years after the victim finally forgives him/her. Still in other situations, he/she may never be able to tell his/her offender personally that he/she has forgiven them. Yet, to reach a "whole" state, it is critical for the victim to make the necessary steps to achieve both stages of forgiveness when the time is right.

The third definition is that of an offender's vantage point. When one commits a wrongful action, he/she ultimately gives up his/her rights to be whole in the community until the community, as a whole, says that his/her rights are restored. This, like victimhood, is a unique state within the community. Additionally, like a victim, offenders can resent themselves for the harmful action caused. We think of penitence, retribution, and repentance, as meeting the contractual obligations to repair harms caused by the wrongful act. It is wrongfully taken as commonplace that, once offenders have met their obligations to the community, they are restored and that is that. In truth, this faulted perception does not offer an understanding of the final stage of how the offender is to move on. That missing mechanism in the equation is self-forgiveness by the offenders for the harm that was committed to others and themselves and their own future. It is the actualization of the offenders realizing that they have harmed others and themselves and that they are ultimately the masters of their own destiny. Once this final stage of forgiveness is reached, then, and only then, will the offender attain atonement for their offense.

This three-fold understanding of forgiveness is what I call Shalom-centric Holistic Intersocial Forgiveness Transformation (S.H.I.F.T.) Theory. This understanding of forgiveness, like the Unbroken Circles [SM] program, is based upon the concept of shalom. The translation of shalom is a state of "all-rightness."[9] A Hebrew word in nature, shalom means peace to the secular world. However, to theologians, especially Christian scholars, the word is really a reflection of perfect peace and harmony, where there is not spot or blemish found anywhere within one's self, other people, or the present situation. S.H.I.F.T. Theory uses this latter understanding of shalom as the driving force to offer a holistic, intersocial, and transformational pathway to healing for all concerned.

Originally, the term shalom was used extensively by early Restorative Justice proponents. Today, its usage is quickly falling away due to the secular applications of Restorative Practices. In our politically correct world, it appears the word seems too contentious to people. Some atheists, Muslims, and others, might take exception to the usage of the word. Out of social fear, personal values, and a host of other reasons, the word shalom and its usage in Restorative Justice practices, is under serious attack here in America as well as in Canada, Great Britain, parts of Europe, and Africa.

I suppose one could use something from another culture more in keeping with America's past. One suggestion may be the Cherokee term of "nv-wa-do-hi-ya-dv" or placing things back in a state of "harmony."[10] However, I doubt very seriously that many people could properly pronounce, let alone, use this term from a quickly dying American language-base.[11] I do not see the use of any other minority-rooted term coming into common usage. Indeed, almost every word and term fails to meet the tests of easy identification, understanding, and acceptance like that of shalom. I contend that shalom is an already known and used word that is readily understood by most of secular society. Therefore, despite its root origins, its place in justice dealings is not only merited but also actually beneficial. It is one simple word with tremendous impact and understanding tied to it. In addition, as a part of S.H.I.F.T. as well as Unbroken Circles [SM], it acts as a guide and governor to set a pathway to peace, healing, and ultimate transformation. On this path, the victim, offender, and broken community transmute and transfigure into a whole and unblemished state.

## Circles

One of the many enduring features of Unbroken Circles [SM] is that it uses old practices and paradigms, common to many cultures across the world, creating a new paradigm shift in contemporary society. In particular, the use of a circle to come together as a group is a centuries old practice. For example, American Indians met in a circle to discuss issues such as which direction the tribe should take on an issue or how to deal with a problem. People today use circles when there are problems, to commune in fellowship, to generate ideas, and for a whole host of other purposes. If for no other reason than dynamic design, circles allow everyone to be included, be equal, and engage their fellow person.

In the field of education, the use of circles is not a new idea. In fact, out of all the various Restorative Practices, circles are probably the most identifiable and easiest to understand for the common layperson. As they pertain to Restorative Practices, "Circles provide an orderly and reflective process that reinforces positive values."[12]

In the Unbroken Circles [SM] program, circles are to the program what bedrock is to a building. Unbroken Circles [SM] uses circles not only as a mode for introducing students to Restorative Practices but also as a way to build whole schools, communication development, promote good citizenship, promote collective collaboration, and much more.

Researchers and practitioners have studied and developed circles in, and for, various uses. Circles can be used for daily classroom discussion, making peace, talking out issues, healing, and much.[13] Amstutz and Mullet best describes circles as being when,

...chairs are placed in a physical circle. One or two facilitators, often called keepers, lead the meeting. A talking piece is passed, usually clockwise, and only the person holding the talking piece is authorized to speak. People may pass the talking piece without speaking if they wish, and only one person speaks at a time. After introductory comments, often including a discussion of values underlying the process, the keeper poses a question or a topic, and then passes the talking piece. Circles usually involve a number of rounds. Since only one person speaks at a time and participants have a chance to reflect on others' words and what they themselves will say, circles provide an orderly and reflective process that reinforces the underlying values of restorative discipline and peaceable schools.

Though circles vary from region to region, the aforementioned description seems to be true for almost all contemporary circles. Another key element of circles is the participants usually gather in a circle because they want to be connected to each other in a positive manner. Participants value each member of the community (circle), and each person has a right to his/her beliefs. Despite differences, each person in the community usually shares some core values with the rest of the members in the community.[14]

Circle Keepers are probably the most misunderstood role of the process. Many people have misconceptions of what a Circle Keeper is and what they can or cannot do. Circle Keepers do not need to be specially trained as mediators and other conflict resolution practitioners. Being a Circle Keeper is not a position of power, but rather the position of Circle Keeper is one the community trusts to safeguard the values and guidelines of the process. This means that a Circle Keeper can be a teacher, a teacher's aide, a school resource officer, administrator, volunteer, or anyone else that is fair and willing. Circle Keepers are facilitators and protectors of the process; they do not control the circle. Their unbiased nature, along with their training, allows for a neutral ground in the circle holding together two or more opposing parties or ideas. Circle Keepers are well trained in knowing how and when to: open and close circles, take breaks, interrupt, and urge people to follow the guidelines of the circle. Most importantly, aside from ensuring the integrity of the process, Circle Keepers make certain that every member of the circle is a participant rather than just an observer.

Though many practitioners say that the use of talking pieces is inherent to indigenous tribes, this is not to say that all tribes have historically utilized a talking piece in their circle processes. Rather, talking pieces have evolved over the years as a way to keep order. Talking pieces are any object of focus (e.g., feather, stick, shell, eraser, and marker) that is accepted by the group. Usually, a talking piece will have some special meaning or tie-in to the group. However, it is not required that the talking piece have a special connection or that a talking piece even be used, though its use is highly suggested. The most important concept to understand is that the talking piece be recognized for what it represents in the nature of order and civility. The benefit of using a talking piece is that its use affords listeners an opportunity for reflection since participants has to wait for the talking piece to come to them before they can talk. Best of all, it affords the individual a guaranteed voice in the circle without worry of competition with others or engaging in open debate that may distract from their intended line of thought.

It is important for participants to understand the guidelines of the circle. Again, Amstutz and Mullet do a superb job in outlining core values that are inherent to all contemporary circle processes. Participants should be respectful to others even though they may not always agree with each other. Only the person with the talking piece has the right to speak. Speakers must always be honest and only speak for themselves. Speakers should keep their comments brief and to the point so that others may have a chance to speak. Not everyone that receives the talking piece has to speak since one can always pass. Solutions offered should not be judged in terms of right or wrong. Most importantly, the participants should respect the confidentiality of the circle.[15]

The Unbroken Circles [SM] program understands there are a number of ways that circles can be used. For the purposes of basic understanding, only a few methods will be addressed; however, it should be understood that any school using the Unbroken Circles [SM] program may modify the circles process, under the supervision of a trained professional, to meet the needs of the situation. Again, for the purposes of core competencies, only morning, mid-day, and end of day circles will be addressed since these circles build the most and can have the most impact on students as a whole. Schools, under the supervision of a trained and certified professional, have the ability to add or take away circle sessions as they see fit.

Starting the day off on a good foot is a precursor to meaningful education. Since the advent of the public school system, educators have urged parents and students to do things that would help the student to get his/her morning off to a good start. A good night's sleep and a hearty breakfast are things that have been suggested over the years. Now, some schools are saying that a morning circle session should be added to that list. Morning sessions are a great way to build the Community of Care (class) while also relieving stress, learning communication skills, and collectively collaborating on meaningful ways to solve various issues and problems. Usually, the Circle Keeper (i.e., school resource officer, teacher, and aide) gathers the students in a circle and has the students go around the circle saying one nice thing about the person to the left of them. Once the student has said the one nice thing, he/she cannot use that comment ever again in the circle sessions to refer to that same person. By doing such, the students are forced to engage each other and learn more about the members of their own Community of Care. From there, the Circle Keeper may ask questions about how the students are feeling, what happened to them over the weekend, what is happening in their lives this week, or other questions.

Mid-day sessions are a great way to diffuse growing issues, as well as stress, which may be happening during the day. Maybe a child is worried about a test, a bully has threatened him/her, or the child needs help of some kind. As with the morning circles, the Circle Keeper urges the children to say a nice thing about their neighbor. Continuing, the Circle Keeper may wish to ask if anyone has anything to share. Sometimes, it may be beneficial for a Circle Keeper to ask direct questions about behavior changes in a given member of the circle.

End of the day circle sessions provide a method to keep stress from growing and affecting the rest of the day for the group members. Again, like with the morning and mid-day sessions, students are urged to say something positive about their neighbor and to bring up issues of concern. Here, the use of storytelling or jokes may be a beneficial tool for the Circle Keeper to employ. The goal of the end of day circle sessions is to solve problems that have happened, thwart problems before they occur (i.e., a fight after school), relieve tension, and afford students an opportunity to engage in community building.

Truly, any one of these circle processes being deployed on a daily basis will help in some manner. However, the driving force behind any successful Unbroken Circles <sup>SM</sup> program is that all three circles are used on a daily basis together. Obviously, this may not be feasible. Schools may opt for using the process once a week or so. This too, is better than nothing, but it is strongly urged that at least one circle program is used on a daily basis with other types of circles happening every other day or so.

## Sample Circles Lesson Plan (Middle School)

**TEXT:** Mikaelsen, Ben (2001). *Touching Spirit Bear*. HarperCollins Publishers:New York, NY

| WEEK | LESSON PLAN |
|---|---|
| 1 | Discussion of Japanese Proverb and Ch. 1-4 |
| | ☐ What do you think the proverb means? |
| | ☐ What was your first impression of Cole? |
| | ☐ What was your first impression of Garvey? |
| | ☐ What did you think of Garvey's cake demonstration? |
| | ☐ What is your impression of Peter? |
| | ☐ What will it take to make Cole behave? |
| 2 | Discussion of Ch. 5-7 |
| | ☐ Why was Cole scared to be alone (p. 43)? |
| | ☐ Why did Cole not regret his actions? |
| | ☐ What do you think of Cole's parents? |
| | ☐ Can silence be hurtful (i.e., the mom's silence about Cole being abused)? |
| | ☐ Is the spirit bear real? |
| 3 | Discussion of Ch. 8-11 |
| | ☐ Why did Cole attack the spirit bear? |
| | ☐ Why did Cole's attitude change towards the baby birds? |
| | ☐ What do you think will happen to Cole? Why? |
| 4 | Discussion of Ch. 12-13 |
| | ☐ Why did the spirit bear come back? |
| | ☐ Why didn't the spirit bear attack Cole again? |
| | ☐ Was Cole worth saving? Why? |
| | ☐ Why did Cole throw away his proof—the hair of the spirit bear? |
| | ☐ Would you have thrown away the hair? Why? |
| | ☐ Is Cole a changed person? Why? |
| | ☐ Did your impressions of Cole change? Explain. |
| 5 | Discussion of Ch. 14-15 |
| | ☐ Did Cole revert to his old self when he was safe from the bear? |
| | ☐ Were the members of the Circle Justice right to question Cole so much? |
| | ☐ What do you think of Edwin? |
| | ☐ How has Cole changed from Chapter 1 of the book? |
| | ☐ What is your impression of Cole now? Explain. |
| 6 | Discussion of Ch. 16-21 |
| | ☐ What did you think of Edwin's lesson with the pool and the rock? |
| | ☐ What is the importance of feasting? |
| | ☐ What was the importance of Cole building his lodging? |
| | ☐ Are the dances silly? Why do you feel this way? |
| | ☐ What was the importance of the spark plug? |
| | ☐ Had Cole known that the spark plug was back in, would he have left? Why? |
| 7 | Discussion of Ch. 22-24 |
| | ☐ What is the significance of the totem pole? |
| | ☐ What did Cole's dance of anger symbolize? |
| | ☐ What do you think of Peter's actions? |
| | ☐ Is Cole changed? |
| 8 | Discussion of Ch. 25-28 |
| | ☐ What did you think of Peter's transformation? |
| | ☐ What did you think of Cole not striking back at Peter? |
| | ☐ Do you think that the boys are permanently changed? Why? |
| | ☐ How did you feel about the book? |
| | ☐ Has the book shown you an alternative way of handling problems? |
| | ☐ Circle Justice is real. Do you think that it works? |
| | ☐ Why do we meet in a circle to discuss this book? |
| | ☐ Have you changed since you first read this book? How? |

Circles are traditionally used to talk about whatever the group wishes to discuss. It is common for the Circle Keeper (i.e., teacher) to employ a study lesson as part of the circle, helping the students to understand how core concepts work. In this case, the suggested study lesson talks about a book where circles help a troubled boy and his victim make amends. The usage of weeks allows the Circle Keeper to involve the students in the discussions and the readings. Depending on the adopted schedule for Circle sessions, a Circle Keeper may have a schedule like the one above or go with a revolving schedule. The key is to make it engaging for all involved. Bored, disconnected students do not talk and, ultimately, will not learn as well. It is critical for the Circle Keeper to look for compelling materials whenever it is necessary and beneficial to the Circle. To keep things as inclusive and collaborative as possible, the Circle Keeper may ask students to suggest books, movies, and even news articles for usage in the circle session. Educators should always be mindful that what is compelling to an adult may not be necessarily compelling to students. When students get to participate in the growth and development of their Circles, they undergo a sense of "buy-in." They become owners of the Circle. This makes for a stronger, more dynamic, and effective Circle.

# Sample Circles Lesson Plan (High School)

**MOVIE:** *Firelight* (2012). Hallmark Hall of Fame Productions

| DAY | LESSON PLAN |
|---|---|
| 1 | Discussion of the movie to the parable of the prisoners in the cave<br>    How does Caroline end up getting arrested? Who sold her out and why?<br>    How many years did she get at the special facility? Is that a lot for the crime? Why?<br>    How do relationships affect our future? What relationships affected Caroline's future?<br>    Why was Caroline called "Butterfly" and what is it supposed to mean?<br>    Terry and DJ both warn Caroline about Pedra. Why does Caroline not listen?<br>    Explain the Voltaire comment and how it related to DJ's explanation of redemption and reality.<br>    What does DJ turn to in order to see things how they should be? Do you have such a thing?<br>    What is "The Cave" parable a metaphor of? Why did Terry tell the parable of "The Cave" to Caroline? |
| 2 | Discussion of the movie to just past the butterfly catching scene where Caroline is asked to consider Crew 9<br>    How did Nelson Mandela make it through 27 years of prison? What does his explanation mean?<br>    Why was DJ worried about the cigarette burns? Who does it remind DJ of?<br>    What is the importance of Crew 9?<br>    What is the importance of DJ teaching Caroline about "social graces?"<br>    What is the quote from Vince Lombardi and why is it important to Caroline? How do you value the quote?<br>    What does Caroline ask Terry as payment for the picture? Was it wrong for Caroline to charge Terry? Why?<br>    What did Terry do to save her friend? Why?<br>    What did the girls do for Terry? Why? Did Terry's character have anything to do with why the girls all were trying to help her?<br>    What is the importance of trying new things? How would it help Caroline? How about you? |
| 3 | Discussion of the movie to just after Keisha leaves the facility<br>    Who tells the prisoners in "The Cave" parable about the hoax? What is their reaction?<br>    How is "owning responsibility" different, or the same, for the girls at the parole hearing?<br>    How did the character of Terry's heart change between the March incident and the parole hearing?<br>    Terry was denied parole based off of a perception. How hard is it to change perceptions? Why? How did a single perception change Terry's own self-perception?<br>    Why are goals important for Keisha? Why does DJ tell Keisha to remember Crew 9 when the detention center and all of the experts said to forget everything?<br>    What does Terry's comment to Keisha about "deserving" parole mean to you? Do we sometimes need to be made known that we deserve something? Do you do this? Has anyone ever told you this before? |
| 4 | Discussion of the movie to the end<br>    Why do people sometimes get mad at other people when they are trying to help them? What does it say about the person in need? What does it say about the person trying to help when they still want to help? Why do you think this interlay happens?<br>    Caroline refused to leave Protective Custody despite Terry offering her a way out. Why do you think she wanted to stay in a cage rather than enjoy the freedom that Crew 9 offered?<br>    What does it mean to be "part of the solution?"<br>    What was the importance of the "standoff" when Pedra and her crew with that of Crew 9?<br>    What does "owning one's self" mean and why is it important?<br>    For former offenders seeking atonement, how important is it for them to be able to distinguish between how they used to act from the person they are today?<br>    Punishment vs. Rehabilitation is a unique paradigm shift. What are the differences between the two? Can they look similar? How can the two fail? How can they succeed? What is your preference between the two and why?<br><br>Homework Assignment: Study the discussion topics (Day 5) and be ready to talk about them |
| 5 | Discussion questions<br>    In the 1990s, Professor John DiIulio, Jr. posited a concept called the "super predator." Over the years, this concept was deemed a myth by multiple academics and government agencies. What is the "super predator" myth and why is it dangerous for youth? How does it relate to Terry's first parole meeting? Do you still see it in play in your own life? If so, how?<br>    Researchers, in the State of Florida, found that, in most of the nation's schools, lower performing students get suspended longer than higher performing students. At present, about 857 students drop out from school each hour of each school day. What is the "Test-to-Prison Pipeline" theory and how valid do you think it is? How do you think this theory applies to juvenile delinquents and youthful offenders Do you see it in play in your own life? If so, how?<br>    What are problems that you see in your own school? Your own community?<br>    You know some of the problems that affects youth. What solutions do you propose? |

As was stated earlier, books are not the only resource that can be used. This high school circle lesson plan shows a popular television movie used as a circle lesson discussion. Again, many sources are used to convey basic core concepts and clarify understandings. However, for the sake of practicality, the use of news clippings, books, and movies are commonly employed. News stories, shared incidences, etc., are contemporary windows of opportunity to introduce, integrate, and refresh concepts and understandings while keeping student bonds and discussions strong and dynamic.

## Peer Mediation

Almost as identifiable as circles is the use of peer mediation in the school system. Peer mediation, however, has a fickle past. There were periods of support and disfavor following waves of success and need, along with economic trends. With over four decades of utilization in America, it has a sound track record for helping juveniles. However, most Americans have a very limited understanding of mediation, and its use in the school system is not well supported. The improper application of the programs and lack of basic core competencies concerning mediation's application and benefits often meant that programs suffered funding shortages due to economic hardships, or when the program achieved target goals and lowered conflict. Ultimately, administrators saw that schools that implemented the program had low conflict levels. If cuts needed to be made, teachers pointed to peer mediation programs as a unnecessary function acceptable to cut. Peer mediation was cut, and conflicts rose in following years. Then someone remembered that the school used to have a peer mediation program that worked. Such patterns of waxing and waning support cannot be tolerated in the Unbroken Circles [SM] program.

The purpose of this section is to place peer mediation in a Collaborative Justice setting and give it new form and functionality as a Restorative Practice. Its role in the Unbroken Circles [SM] program is critical and should never be overlooked or understated. With the exception of circles, it touches the lives of more students than other elements of the program and is a primary tool, keeping problems and dilemmas from escalating out of control. It teaches students core competencies and values regarding Collaborative Justice and Restorative Practices. In addition, for the peer mediators involved in the program, they learn a skill set they may later develop to establish a very lucrative practice in government, commercial, private, and even international venues. With that said, let's look at what peer mediation is and what it entails.

Dr. Don L. Sorenson, author of *Conflict Resolution and Mediation for Peer Helpers* describes in his book that,

Mediation is the process of intervening in the lives of others to help them resolve conflicts. Mediation provides an opportunity for persons who are in conflict to listen to, to understand, and to respect the views of others. Communication between the disputing persons is improved and cooperation is sought for solving a common problem. The conflict is defined as a win/win situation and a mutually satisfying solution is agreed upon and implemented.[16]

Though the definition used by Dr. Sorenson is accurate, a better definition of peer mediation is:

Mediation is a communication process in which the people with the problem work together, with the assistance of a neutral third party, cooperating to resolve their conflict peaceably…The mediator is the neutral third party. When students serve as mediators to assist other students, they are called peer mediators…Mediation is an approach to resolve conflict in which the disputants—the people who disagree—have a chance to sit face-to-face and talk, uninterrupted, so each point of view is heard. After the problem is identified, the disputants created options for mutual gain, and chose a win-win situation. They then finalize an agreement to behave in some way from that point forward.

So, with a general understanding that peer mediation is a tool to resolve conflicts, one is inclined to ask, "Where are these conflicts coming from?" One may say that "Most every dispute between people involves the attempt to meet certain basic needs for belonging, power, freedom, or fun" or that "Differences in values…result in conflicts" but is this really the case?[17]

Richard Cohen, author of *Students Resolving Conflict: Peer Mediation in Schools* may agree, but he also notes that other factors may be involved. In his book, Cohen addresses five reasons why conflicts are occuring at a steady pace in our school systems, to wit: The environment of the students' homes, Economics, Violence, The Media, and Race. At home, Cohen notes;

"More than one-half of marriages end in divorce, and two-thirds of all American children live with a single parent at some time before the age of eighteen. Fully 42 percent of fathers fail to see their children in the wake of divorce, and one quarter of all school-aged children grow up with little or no contact with their fathers. Children today spend ten to twelve hours less time with their parents each week than children in 1960."[18]

Obviously, Cohen's research indicates that the breakdown of the family unit is hurting our children. Quite possibly, a reason for the correlation between growing school violence and deterioration in the family unit may be that less time with parents leaves the child lacking the appropriate skills required to interact properly in society.

Could there be something else at play concerning the breakdown of the family unit or just of the state of the contemporary family in general? To answer the question, Cohen says that economics has a great deal to say about the status of the family unit, to wit:

Male wages fell 20 percent between 1973 and 1990. More than half of all Americans have fallen behind inflation and experienced a decline in their standard of living since the early

1980s. The annual income of 36 million Americans (one in seven citizens) falls below the threshold the federal government uses to define poverty. Many more hover just above that threshold. Twenty percent of all American children—and 50 percent of African American children—now live in poverty. The United States is the only industrialized country where the number of poor children has increased significantly in recent years.[19]

Thus, one can assume from Cohen's research that this dire economic landscape is causing parents, single or otherwise, to spend more time working than with their children, fulfilling basic needs. As stated before, inattention from parents may leave the child lacking skills. Shortages of money may also leave a child want of basic needs as well.

On violence, Cohen notes that "More than 20,000 Americans die in homicides every year, far more than in any other industrialized nation" and that "Firearm murders of youngsters more than doubled between 1984 and 1990." What is worse is that Cohen's research indicates, "Americans eight to fifteen years old spend approximately four hours watching television daily… Those same children will have witnessed 200,000 acts of violence on TV by the time they are sixteen."[20] From this, one assumes a reason for the growing trend in violence in schools is that the nation is becoming more violent. Quite possibly, children are acting out what they see in real life, on the news, or on their favorite television shows.

Another issue that Cohen touches upon is that of race. Though Cohen briefly touches upon this subject, with a decidedly African American bias, he does bring up some astonishing food for thought on why racial tension may be growing. For instance, Cohen notes that "Almost two-thirds of all African American children still attend predominately segregated schools—African American males born in 1989 face a 1-in-27 chance of being murdered—The infant mortality rate for African American children ranks twenty-eighth worst among all countries."[21]

Though Cohen's research only shows figures related to African Americans, it may be a litmus test of how the disparity of the races may be attributing to violence in schools.

Obviously, any single issue raised by Cohen could explain why violence is rising in schools. However, when combined, Cohen's findings paint a grim picture of America. What is more troubling is that there may be little communication between these diverse groups. This lack of communication, along with the need to fulfill needs and wants, leads to conflicts. So, what can be done? Peer mediation may be an answer to this quandary.

Generally, peer mediation can be broken down into two categories: 1) Classroom only models and 2) School-wide models. As Dr. Leah Davies notes,

A classroom model often involves the children in one or more grades who are all trained in conflict resolution skills. In addition, several students are selected to receive additional peer mediation training. Those students serve as peer mediators in their own class or in other classes at their grade level or with younger children.

Dr. Davies contrasts this with the school-wide model in which she notes,

> In a school-wide program, students representing various grade levels and groups are chosen to participate in training. Those who successfully complete the course serve as school-wide peer mediators for a year. The mediations are scheduled and conducted in a designated area with minimal adult supervision.

As Dr. Davies describes peer mediation:

> Usually a teacher or school counselor, who has training in mediation skills, serves as a program coordinator. Since peer mediators are role models for other students, it is important to choose them carefully. In some programs, mediators are selected by their classmates after engaging in a discussion of the qualities of a good peer mediator. While no single quality predominates, many mediators exhibit high levels of trustworthiness, helpfulness, and respect for individual differences. Self-referrals as well as those made by teachers, counselors, and other staff are considered. A cross-section of students representing the ethnicity, socioeconomic level, grade, and gender of the school population are chosen for the intensive training. Since these students miss some class time, they need to be willing and able to make up assignments....

> The conflicts that lend themselves to peer mediation include interpersonal disputes like friendship issues, verbal harassment, spreading rumors, physical aggression, or other bullying behaviors. Assault or other criminal activities are not referred for peer mediation... In formal mediation a peer mediator or a team of two mediators meet at a scheduled time and place with the disputants. The sessions vary in length depending on the nature of the conflict and some may be conducted over several days. Sessions take place during class time, recess, lunch time, or after school. The program coordinator follows up with the parties to ensure the agreement is working.... If a dispute occurs in the hall, cafeteria, or on the playground, peer mediators may engage in informal mediation. During these transition times, mediators are often available and identified by arm bands, vests or badges. When an altercation occurs, students are taught to seek out a peer mediator to facilitate a solution to the problem.[22]

Truly, peer mediation is one of the most in-depth Restorative Practices at both the student and faculty levels. For that reason, the appendices of this book have resources to help peer mediation coordinators with that portion of Unbroken Circles [SM]. Coordinators are urged to undergo a rigorous mediation-training program, much like what adult professional mediators complete with state-based mandatory training programs. Coordinators are also urged to seek out well established manuals, such as Mr. Schrumpf, et al's manual, and supplemental literature, such as Dr. Sorenson's and Mr. Cohen's books, so that students can learn more refined lessons such as "perceptions" and "enabling words", among others.

# Peer Mediation Training Exercise

*Below is a tentative peer mediation training exercise to help program participants better understand the dynamics of peer mediation. Such exercises are used by many training and certification programs in order to give participants an appreciation of subject matter contents in a near "real world" mock up environment. The story is typical of what one might find in a high school. Copies of the players list should be cut and doled out to participants so that they are unaware of what the other players know. Later, a discussion should be conducted to let all parties know what information each player had and to afford participants opportunities to reflect upon where they could improve, as well as what they were feeling during the process. The part of Ms. Hendrix is very important in the discussion because this person does not have any information. Therefore, she can reveal how she felt and what she saw as a true third party neutral in the training mock-up.*

## The Case:

Tom and Marco are both exceptional students. Marco is a star athlete with brains to match. Tom is more introverted but his test scores have him in line to go to college on a full-ride scholarship. Tom is a fairly new student to the school and little is known about him as he likes to keep to himself. Marco is a native of the area and is extremely well known. This morning, Coach Nielson found the two boys shoving each other. Despite having tears in their eyes and puffy, red faces there was no evidence that the boys ever struck each other. Later, witness accounts confirmed this. Dean Wright received the case from Coach Nielson. Mr. Wright has evaluated the case and, based on the foundational principles of ***Unbroken Circles*** *SM* ***for Schools: Restoring Schools One Conflict at a Time***, which the local School Board adopted, he transferred the case over to the school's Peer Mediation Corps. After being notified of the mediation session, both boys are now here to talk with Jerry, a peer mediation volunteer, who is accompanied by the program's sponsor, Ms. Hendrix.

## The Players:

## Jerry

You are the peer mediator. Most schools will develop an opening statement that all mediators are to follow as well as standard procedures for starting a peer mediation session. For the purposes of this training exercise, you will want to introduce yourself to the boys as well as Ms. Hendrix. You may want to offer the boys a cup of water to ease tensions. Give the boys pen and paper and sit them at a table. While a round table is preferred, you can use a rectangular table so long as you are sitting at the end and the boys are seated across from each other looking face-to-face. Open the session by saying something like, "Hello! As you know, I am Jerry and Dean Wright has referred this matter to peer mediation. Ms. Hendrix is here to observe this peer mediation session. Peer mediation is a confidential process. This means I cannot tell anyone what is said after this mediation is over with. The only record of the final outcome will be when we memorialize the mediation agreement. This is an agreement that we will jointly draft and sign. This process is based on openness and mutual respect. My role in this process is merely as a third party neutral. This means that I cannot make decisions or verdicts. When you came in, I gave you both a pen and some paper. Please use this to write down any questions or comments you may have while the other party is speaking. This allows everyone to have their fair say. From time to time, I may deem it necessary to ask a party to step outside into our waiting room while I talk with the other party. This is called a caucus. A caucus is a confidential discussion between a mediator and given party of a mediation. This means I cannot tell the other party what you tell me in caucus unless you specifically give me permission to do so. For the sake of fairness, if I call a caucus with a party, I will also caucus with the other party as well so that each person has their say. Remember, this is your conflict and together it is my hope that we can reach a mutually agreeable solution. Does anyone have any questions?" From there, you may want to ask if anyone would like to start the discussion or you can turn to the person to your left and ask him, "In our own words, please state what brought you here today and why." During this process, you will be looking at body language. You will also need to ask probing questions to keep discussions moving along. When a person is done speaking, you may want to do a synopsis such as, "From hearing your account of the situation, I take it that you feel . . ." Rephrasing allows you to use words that reassures, empowers, neutralizes negativity, and clarifies situations or concepts. Remember, the truth is a three-edged sword with both sides having their own account but the truth is often the side less revealed. Part of peer mediation's function is to better reveal truths in a conflict. If you do a caucus, be sure to let the party know to stay in the waiting area until called back in. Remember to give both parties equal access to having a caucus. Make sure that, after a caucus session is about to wrap up, that you ask the party if you can have partial or full permission to reveal what was said. This can be done by saying, "From time to time it may be necessary for me to reveal what was said in the caucus. At this time, I would like your permission to disclose what was said here should I find it necessary or beneficial to the two of you reaching an agreement. Is there anything that you would object to me sharing with the other party? What do I have permission to tell the other party?" If the situation calls for it, never be afraid to suggest another school-provided service as an option to put in an agreement. This may be a trash pickup day, tutoring, or even peer counseling. At the end, you will draft a "Mediation Settlement Agreement" which says how the parties agree to handle the situation and a deadline (if necessary) for when actions should be done. The parties will then sign off on the agreement. In the back of this book is an Appendix section. Appendix H, Appendix I, and Appendix J are three forms that the peer mediator will usually have at a session. Appendix J is the mediation agreement form. If special services or conditions warrant, or if you need more space to write the conditions of the settlement, write "See Attachment A" in the blank agreement section, then take a blank sheet of paper and write "Attachment A" at the top, below that write the agreement and any special conditions that apply, below this you will want all three of you then initial the bottom "Attachment A", and then everyone would sign the agreement. By doing this, the attachment is now incorporated as a part of the agreement.

## Marco

You are a star varsity athlete as well as an A-student. Because you were raised in this area, you are well known by everyone in the school. Your sports prowess has also boosted your popularity at school but you don't ever want to be known as just another dumb jock. You hold intelligent people in high regard and try to surround yourself with them as often as you can. This is why you have repeatedly tried befriending Tom. He is a new kid, very introverted and removed from the other students, but he is also highly intelligent. You both love science and you think that you two could be fast friends if he would just give you the chance. After the third straight week of trying to be cordial and him running away, you just lost it. You figured that he saw you as just another dumb jock so you shouted out to him, "Go ahead and run away you little mama's boy!" That is when Tom turned around with tears streaming down his face. He came running back to you saying, "I'm not going to take anything off of a dumb jock with a Joe Six-Pack for a father!" That is when he shoved you. It surprised you how strong he actually is. With tears streaming down your face, you shoved him back as hard as you could. Shortly thereafter is when the coach came to break up the fight. What Tom does not know is that your father divorced your mom when your were in middle school. Playing sports was her idea to keep a positive male influence in your life. Your dad is a scientific consultant who travels frequently out of the country with the military, NASA, and other government agencies. No one knows how much you miss your father and how you try to use your intelligence to gain his attention. Another issue that no one knows about is your mother and your fears that something may be going on with her. She stays out of the home for hours on end. Sometimes, you even find her passed out on the couch when you wake the next morning. Every once in a while, a utility company has been known to cut off the water, power, and even natural gas. A time or two the only hot shower or meal you got was at school. She won't talk to you about what is going on and she won't let you take a part time job to help out with the bills. Her only goal is for you to get a sports scholarship and do well. This incident could ruin your chances at getting a scholarship if you get expelled. It is all becoming too much for you to bear. None of your so-called friends are that close to you where you feel you can honestly talk with them. Maybe that is why you tried so hard to reach out to Tom because he acts like he doesn't have a friend in the world.

## Tom

You are the new kid in school. You have been deliberately avoiding Marco like a plague. However, when he said, "Go ahead and run away you little mama's boy!" something turned on inside of your head and you just snapped. It really is kind of foggy now how everything happened afterwards. You do remember running towards Marco, shoving him, and saying something that you can't even remember now. Your lack of memory on this issue is now troubling you because, until now, you have had a near-eidetic mental recall. Because you are new, and keep to yourself, no one really knows that much about you . . . which you seem to like. No one knows that your dad used to be a well-paid research scientist. People also do not know that your mother was killed by some drunk football players one night after they were celebrating winning the regional championship. Your dad ended up losing everything shortly thereafter. This move was your dad's idea to start over with a new life. The problem is that you don't want to start over but you know that you can't go back either. You are stuck. Your dad doesn't speak to you about anything that matters to you. You have no one to talk to. And, to top it off, you are living in a small, low-rent apartment rather than the 3,500 square foot home and 20 acres that you are accustomed to. Your clothes are from thrift stores and meals are usually out of a box, a can, or from a cup that you pour boiling water in. Prison inmates get better food! To you, Marco represents the boys that killed your mother. In truth, you think you would like Marco but you can't bring yourself to talk to him because of all of the emotions you are feeling. Plus, you feel like you two have nothing in common and you are embarrassed by your home, clothes, etc. In your old school, you were pretty popular and even the president of the student body. You are not the person you used to be and you definitely are not wanting to be the person you are now. If this peer mediation goes sour, you can see yourself losing your entire future since your dad no longer can pay your college.

## What to Do:

Each player has a slip that tells about his or her character. The players should be given a few minutes to understand their character's point of view and understanding. The person playing Ms. Hendrix will read out the information about the case but she will have access to no other aspect of the case or the motivations of the characters involved. The characters will all have paper and pen to jot down notes as the mediation session progresses. It is important for the players to understand that what they are doing is very similar to what professional mediators do in the real world to resolve various issues. The peer mediator will help lead the discussions along. She must remain neutral. Parties usually are hesitant to reveal data. As a neutral, the peer mediator will have to use psychology, body language, intuition, personal experience, and other such tools to help forge in-roads to new information from the opposing parties in hopes that it will help to create agreement and understanding.

Jerry's performer has the instructions for how to seat everyone and how the session should take place. Sample forms are found in the Appendix section of this book for Jerry's performer to use.

When role players for Tom and Marco speak, they need to remember that they have data that only they know about. It is up to the skills of the professional and the process to reveal hidden information. Data revealed, as in real life, normally is only done if the person feels it would be beneficial. While it is okay for the performers to display realistic feelings, they should also stay somewhat cordial and adhere to the rules of not interrupting each other. If a player thinks that there character would not answer a question, it is okay to politely decline to answer or to somewhat dodge the question. It is the duty of the peer mediator to find ways to get the two parties to talking in a cooperative fashion and to take ownership of their conflict.

After the role playing session is over, have everyone gather in a circle and talk about their feelings. Was the set up a little odd?  If so, why? How did the individual people see the individual characters? Did perceptions change at all? How true to life do you think this situational scenario was? It should be noted that the scenario was made up by meshing up a host of common traits found in juvenile cases across the country. What did everyone think of the secrets and hidden thoughts? Do secrets and hidden motivations, or just an unclear perception for that matter, color how we act and behave around people? Did anyone have any knowledge that he didn't reveal? What would it have taken to reveal the hidden data? Do you think that the hidden data would have helped any? In real world mediations, the majority of cases rarely have anything to do with the stated reasons for the mediation session. That is to say that there is always some underlying conflict that is hidden and separate from the stated conflict that seems obvious to everyone. What could have been done better by the participants to resolve the issue at hand? What percentage of school-based problems do you think could be handled through peer mediation? How could something like a Peer Mediation-based program help a Community of Care?

# Conferences/Panels

Conferencing has to be the most misunderstood aspect of Restorative Practices. In America, a conference usually means a parent-teacher conference where the child is excluded from the conversation while the child's behavior or progress is being discussed. This type of conference is a far cry from what conferencing means in other parts of the world, like New Zealand, where juvenile conferencing is mandated by law.

A brief understanding of conferencing can be found in the February 2001 issue of the Office of Juvenile Justice and Delinquency Prevention's *Juvenile Justice Bulletin.* In this issue, the use of family in conferencing is described as follows:

> Family group conferencing is based on centuries-old sanctioning and dispute resolution traditions of the Maori of New Zealand. In its modern form, the model was adopted into national legislation in New Zealand in 1989, making it the most systemically institutionalized of any of the four models. In South Australia, family conferencing is now widely used in modified form as a police-initiated diversion approach known as the Wagga Wagga model. (Developed by the Wagga Wagga Police Department, this model uses police officers or school officials to set up and facilitate family conferencing meetings.) Conferencing is also being used in U.S. cities in Minnesota, Montana, Pennsylvania, Vermont, and several other states and in parts of Canada. (The Wagga Wagga model is the primary approach that has taken hold in North America.) A variety of offenses have been resolved through family group conferencing, including theft, arson, minor assaults, drug offenses, vandalism, and, in a number of states, child maltreatment cases. In New Zealand, conferencing is used in the disposition of all but the most violent and serious delinquency cases. Family group conferencing involves the community of people most affected by the crime—the victim, the offender, the family, friends, and key supporters of both, in deciding the resolution of a criminal or delinquent incident. The affected parties are brought together by a trained facilitator to discuss how they and others have been harmed by the offense and how that harm might be repaired.[23]

These statements tell us a little about the history of family based conferencing, other types of conferencing, and what it can be used for. They do not address how conferencing is to be carried out or what is involved. Moreover, a very broad picture of conferencing is painted. Truly, something is missing. If we look at the Unbroken Circles [SM] model from a "continuum of discipline" perspective, the program ranges in severity from very mild circles all the way to the very dire Circle Justice, which will be discussed in detail later. Conferencing is thus used for specific problems that are just beyond the capabilities of peer mediation yet just under the standard purviews of Circle Justice. Offenses suitable for conferencing are those where a student is about to be suspended or expelled, when a student has had repeat referrals to the dean's/principal's office, addiction issues, risky behavior/risky lifestyle issues, and even some first and second time misdemeanor offenses. Many of these types of issues are similar to what the local Teen Court hears;

consequently, conferencing occurs in conjunction with, or as a replacement for, teen courts. Like teen courts, conferencing in the court system relies heavily upon the practice of diversion with informal (discretionary) diversion by officers favored over programmatic (trial-ordered) diversion.

Similar to conferencing is the use of panels. Panels, rather than conferencing, are used in America and the rest of the world as a diversionary program in many court systems that employ a Restorative Justice perspective. Panels are different from conferences in that they do not include families, stakeholders in the community, etc. A great example of the panel system can be found in the Restorative Justice Panel system of the Burlington, Vermont Police Department. Here, the city's police have panels employing the use of three to five volunteers meeting with victims and offenders about cases. According to the City of Burlington, "The Panel's mission is to hold an offender accountable for the effects of their actions on others. They discuss the circumstances and impact of the crime and ways the offender can avoid making similar mistakes in the future." Like conferencing, these panels only handle low-level offenses that are typically found to be ideal for diversionary programs. The city notes,

> "The Panel, the victim and the offender decide together how the offender will make amends and repair the harm they caused. The reparations should be related to the crime and improve the community. Many people write letters of apology, do community service, repair damaged property or pay for damages they caused. Other times people do something they are good at or like to do. For example: a musician held a fundraiser for a non-profit daycare center, another woman made potpourri vases for a local senior citizens center, and a computer programmer helped the Community Justice Center improve its database. Once the group has agreed on the reparations to be made, a Restorative Justice Agreement is filled out and signed by all. The offender has 45 days to complete his or her commitments. The full group comes back together a few more times to review progress, solve any problems, and celebrate successful completion." According to the city, "The Burlington Community Justice Center sees an average of 300 cases a year. The Burlington Community Justice Center currently has four Panels meeting with adult offenders and one Panel that meets with youth offenders each week. Members are volunteers who make a two-hour weekly commitment for at least a year. They receive training and support from the Department of Corrections and the Community Justice Center."[24]

Whether funds allow a school, or judicial system, partnership with the school district to use conference or panels is really an issue of need and economics. In our highly legalized society, panels and conferences can be used as a diversionary method, taking the offenders out of the court system and giving them a chance for redemption and keeping a clean record. What is all of this talk about diversion? What is "diversion?"

Diversion is described as a method of steering offenders out of the criminal justice system by putting them in appropriate habilitation/rehabilitation programs to get help. Diversion can be requested by attorneys or ordered by a judge once charges have been filed. By not filing charges, a police officer can use discretionary powers to divert an offender to a program.[25] The latter is often more favorable when dealing with youth since the child has not been formally charged. Thus it will not show up on his/her permanent record when going to enlist, seeking employment, or seeking funding for college.

A panel versus a conference is a matter of need, preference, and economics. While conferences are preferred, panels are mentioned as a suitable substitute. In sophisticated programs, a school could set up panels leading to conferences. Panels are far less detailed than full-blown conferences, and, therefore, offer student volunteers and faculty the chance to work lower level panels and then, if required, the same panelist members can also serve in higher level conferences as interested stakeholders to keep continuity within the overall program. In either case, the setup for a conference or panel is very similar to that of a circle but with more formality than that of peer mediation. In fact, very often Restorative Justice Practitioners opt for a circle process. The dynamics and setup of conferences differ, depending on which of the many styles available the practitioner wishes to utilize. For instance, Wagga Wagga trained practitioners may utilize Reintegrative Shaming Experiments (RISE) based tactics with a school resource officer as the facilitator. By contrast, an England/Wales trained practitioner would probably be a school resource officer, but he/she would not use RISE.[26] The Unbroken Circles [SM] model highly suggests the use of Reintegrative Shaming.

Since the use of police officers has led to serious controversy in the past overseas, it is suggested that the facilitator be a state, county, district, or city, certified practitioner with at least twenty hours of Restorative Justice and formal conferencing training documented. This does not preclude school resource officers from being conference facilitators; rather this requirement acknowledges that a given standard has been set by the school delineating appropriate actions/behaviors and providing an added umbrella of immunity from legal prosecution. School resource officers, in addition to teachers and other education staff throughout the school district should be urged and encouraged to obtain the required minimal training. The purpose is to accrue a pool of facilitators to draw upon rather than just a handful in the school. This prevents resources from being "worn out" and allows a level of neutrality that is lacking in many contemporary Restorative Justice Programs using a community-intensive model.

The Unbroken Circles [SM] program acknowledges there are a diverse set of conference styles available. All conferences in a given school, or school district, should embody certain characteristics.

1) Participation in the conference should be voluntary.

2) Stakeholders should be involved.

3) Safety for all parties should be secured.

4) The process should be unbiased and fair.

5) Family of the offender and victim (if there is one) should be included in the process. Family members of the offender should be those family members that the offender looks up to and respects.

6) Positive friends of the offender may be included.

7) Supportive friends of the victim may be included.

8) All participants are subject to full disclosure of what will happen and be expected of them beforehand, with adequate time allotted in advance for any answering of questions and redress of issues.

9) The offender must admit guilt.

10) The process must be solution oriented, and the participants must speak in turn and be cordial.

11) An agreement must be reached; the agreement must be within the offender's ability to carry out, and the process must take into consideration habilitation/rehabilitation for the offender.

12) The victim (if there is one) should be the primary beneficiary of any reparations. The offender needs to make reparations to the victim (if there is one).

13) There should be consequences attached to the agreement for failure to comply, with a time limit set for reasonable completion of the agreement.

14) Oversight should be taken into consideration.

15) The contents of the conference should be held confidential with exception given to the specifics of the agreement and where otherwise required by law.

Taking into account that varying practices often demand varying setups, a suggested default setup format for an Unbroken Circles $^{SM}$ conference is:

1) A series of chairs placed in a circle.

2) Microphones and speakers strategically placed to facilitate proper communication.

3) The facilitator sitting with his/her back towards the primary exit. A secondary facilitator (if required or available), sitting across from the primary facilitator. Any additional facilitators (if required or available), are to sit equidistant from the primary and secondary facilitators.

4) Radiating from the left of the primary facilitator should be the friends and relatives of the victim, and the victim (if applicable).

5) From there, it should radiate out to the friends and relatives of the offender, and the offender themself.

6) Any neutral stakeholders (e.g., school officials, clergy, court officials, and officers) should be strategically placed between friends of the victim and friends of the offender.

Like with classroom circles, a talking piece may be used but is not necessary. The process should start with introductions, starting from the left of the mediator and going around the room. Several rounds should occur with the main rounds of concern being Introductions, Story of the Crime/Offense, Impact of the Offense, Addressing of Needs and Wants, Problem Solving, Issues Identification/Deliberation, Agreement and Conclusion.

As shown earlier in this chapter, role playing scenarios are critical, and any school employing a Collaborative Justice Program using conferences/panels should use multiple scenarios of varying degrees so participants trained can garner a greater appreciation for the set-up and core competencies of such tactics. Depending on the situation, set ups and equipment needed will vary, as well as the size and makeup of the group. For this reason, it is strongly suggested that a professional in conferences and panels be used for both training and as-needed consulting purposes.

# Circle Justice

In their book, "*Youth Offending and Restorative Justice: Implementing Reform in Youth Justice*," Adam Crawford and Tim Newburn write:

> Circles were first adapted from indigenous practices of First Nation people in Canada…The expansion of circles owes much to the re-emergence of tribal sovereignty on North American reservations. It has also been encouraged by the desire to keep down the numbers of aboriginal young men in prison. Circles are similar in many ways to conferences in that they seek to include the participation of affected parties beyond the victim and offender. However they tend to incorporate a broader notion of community participation than do most conferences… A common aim is to draw extended family and community members into the process of finding resolutions and redress to crimes… The idea is to assemble actors with the closest relation and social interdependencies to the principle disputants, most notably with a view to bringing together those people with the best chance of persuading the offender of the irresponsibility of a criminal act. There is also an emphasis upon ritual within circles. There is a 'keeper of the circle' whose purpose (like a mediator or facilitator) is to ensure inclusive dialogue and the integrity of the process. There is usually a 'talking piece' —which will often take the form of a feather —that is passed around the circle, only permitting the person holding it to speak. Circles seek to connect with, and allow space for, the spiritual and emotional aspect of aboriginal and indigenous cultures…Circles may involve multiple meetings in relation to a particular offender… Circles tend to take one of two forms: either 'healing circles' that have as their focus the disposition of situations and 'sentencing circles' that have a quasi-judicial capacity in that they make recommendations to judicial authorities for actual case disposition.[27]

Though healing circles are a valid American Indian practice, it is understood that such practices may seem alien for a community not accustomed to the ways and culture of American Indians. As such, for our purposes, and the practicality of the program, the topic of healing circles, as it pertains to Unbroken Circles [SM] would be only at the request of the victim or offender, with clergy present—if desired by participants and stakeholders—full disclosure beforehand, and proper counseling sources readily available. The holder of the process should be an individual trained in American Indian healing, such as a Cherokee Di-da-nv-wis-gi (Holy Man) or U-gu (Chief) and/or a religiously open-minded facilitator specifically trained in conferencing in this manner. Such a special event, depending on the law particulars of the wrongful offense and wishes of the school board, may necessitate the circle be held outside of school property. Some school boards may not be able to sanction these type of healing circles, in any shape or form, for legal reasons. Thus an outside location and facilitator in the community, apart from the school system, would need to be found.

For these reasons, public school officials may not be able or willing, to host, endorse, or suggest such a process. Nevertheless, healing circles can have profound transformative attributes that should be explored as an offering by a non-school affiliated non-profit partner. For those interested in developing such a program, an effective healing circle process should:

1) Embody full disclosure.

2) Establish safety for the victim.

3) Give the victim the ability to confront the offender safely.

4) Give support to the spouse/parent/child of the victim/offender, support the family of the victim/offender, and support the community,

5) Have proper assessment beforehand by trained professionals, with in-depth private counseling of the offender, in-depth private counseling of the victim, and group counseling with the families, well before the healing circle takes place.

Healing circles may take many sessions, with routine review circles occurring every six months for five years. Usually, when an offender has made amends, there is a cleansing or reintegration circle held to welcome the offender back into the fold as a fully vested member of the community.[28]

Sentencing circles are different from conferences and healing circles. The role of this circle is to determine the sentence of the offender so that (s)he can make amends for his/her crime. There are also many types of sentencing circles available. As Crawford and Newburn describe,

"Sentencing circles tend to be used in relation to serious offenses that warrant the significant investment of effort they entail. Circles may take a number of hours and may spread over a number of days. In addition to the parties affected by the crime, the judge, prosecutor, defense counsel police, and court workers may participate. Circles are sometimes held in courtrooms and may split into an inner and outer circle with the direct participants, victim, offender and their families, as well as justice professionals who may be called upon to provide the information in the outer circle."[29]

As with healing circles, sentencing circle processes have the same requirements for disclosure, victim safety, support, and assessment. Ultimately, the main difference between the two is the purpose, tone, and constituency makeup of the stakeholders in the process. Sentencing circles may take many sessions with a judge present to take "disposition"—a legal term, referring to the change in custody of a case. Subsequent review circles are generally held every six months for five years. Usually, when an offender has made amends, there is cleansing or reintegration circle held to welcome the offender back into the fold as a fully vested member of the community.[30]

Since laws that come into play in a sentencing circle vary, it is unwise for any set program to deviate from the Unbroken Circles [SM] Program. However, certain traits and considerations should be seriously contemplated when developing a specific Circle Justice program. The State Attorney's Office and the Public Defender's Office need to be mutually involved in the development of the program to meet general legal needs. Judges who may be associated with cases held by Circle Justice groups should be involved in the development of the program to meet certain judiciary needs. The Sheriff's Office should participate in the coordination of the program to meet certain safety and transport-of-prisoner considerations. Counselors should be identified for participation in a counseling pool. Likewise, evaluators should be identified for inclusion in an evaluator's pool. Circle Justice facilitators should be identified and placed in a facilitator's pool, and appropriate academics should be called upon to assist with various training and research needs.

It is highly recommended that, due to a lack of research on individual tribal practices concerning Circle Justice, facilitators be well versed in the Ojibwa Community Holistic Circle Healing Program developed in Hollow Water, Manitoba, Canada.[31] If possible, local tribes, using a similar program extensively as a part of their culture, should be considered for inclusion. Though rarely found in other cultures, if a group wishes to use the Circle Justice practices of another culture, such a request should be reviewed by a trained facilitator and a cultural ambassador from that community. This is to ensure that any necessary changes and revisions do not compromise the overall intent and function of what Circle Justice sessions are supposed to be. Moreover, due to legal reasons, the training of facilitators may need to be evaluated to meet demands of the State Attorney's Office, Public Defender's Office, and judge(s). Such training requirements may include that the facilitators be certified mediators with forty hours of additional training in Restorative Justice and Circle Justice Practices.

## Discussion

The Unbroken Circles [SM] proposed model of Collaborative Justice is based on years of research and application. It meshes both Restorative Justice and Conflict Resolution practices—two fields that recently have been at loggerheads with each other. Both sides, ironically, have sectors that are increasingly becoming more like the other in form and practice. Collaborative Justice realizes this truth and embraces the benefits of the two opposing sides.

Not all practitioners are trained to handle a Collaborative Justice Program. For instance, even within the field of Restorative Justice, there are practitioners who have absolutely no understanding of the intricate nature of "shame" as it pertains to Reintegrative Shaming. Additionally, most Conflict Resolution specialists do not recognize three-quarters of the tactics employed in this book. Therefore, they have no appreciation for the various nuances of stigmatic shame versus Reintegrative Shaming. Be careful that your school uses a professional trained in Unbroken Circles [SM,] and that the professionals have core competencies in all of the elements espoused and utilized by the Unbroken Circle [SM] Program.

Values and beliefs also play in the success and processes of the program. Values and beliefs are different from program axioms. There are a number of people trained in theories or techniques but do not necessarily pair them well with their practice. The Unbroken Circles [SM] is a well-researched program with successful case histories to draw on including usage of peer mediation, circles, etc. throughout North America and the rest of the world. However, sometimes there is a potential consultant saying Restorative Justice is totally a Native American or a total Maori system of justice dealing. Some think it is a Hebrew system found in the Bible. This is not the case. While pieces and parts come from different cultures, the combined practices of Unbroken Circles [SM] are a new method intended for the needs of our contemporary society. Yes, the program axioms are age-old in some respects, but the mixing and mingling, using one's strength to fortify the weaknesses of another program, gives the Unbroken Circles [SM] Program a distinct vantage point.

This is the only Collaborative Justice Program on the market allowing schools to decide what is best. While the name, Unbroken Circles, [SM] is a protected name that can only be used under an authorized contract, the core components of the program are in the public domain and are not proprietary material. This allows the school, or school district, tremendous flexibility. In the end, the ultimate power to change the school is given back to the school along with tools that have a proven track record.

From this point on, the remainder of the book concerns itself with implementation. Very few references or diagrams are used. The second section of the book is about the application of the program rather than details of the program. Compelling issues like Broken Windows Theory are addressed to illustrate how schools can further curb conflict by keeping walls painted, fixtures repaired, and so forth. As with S.H.I.F.T. Theory, the Unbroken Circles [SM] program employs a holistic approach. Multiple layers of psychology and criminology theories are used in conjunction with the four pillar practices in order to create a revolutionary program that gives schools the desired results they seek, if properly employed.

# References

1.    Amstutz, L. and Mullet, J. (2005). *The Little Book of Restorative Discipline for Schools: Teaching Responsibility; Creating Caring Climates.* Good Books:Intercourse, PA

      Bazemore, G. and Walgrave, L. Eds.(1999). *Restorative Juvenile Justice: Repairing the Harm of Youth Crime.* Criminal Justice Press:Monsey, NY

      Bazemore, G. and Schiff, M. Eds. (2001). *Restorative Community Justice: Repairing Harm and Transforming Communities.* Anderson Publishing: Cincinnati, OH

      Bazemore, G. and Schiff, M. (2005). *Juvenile Justice Reform and Restorative Justice: Building Theory and Policy From Practice.* Willan Publishing:Portland, OR

      Crawford, A. and Newburn, T. (2003). *Youth Offending and Restorative Justice: Implementing Reform in Youth Justice.* Willan Publishing:Portland, OR

      Hayden, A. (2001). *Restorative Conferencing Manual of Aotearoa New Zealand: He Taonga no a Tatou Kete (A Treasure From Our Basket).* District Courts of New Zealand: Wellington, NZ

      Johnstone, G. Ed. (2003). *A Restorative Justice Reader: Texts, Sources, Context.* Willan Publishing:Portland, OR

      McLaughlin, E., Gergusson, R., Hughes, G. and Westmarland, L. Eds. (2003). *Restorative Justice: Critical Issues.* Sage Publications:London, UK

      Roche, D. (2003). *Accountability in Restorative Justice.* Oxford Press:Oxford, UK

      Zehr, H. (1990). *Changing Lenses: A New Focus for Crime and Justice.* Herald Press: Scottdale, PA

      Zehr, H. (2002). *The Little Book of Restorative Justice.* Good Books:Intercourse, PA

2.    Dellaportas, S. (2011). *Accountants in Prison: Reintegrative or Stigmatic Shaming.* AFAANZ 2011 Conference. Paper 90. Accounting & Finance of Australian and New Zealand (AFAANZ). Retrieved on 1/16/2012 from http://www.afaanz.org/openconf/2011/modules/request.php?module=oc_proceedings&action=view.php&a=Accept+as+Paper&id=90

3.    Campbell, H. & Revering, C. (April 2012). *Holding Kids Accountable: Shaming with Compassion.* CYC-Online. The International Child and Youth Care Network. Issue 39. Retrieved on 1/28/2013 from http://www.cyc-net.org/cyc-online/cycol-0402-accountable.html

4.    Victoria University of Wellington Institute of Criminology (September 2001). *Revisiting Reintegrative Shaming.* *Criminology Aotearoa/New Zealand* Newsletter, September 2001, No. 16. Institute of Criminology. Victoria University of Wellington: Wellington, New Zealand

5.    Dictionary.com (2013). *Retribution.* Retrieved on 1/25/2013 from www.dictionary.com

6.    Dictionary.com (2013). *Repentance.* Retrieved on 1/25/2013 from www.dictionary.com

7.    Dictionary.com (2013). *Atonement.* Retrieved on 1/25/2013 from www.dictionary.com

8.    Dictionary.com (2013). *Forgive.* Retrieved on 1/25/2013 from www.dictionary.com

9.    Zehr, H. (1990). *Changing Lenses: A New Focus for Crime and Justice.* Herald Press:Scottsdale, PA

10.   Florida Tribe of Cherokee Indians (2012). *Cherokee Language.* Florida Tribe of Cherokee Indians:Milton, FL

11.   US Government Accounting Office (2012). Native American Sterilization Program Data to 2009. US Government Accounting Office: Washington, DC

      US Bureau of Indian Affairs. Native American Tribal Recognition Laws. US Bureau of Indian Affairs: Washington, DC

Johnson, K (6 May 2013). *Ken Johnson: At Least Let Us Recognize Florida's Tribes. Tallahassee Democrat Newspaper*. Gannett: Tallahassee, FL

12. Amstutz, L. and Mullet, J. (2005). *The Little Book of Restorative Discipline for Schools: Teaching Responsibility; Creating Caring Climates*. Good Books: Intercourse, PA

13.

Amstutz, L. and Mullet, J. (2005). *The Little Book of Restorative Discipline for Schools: Teaching Responsibility; Creating Caring Climates*. Good Books:Intercourse, PA

Bazemore, G. and Walgrave, L. Eds.(1999). *Restorative Juvenile Justice: Repairing the Harm of Youth Crime*. Criminal Justice Press:Monsey, NY

Bazemore, G. and Schiff, M. Eds. (2001). *Restorative Community Justice: Repairing Harm and Transforming Communities*. Anderson Publishing:Cincinnati, OH

Bazemore, G. and Schiff, M. (2005). *Juvenile Justice Reform and Restorative Justice: Building Theory and Policy From Practice*. Willan Publishing:Portland, OR

Crawford, A. and Newburn, T. (2003). *Youth Offending and Restorative Justice: Implementing Reform in Youth Justice*. Willan Publishing:Portland, OR

Hayden, A. (2001). *Restorative Conferencing Manual of Aotearoa New Zealand: He Taonga no a Tatou Kete (A Treasure From Our Basket)*. District Courts of New Zealand: Wellington, NZ

Johnstone, G. Ed. (2003). *A Restorative Justice Reader: Texts, Sources, Context*. Willan Publishing:Portland, OR

McLaughlin, E., Gergusson, R., Hughes, G. and Westmarland, L. Eds. (2003). *Restorative Justice: Critical Issues*. Sage Publications:London, UK

Roche, D. (2003). *Accountability in Restorative Justice*. Oxford Press:Oxford, UK

Zehr, H. (1990). *Changing Lenses: A New Focus for Crime and Justice*. Herald Press: Scottdale, PA

Zehr, H. (2002). *The Little Book of Restorative Justice*. Good Books:Intercourse, PA

14. Amstutz & Mullet, 2005, pgs. 52 & 53

15. Amstutz & Mullet, 2005

16. Sorenson, D. (1992). *Conflict Resolution and Mediation for Peer Helpers*. Educational Media Corporation:Minneapolis, MN

17. Schrumpf, F., Crawford, D., and Bodine, R. (1997). *Peer Mediation: Conflict Resolution in Schools (Rev.) Student Manual*. Research Press:Champaign, IL

18. Cohen, R. (2005). *Peer Mediation in Schools: Students Resolving Conflict (Grades 6-12)*. Good Year Books:Tucson, AZ

19. Cohen, 2005, pg. 4

20. Cohen, 2005, pg. 5

21. Cohen, 2005, pg. 5

22. Davies, L. (2006). *Solutions Through Peer Mediation*. Retrieved 5/19/ 2006 (Verified as active again on 2/3/2013) from http://www.kellybear.com/TeacherArticle/TeacherTip13.html

23. Bazemore, G. and Umbreit, M. (February 2001). *A Comparison of Four Restorative Conferencing Models. Juvenile Justice Bulletin*. Office of Juvenile Justice and Delinquency Prevention:Washington, DC

24.  Burlington, Vermont (2013). *Restorative Justice Panels.* Retrieved on 2/3/2013 from http://www.burlingtonvt.gov/CJC/Restorative-Justice-Panels/

25.  Worrall, J. (2006). *Crime Control in America: An Assessment of the Evidence.* Pearson A&B:Boston, MA

26.  Crawford, A. and Newburn, T. (2003). *Youth Offending and Restorative Justice: Implementing Reform in Youth Justice.* Willan Publishing:Portland, OR

27.  Crawford & Newburn, 2003, pgs. 32-33

28.  Morris, A. and Maxwell, G. Eds. (2002). *Restorative Justice for Juveniles: Conferencing, Mediation & Circles.* Hart Publishing:Portland, OR

29.  Crawford & Newburn, 2003, pg. 34

30.  Morris & Maxwell, 2002

31.  Morris & Maxwell, 2002

# Section 2

# 2.1

## Caring Shows - Critical Concepts Review

In the field of Criminal Justice, there are two concepts referred to under the terminology of Community Control or Community Crime Prevention. The idea of Community Control is to show that the community cares so criminal activity either never starts or it is displaced elsewhere.[1] One of the key concepts used by this methodology of crime prevention is the Broken Windows Theory while the other concept is the Palo Alto Car Experiment.

Broken Windows Theory implies that crime, at least in part, is based on the lack of care exhibited by a community. Areas with unfixed, broken windows in buildings and homes also tend to have higher levels of crime. When the windows are fixed, and the appearance of care by the community is demonstrated (i.e., new paint on buildings, grass cut, etc.) then the level of crime experienced goes down.[2]

The Palo Alto Car Experiment is the precursor to and reinforces the Broken Windows Theory by showing how deliberate actions to lower perceptions of care can provoke crime to happen. Already you have learned how, in 1969, a psychologist, named Philip Zimbardo, took a 1959 model Oldsmobile and placed it in two different cities, representing two disparate socio-economic classes. Once a sufficient lack of care was shown, the experiment revealed that all societies inevitably break down and resort to crime.[3]

This book does not go into all the theories and contentions made by Zimbardo or Wilson, regarding Palo Alto and Broken Windows. However, it is important to note how psychologists and Criminal Justice academics have long correlated and supported the notion that crime is, at least in part, related to the level of care that a community exerts to keep the buildings and landscaping all neat, clean, tidy, and in working order. This concept is the easiest mechanism to enact, the most effective control, and the one most underutilized by any crime prevention program.

In a traditional school system, you are in a community that Restorative Justice Professionals refer to as a Community of Care. Sometimes, based on size and involvement, Restorative Justice Professionals will refer to such a Community of Care as either a Macro Community or a Micro Community. The students who come to said school are there for most of their waking day. They are exposed to peers and people in the community. For many students, there are other influencers and stakeholders in their Community of Care such as tutoring institutions, dance classes, sports teams, churches/synagogues/temples, etc. Some schools are "last stop" schools for troubled students with criminal backgrounds. Here, the students may not share as many community "stakeholders" as traditional students, but they still have the court system, probation officers, or the state Juvenile Justice agency. However, whether the child is a traditional student or a student with a criminal past, he/she is going to a school that can be a Community of Care with profound, life-changing powers. A poorly kept school, which is dirty, graffiti-ridden, disorganized, and generally disheveled, serves as a social indicator that it is okay for the student to commit acts of vandalism or crime within the community. It is a blaring, "Please commit crime here" sign put out in front of the student body each and every time they see litter throughout the halls, graffiti on lockers and in bathrooms, and broken fixtures.

## Zero Tolerance

Understanding and using Broken Windows and Palo Alto as a guide, it should be apparent to any school administrator that the first and foremost action to implement with the Unbroken Circles <sup>SM</sup> or any other crime prevention program, is to initiate a Zero Tolerance Graffiti/Desecration Policy. This policy would focus on ensuring student exposure to broken fixtures, graffiti, chipped/fading paint, and litter is as minimal as possible. Mind you, this is not proposing a punitive policy. Rather, this is a policy meant to safeguard and strengthen the Community of Care the school represents to the students.

Starting such a policy is relatively easy. It begins with a simple policy change by the school principal stating that no graffiti will be allowed, trash should be picked up and properly disposed of, and that every fixture should be working properly with no sign of wear, vandalism, or disorganization showing. The hard part is the follow through.

Such a policy is not merely an administrative decision. Rather, it must be a whole school embracement of a concept. Teachers must make sure the same policies go to their classrooms as well—even if it means personally sweeping the floors before and after class. However, no such change will take place if the administration does not embrace this concept and demonstrate it on a daily basis.

Think of it this way; there is a piece of paper in the hallway. The principal comes by, says "hello" to a few students, notices the paper, and walks on by. What are the students and faculty to think? Now, let us imagine that instead of walking by, the principal picks up the trash. What do you think the students and faculty are to think? It is simple human psychology; subordinates will only place value on the things that the leader places value. If the school is so important that the principal is willing to play janitor, then the students and faculty will know that the school must be so important to them that they are willing to play janitor as well.

Once this concept has taken root, the administration needs to set up a system where students and faculty can report issues for the upkeep of the school. Naturally, the school should not be in the position where anyone can call a maintenance person to repaint a bathroom or hallway—that can get rather costly. Therefore, it is up to the administration to set up a workable plan, based on the school and its needs, where students and faculty have input and can alert officials of a need to keep the school presentable as a source of pride. In addition, it is critical for the administration to quickly evaluate and act upon such complaints. After all, what are the faculty and students to think after they have notified someone about a graffiti-ridden bathroom for weeks on end with no resolution? Thus, it is critical to keep evaluation and engagement at the forefront so that no more than a few minutes pass without some action being taken.

It is also good to post signs in the school about the policy and to have the zero tolerance policy prominently posted on the school's website. The policy should be brief but concise. It may even be advantageous to the school to state it is based on the Palo Alto Car Experiment and Broken Windows Theory research and that the policy is the school's affirmation to the students, faculty, and community that it is a place of care and proper stewardship. The policy should be specific, stating that any noticeable wear, graffiti, or desecration of school property will be fixed promptly and that all visitors are encouraged to notify faculty/staff should attention be drawn to a point of concern, improperly placed trash, etc. Moreover, the policy should be empowering in its wording to let even students know that they are a part of a Community of Care and that they have a right and duty to keep their school looking the best it can and be in proper working order.

## References:

1. For more information, please visit http://www.solutionsforamerica.org/thrivingneigh/crime-prevention.html

2. Wilson, J. and Kelling, G. (March 1982) The Police and Neighborhood Safety: Broken Windows. The Atlantic Monthly, pp. 29-38. Atlantic Monthly Group: Washington, DC

3. To learn more about Dr. Philip Zimbardo and his studies on crime, please visit:

   https://www.criminology.fsu.edu/crimtheory/zimbardo.htm

# 2.2

## Inclusion

After lack of participation from administration, the next greatest reason why any conflict control program fails is a lack of inclusion. As Americans, we all love to talk about democracy and every person having his/her say. However, the truth is that we, as Americans, often times rarely have a say. In fact, the whole idea that America is a democracy is a myth perpetuated by politicians and places of education. America is in fact a republic form of government. This means, in addition to the elected representatives, we also have appointed and hired representatives. Think about it for a moment; when is the last time you had a voice in who the next dogcatcher was or who the next Supreme Court Justice was? The reason why you never had a say in such matters is our republican form of government.

Indeed, the average American usually has little say for how their taxes, children, and land are handled and treated by the various layers of government (i.e., federal, state, regional, county, municipal, etc.). For the most part, many Americans like our republican form of government because we simply do not have the time, resources, or even care to properly determine whom the next dogcatcher should be, set standards for the grading of eggs, or determine regulations on the "cottage foods" industry. That does not mean, however, that such a mentality should be the norm when developing a program to change the structure of a school. Yes, school officials have a legal right, yet sometimes having a legal right does not mean that one has a moral or ethical right to do something. Even in our republican government, some things are so life changing and important that constituents and stakeholders are frequently included in the discussion and planning.

In fact, studies have shown repeatedly that inclusion by stakeholders in the implementation and direction of a life-changing program, often results in heightened functionality of the program as well as the general level of acceptance that the impacted group(s) has towards the program. With the Unbroken Circles $^{SM}$ Program, it is even more critical that inclusion be available to students, faculty, and staff.

To best meet the needs of the school and facilitate full inclusion, some hard decisions need to be made by administrators as to how break out groups, surveys and committees are set up, and who is to participate in the groups. After all, one would not necessarily want kindergarteners having a say in such a program's development, but some middle school, and most high school aged students have sufficient cultural sophistication to know how they are expected to act, where points of conflict may exist, and ways they would be responsive to having those points of conflict resolved.

For some age groups, it might be best if teachers survey students about how safe they feel at school, how fair they deem current disciplinary actions to be, and how responsive they would be to having peers more involved in dealing with disciplinary actions. Encouraging teachers to talk about the benefits of Conflict Resolution practices and/or teaching about Alternative Dispute Resolution practices in relation to the status quo is advantageous. Administration could allow the Student Council or Student Government Association (SC/SGA) leaders to hold general assemblies and/or set up their own surveys and commentary boxes. Of course, such actions are subjective decisions that the school must make based on the age and maturity of the student population in relation to the desired goals and outcome of the program.

With teachers, as well as other faculty and staff, having professionals host a discussion may be advantageous. Many school professionals have never heard of Restorative Justice, Alternative Dispute Resolution, or Conflict Resolution. Having an honest, open discourse about what each concept is, how it works, its benefits, its limitations, and how it can be applied, empowers the professionals with new knowledge and understanding. It demystifies unknown aspects and concepts while giving them a voice so that they may express their concerns and desires. Such open discussions often create inroads to alleviate and reduce feelings of apprehension and hesitance that professionals may initially have of a proposed policy change.

Parents, on the other hand, can be a bit challenging at times—as can be vouched for by any teaching professional. Students come from various backgrounds, from families who are seldom involved with the student's life to families that are highly involved. Some students don't have a traditional family setting and may have an elderly grandparent raising them along with other children. Due to a changing society, many families require parents to work more than one job. It is a national travesty that many students go home every day to an empty house with little to no food. Thus, special care needs to be taken to involve parents/guardians to the best of the school's (as well as the parents'/guardians') abilities. This may mean employing the help of the Parent Teacher Organization or Parent Teacher Association (PTO/PTA) officers, local community church leaders, and local extracurricular activity instructors (i.e., dance teachers, drama teachers, band directors, coaches, etc.) to help get the word out about the proposed changes. They can also act as a resource, or emissary, between taxed parents/guardians and the school. Making sure that the PTO/PTA officers, extracurricular instructors, and local church leaders all work together can be challenging. After all, they do truly love the kids and want the best for them, or they would not be spending so much time trying to help the children. However, they all have different goals and different vantage points that can sometimes color perceptions, get in the way of understanding base concepts, or prove as a point of conflict in how best to implement something, to correct for a perceived problem. Therefore, it may be beneficial to have them come together as an advisory board, or panel, with a school administrator or other official as an ad hoc member, to keep the group on track.

In a world where committees seem to exist everywhere, some people groan at the idea of a special committee being set up to investigate a policy/program change. However, once there is a decision to accept a given change, committees can be a fountain of knowledge and guidance on how best to develop and implement a proposed program. It takes the burden off administration, and it provides inclusion for all parties involved. Ideally, a well-structured committee should be formed of members who come from administration, faculty/staff, parents/guardians (i.e., PTO/PTA), Conflict Resolution professionals (i.e., Johnson Institute), and the student body (i.e., SC/SGA). Within such a committee, sub-committees should also exist to address the needs, implementation, and practicality of any proposed procedural changes.

For instance, one sub-committee would work on the design, function, and makeup aspects of a board or panel that addresses high-level offenses. Still another sub-committee would look at a board, panel, or circle that will be handling medium level offenses. A third group would develop a peer mediation program that is workable and functional to the needs and goals of the school. Finally, another group would determine how best to set up daily class circles.

Nothing says that a member of one sub-committee cannot serve on another sub-committee as well. In fact, it is common for committee or board members to serve as an advisor and member to sub-groups as the need arises. The trick to using committees is to make sure that any meeting is functional, productive, and ultimately beneficial to the process and program. Please note, the best committees are composed of both professionals and lay persons so that all issues can be resolved in a meeting before they ever happen in real life.

As a whole, the committee should look into core concepts for all established boards, panels, and circles, to identify with. For instance, this book talks a great deal about Communities of Care, Macro Communities, and Micro Communities. However, from the school's standpoint, it is very important not to use vague language and instead identify who is and isn't a stakeholder at a given level of a Community of Care. After all, one would not want to have the local church pastor or baseball coach, serve in a daily class circle as a stakeholder. For the same reason, in an act of serious school vandalism, it might be beneficial to involve a student's coach or pastor, as a stakeholder in a high-level offense's board or panel meeting. Having those terms properly identified and defined for the usage of specific components to the overall plan is critical to the viability and success of the program.

Again, it is all about the school working things out to fit the needs of the school. Unbroken Circles <sup>SM</sup> is not a "one size fits all" approach to resolving school-based conflicts. Rather, look at it as a toolbox from which stakeholders can take out and use what tools best fit their needs, goals, and objectives. The program is only as successful as the community makes it. Moreover, at the bottom of it all lies the fact that inclusion needs to be the primary concern at all levels of discussion, development, implementation, and review.

## Taking the Ball and Running with It

Inclusion is one thing, but education is a horse of a different color. Education has the power to persuade, inform, and even help guide a person through a given topic. While education may involve inclusion, the subject matter and course guidelines are predetermined and frequently pre-established to give a specific vantage point.

In a school, students are used to being taught whatever and however, the school system deems fit. If done right, the education given to the students enriches their lives and provides a resource they can use for higher-level activities as they develop. We already do this as a society with algebra, biology, social studies, and history, so why not include Conflict Resolution practices that reinforce the Unbroken Circles SM Program adopted by the school?

Something that the school's instructional staff may desire to do is to set up classes that empower students to learn how to resolve disputes in a civil manner. This may involve role-playing. The act of role-playing is a tried and true technique used by many states in the education and certification of mediators and other Conflict Resolution professionals.

Another thing that the instructional staff may want to address is the hierarchy of Conflict Resolution methodologies, as the school sees and employs them, for the proper addressing of conflicts. Teachers should be shown how similar methodologies work elsewhere in the world (i.e., the use of panels in New Zealand vs. America). This is especially important so they may compare how different cultures handle similar situations. It is easy to integrate such a program into a social studies setting.

However, like the picking up of trash discussed in Chapter 2.1, some concepts are foundational to the program's success. With students, especially today's students who exist in a low impulse gratification world, it is imperative to teach them to take responsibility for their actions.

One way to do this is for the school to adopt a P.R.I.D.E. component to the daily curriculum. P.R.I.D.E. is an acronym, which stands for the taking of Personal Responsibility In One's Daily Efforts. Personal pride comes from a heart that embraces a concept of P.R.I.D.E. It says, "you and you alone are responsible for your actions." This is a profound statement and belief that runs contrary to a worldview, where everyone is a victim and no one should be held accountable. More than that, though, it changes the definition of a wrongful action from being the mere breaking, or lack of compliance, with a given policy or rule to one's unwillingness to be accountable for their own actions and respectful of the will of the community that they exist in.

With P.R.I.D.E., if anyone loses their say in the community—it is because they gave it up of their own accord. For the politics and government teachers, it refocuses the core class discussion from America not living up to its promise by shutting out its people to Americans not living up to their duty to maintain the promise by staying perpetually involved with the actions and focus of our mutual government. For social studies teachers, it reaffirms and contrasts how Americans are alike so many cultures yet so fundamentally different. In regards to the math and science teachers, it places the blame and ownership of the student's education squarely back on the shoulders of the student. Any failing or inability to grasp a concept is because of a student's failure to strive for greatness and reaching out for help to accomplish such a task.

If employed properly and embraced by every stakeholder in the school (i.e., administration, faculty/staff, students), P.R.I.D.E. is a paradigm changing concept in how a school responds to a given situation. It gives everyone a source of pride because they not only worry for themselves but also for those around them—and they know that others are doing the same in return for them. P.R.I.D.E. is the brick and mortar to building a great Community of Care.

## Ownership

There comes a point for everything worth doing, when it is time to move past planning, theory, and conjecture to actual ownership of the situation at hand. We walked through the various methods of planning, discussing, and seeking proper implementation for a program based on the concepts espoused in the Unbroken Circles [SM] Program. Consider the needs of the school as a community and include this during the process. Suggestions are available on possible lesson plans. Developing future lesson plans, and expanding the program should be based upon need and the fluid situation in a given classroom. Now, let's talk about ownership of the program once it's approved.

One way to, publicly and mentally, gain ownership of any given situation is to draft and sign a contract or covenant. In an ideal world, there would actually be different contracts for different stakeholders. Administration would have one that they would publicly sign stating that they will recognize the authority of the community in the handling of disputes and that they will temper their involvement to best administrate the needs of all parties concerned. Outside stakeholders (i.e., churches, civic clubs, etc.) would then draft a resolution affirming their recognition of the school as a member of the community and affirming the outside group's commitment to helping the school resolve conflicts in a peaceful manner so it is a source of strength and pride in the greater Community of Care. Non-instructional staff could execute a compact affirming their influence on the look and functionality of the school and the impact on the attitude of students. A similar styled compact, drafted by instructional staff, would affirm their commitment to the process, adopted programs, and adherence of P.R.I.D.E. for the betterment of all involved. Through the SC/SGA working in collaboration with the PTA/PTO, a resolution could be rendered affirming mutual intent to embrace the process and programs adopted, while also affirming the adherence of P.R.I.D.E. and promise of daily personal involvement.

When drafting such a contract, or covenant, the wording should not become vague or frivolous. The document needs or requires "teeth." A document should not be so draconian that it becomes a snare to entrap the subscriber or a club to pummel them. Instead, it should be thoughtful and reflect the covenant being made with due consideration for the duties required and the consequences posed, should the agreement be broken. As a mortgage, deed, or other contract it should be a document with the benefits, costs, and duties properly spelled out, remedies considered for minor infractions, and an overall commitment to a higher form of conflict resolution as need merits for greater level offenses and outright breeches of contract.

Naturally, in a well-rounded program, one might consider having the contract/covenant signing as a public event with press and other members of the community invited. In this way, it becomes a statement to the local community that this school is making a commitment as a unified front. It makes a public statement; "Nothing is taken lightly." It publicly reaffirms involvement by all concerned. Moreover, it makes the experience real for all of the parties involved so that it is not just an action done and forgotten but an action that now has a perpetual duty.

# 2.3

## The Overseer

The word, overseer often times has negative connotations tied to it. In science fiction it gives an ominous tone, a perceived taskmaster who lords over (slave) workers and whose pecking order in the overall hierarchy is unknown. However, in a world of budget cuts, people hold multiple functions. I see the term as a person who is ultimately accountable for making sure the process works. If there are any slave-like attributes tied to the person, it is the program itself, not the people. The overseer is charged with making sure it does what it is supposed to do.

Think of my usage of overseer as being an administrator, foreman, or other such official without the reference to a specific title or functionality. Instead, the term is merely generic to refer to a person in charge of the program. Remember, in the Unbroken Circles [SM] Program, I talk in terms of generalities so that the schools can come together with their own definitions and titles and talk in terms of specifics.

## Part Time/Full Time: Working the Job

In today's society, there is indeed a wearing of many hats by workers. Practically every worker has had a time when he or she was doing the work of more than one person. When economies dip, or are uncertain, it is common to find people laboring away, doing the work of four or more people while receiving the same pay for seemingly more frustration. True, it is a sad state of affairs at times, but it is how our capitalist system works. Moreover, in an ideal situation, one's boss should see this dedication and reward it when times are better.

In the field of education, this idea is especially true as teachers take on more and more duties, as well as paying for classroom resources out of their own pockets while budgets dwindle more and more. With that said, starting a full-on Conflict Resolution-styled program is naturally going to give the administrative staff heartburn as proposed cost savings are being thrown up against perceived true costs of implementing a program.

For this reason, all parties involved need to know the benefits and costs of the program using different strategies. In addition, since having someone over the program is necessary, the most practical thing to look at is whether the overseer of the program is dedicated to the program either on a full time or part time basis.

162

Having a program overseer who is only working part time is very cost effective for a school. It allows the school to use a teacher, or other professional in the system, to take on additional duties. The hope is when times get better, this person will be promoted and possibly take over the program and get set on a track to work his/her way up the socio-economic ladder of employment with the school and the school district.

For the same reason, the school can also choose to outsource the part time role to a professional group on a contractual basis. Such a contracted professional might be with a local mediation firm, local mental health counseling service, or local church. These people have a greater sense of duty to the program because they do this every day as a part of their profession. They also have a contract in place that demands their attention and expertise to be devoted to the program's success—something not done often with instructors and staff in a school who are taking on the role as a part time function in addition to other duties.

However, allowing the overseer of such a program to be part time has a host of pitfalls to it as well. Most importantly, there is a compression of priorities when one works such a job only part time. For instance, if the part time overseer is faculty/staff, the overseer not only has to handle the program's problems but also the duties of their primary job. If their boss says that getting students ready for a national testing session is the priority for their main job, then that means that they will have to either intentionally, or unintentionally, cut back on what they are doing with the program so they can carry out their primary role.

By the same token, outsourced contractors, doing part time work in the school or school district, run into similar situations when their boss tries to pick up a larger contract or if ownership or management of the business is changing hands. Ultimately, the priorities of a private contractor can dramatically shift because of business-related events transpiring outside of the school, similar events taking place independent of the school district, or even events taking place in their very own corporate headquarters.

With part time work, there also comes the matter of pay. It is common for entities to throw on the duties without just, monetary compensation. This may be good for the company, but it is not good for the worker. Whether a private contractor or faculty/staff, people are still people and everyone desires to be treated fairly. If there is no just-compensation for the extra duties, it should become obvious that the worker, at some point, will decide to shirk duties so the level of work he/she is doing more fairly (in their eyes) matches up with the pay he/she is receiving. To clean up an old Vietnam era military mantra, "part time work results in very poor performance."

For this reason, my recommendation is to hire a full time overseer, whenever it is appropriate, and permanently assign that person to run the program. The part time approach is fraught with dangers and problems that may cause decay in a perfectly structured program. The way that I see it, you are either committed 100%, or you are not committed at all—anything other than that is just a colossal risk of lost time and resources. However, it is hard to hold such feelings when one is an administrator having to decide which programs not to teach and which teachers to lay-off in order to balance a budget. Therefore, before deciding to go either part time or full time, it is important for all parties involved to evaluate fully, the pros and cons of going each route.

This, however, does not mean that having a full time overseer is without problems. For instance, having a full time overseer is costly. Usually, in order for the school to justify such enormous cost expenditure, job candidates are required to have and maintain certain credentials beyond what would be required of a part time person, in order to get and keep the job. Higher training often translates into a higher salary while the need to maintain credentials and training often equates into even higher costs. Using common business consulting practices for government employee management planning, one can expect about a 1 to 3 ratio of the part time professional salary, to the cost of a full time professional. Such additional costs are taxes, training, insurance, benefits, retirement, etc. For private contractors, the cost ratio is less, at about a 1 to 1.5 ratio because there usually are not retirement and benefit costs paid out; instead, the contractual price covers whatever costs the contracted firm has to pay for their agent. In other words, a school can expect to pay out an additional $150,000 for a full time position where it has been paying $50,000 to a tenured faculty/staff member to do the work part time.

Using the outsourcing model, logic indicates that a school could expect to pay out an additional $75,000 in contracted full time employment for the same contracted part time employment position. That would be $75,000 in overall cost savings in contracted vs. in-house full time worker costs. However, it is not realistic to try to compare the government and business cost estimate ratios equally since most Conflict Resolution professionals can easily make $150 to $300 per hour or more, in the private sector. For this reason, school officials might want to pay $100,000 for a full time job position but instead they might have to pay out a total of $200,000 since the outsourced firm would probably have to pay their agent $80,000 to keep the position filled.

For this reason, outsourcing does not always lead to cost savings. In fact, in the scenario given, the cost was essentially the same since government workers usually take less pay for more benefits while private workers require higher pay and fewer benefits.

Another problem of the full time issue is while it allows full attention placed on the program, there are still internal motivations and perceptions that have to be addressed. For instance, as a program grows, the incumbent may demand more pay because of the office set up, and budgetary issues they have to endure…all of which will be further discussed later on in this chapter.

For the outsourced professional, the desire for more money, and the known real value of their talents in the marketplace, often leads to contemplation of leaving a company to strike out for better opportunities. These are issues and concerns that government workers usually do not exhibit. Therefore, know that the hired professional you start out with may not be the same professional you have at the end of a school year. This is merely a function of overturn—a problem inherent to our free market economy.

# The Role

It is critical to any faculty/staffer to know one's role in the school structure whenever taking on an administrative/overseer function. Without this, the person can feel as if he is in limbo outside of the system. Moreover, in time, improper attitudes can develop as a result.

The easiest and cheapest way for a person to see and know his/her role in an organization is to have an organizational flow chart prominently posted where everyone can see who is over his/her department, which department works with whom, and who is in each department.

When drafting the organizational flow chart, it is important to note whether the department overseeing the program is a subdivision of a larger department or if the department is unto itself a separate entity.

It is also important to spell out which department is under the program and which one isn't. If no department is under the program, which is truly a preferred way of executing the program, note in the flow chart which divisions partner with others in a collaborative effort to execute the program.

Again, remember that the program is the "slave" to the school and not the "master" to any one department or group of people. The usage of collaborations and partnerships should be extensive and help all concerned.

These considerations may seem simple, but they greatly help shape viewpoints and perceptions of the people working in the program to bring change. Remember at all times, that people are people. A plethora of perceptions and opinions will develop if allowed to form. The organizational flow chart, being prominently placed and consistently referred to, serves as just one simple tool to keep everyone of the same mind and goal.

## Duty Bound

Knowing what one's role is can be important to job performance, as can knowing one's job duties. However, before we go on, I want to stop and point out something here that should color the rest of this chapter section.

As a culturalist (a.k.a. social scientist), I often look at the organizational psychology of a group. That is why I say, "people are people," and why I often bring up the base nature of human behavior. It isn't to say, "this is how people will behave" but rather to say, "this is how people can become." Knowing a given duty allows the professional to walk into a job with a given expectation. When additional job duties pile on, due to economics, necessity, or other reasons, having duties properly spelled out gives the professional a tool to effectively air out any grievances and allow all sides to see what is going on. Being the overseer of a school-wide, or district-wide, Conflict Resolution program is a stressful job with a never-ending worker caseload in itself. By giving your program's overseer resources to point out their duties and role allows him/her, as well as others, to keep better focus and talk on an "apples to apples" basis with known standards, policies, practices, and definitions in place to facilitate meaningful communication.

With that said, all concerned should see duties as a set of guidelines on how best to go about the job at hand. These guidelines may be firm or flexible as the situation may call for it to be. Knowing the rigidity of the guideline's nature and function is often as critical as knowing what the guideline is.

For instance, review of the program is critical to keep the program running effectively. When establishing duties for the overseer position, it is critical to ask who will be doing the review of the program and at what level(s) the program will be reviewed. If the overseer is involved in a review process, it should be determined to what end that review should be done, how detailed the review should be, when reviews should be performed, and for what purpose(s).

Another thing to consider is the role of the trainer. Is the overseer a trainer as well? How many trainers/trainees do they oversee? Do they review and/or create the training curriculum? Again, address these serious questions early in the planning phase of the program.

I will reiterate; it is common for a person to work more than one function while at a given job. When a job is already critical and stressful, it is important to consider which functions the overseer will be personally handling as a part of their daily job duties. For instance, we have already talked about training and review being possible job functions. However, look at how stressful the job can grow when duties pile on, like overseeing all peer mediation, heading up higher-level Circle Justice sessions, etc. In an ideal world, the overseer has a staff that handles these additional job functions. Yet, life is anything but ideal. Therefore, always keep in mind alternative solutions to potential problems/issues. One excellent alternative is to have a teacher who is interested in peer mediations, to oversee a club that handles peer mediations. Having a school resource officer or school mental health counselor, might be a great way to enlist help with facilitating Circle Justice or panel sessions for intermediate or high-level offenses. The trick is to be innovative in one's thinking and use available resources in a collaborative mindset to ensure the program is as strong as possible. All facilitators and overseers of programs should be able to carry out their core responsibilities effectively.

Delegation of authority is another issue to look at. We all have been victims of people shifting the responsibility in the workplace. If you have not, consider yourself a very fortunate individual. However, the difference between one shirking unwanted job duties and a person authoritatively handing off job functions is an important line to make. Knowing what duties the overseer can hand off to others, as well as which ones (s)he can't, is crucial to allowing all parties concerned to know where they stand in the greater hierarchy of things.

Similarly, it is critical that all parties know where the boundaries are concerning what the overseer of the program can and cannot do. Ask questions such as, "Should the overseer be allowed to conduct reviews of how effectively teachers do their individual classroom circles?" "If so, will such an evaluation have any effect on the teacher's annual job performance review?" and "Can the overseer ethically allow criticism of teacher body language, word usage, etc.?" These questions and more demand serious contemplation when developing the position of a program overseer.

## The Numbers Game

They say the "devil is in the details." In truth, I have a serious dislike for accounting and accountants. To me, it seems like "bean counters" can suck the life out of anything fun and enjoyable. However, then I have to remember that I am not nine years old and get back to the world of being an adult where "bean counters" can be heroes —in some weird, sick, twisted sort of way.

All kidding aside, budgeting, and number crunching can be rather beneficial to the well-being and strength of an effective Conflict Resolution program. It allows a means of justification and benchmarking for a program while affording a sense of transparency and accountability.

A Conflict Resolution program needs its own budget. This is to say, a true section of the overall budget— not just combined with another department or division's budget. Spell out everything in the budget so everyone understands where the money is going, what is being used, and everything is transparent.

The overseer of any Conflict Resolution program, in addition to maintaining a precise and tightly managed budget, should also be keenly interested in number tracking. There are divisions of schools responsible for keeping track of data. However, I am not talking about such a thing. Rather, these numbers need to be for the sole purpose of monitoring and supporting the effectiveness of the program. Such numbers need to take a look at how many students were touched by the program (i.e., class circles, peer mediation referrals, panel referrals, etc.), how many utilized each specific component, how many were escalated to higher level functions, changes in overall grades of students, dips/rises in referrals, drops/increases in absenteeism, etc. It is beneficial to take the data and break it down by grade level, age, and ethnicity. Over time, if the data collection methodologies are maintained appropriately, one can use historical data to compare and contrast, as well as give trending data.

## The Office

Office space is important for the proper carrying out of the program. After all, the program is essentially a division unto itself. The demands of the program can be enormous at times and therefore require sufficient space and resources. For instance, there needs to be a safe and secure area for files concerning the various aspects of the program. Such files can be varied, ranging from peer mediation files, to grant program files, to statistical and financial data, to secure court-mandated diversionary tracking files. As such, workers need an area to carry out essential job tasks. Because of the unique nature of the program and its impact on the school, all parties concerned (i.e., staff, teachers, students, and parents) need a known office location to visit in order to talk about issues concerning various program aspects.

With that said, nothing quite colors a position like the office space that represents the position. In an effort to balance budgetary constraints with functionality, I have seen one-person offices subdivided into office cubicles with people packed like sardines. This gives the appearance that the program is not important. Then again, I have seen one-person offices totally understaffed and practically a joke as the sole worker was overwhelmed with work. I have also seen small offices collaborate with a secondary office in situations where people were respected and admired. Set-up of the division's working area truly does matter. You need the resources to do the job well, but you also need a reputable base of operations to command respect while being mindful of often-scarce financial funding. For these reasons, set-up can be an extremely tricky matter to get right.

The first thing one needs to look at is the number of people working in the office. Is the overseer the only true worker in the office? As will be discussed in a later chapter, this is a poor idea and should never happen unless necessary. With that said, does the overseer have a staff of any kind? If so, what are their job functions? In an ideal world, the overseer would have his/her own office where there would be a receptionist, a trainer, one or more facilitators, an office secretary to run numbers and process paperwork, and the overseer. As I have said before, the world is anything but perfect. In reality, the actual set up of the office will most likely be the overseer, a trainer that doubles as a facilitator, and possibly a receptionist. It is important to make sure that the setup is a sufficient balance of *lean* and *slack* to afford functionality, while also staying within budget.

As I mentioned beforehand, collaboration is a beautiful thing. Collaboration implies more than one professional mutually respecting each other and working with the other as a unified team to accomplish a singular goal. Collaboration can be extremely cheap—if you are the kind of person who thinks free is always the right price. That does not necessarily mean that collaboration can be easy to maintain. When setting up job positions, remember to look for similarities in basic job functions, job goals, commonalities in thinking. Try not to duplicate duties or functionalities. It is okay for a trainer to also be the facilitator so long as the pairing of the duties makes sense and eliminates slack. A lot of this will also hinge on what the official title of the overseer is and what his/her role is (i.e., an administrator, a facilitator, etc.). Also, don't forget to look at the most valuable resource —the teachers. Often, if approached the right way, teachers are willing to do something that they believe will both help the students and make their lives easier. Again, this is a collaboration that is based on mutual respect and working as a unified team toward a singular goal of making the program a success so all stakeholders in the school are made stronger and better.

## "Cred"

Competition these days, especially in sports, and other elements our nation's youth favor, often involves the notion of "street cred." "Cred" is nothing more than one's credibility or authenticity. In the world of professionals, "cred" is essentially the license, certifications, and other credentials that are believed to be what makes that professional worthy and skilled enough to do what he/she does.

The problem with Conflict Resolution studies, especially in America, is that certifications and licensure is spotty at best when it comes to legitimacy and necessity. In addition to private companies, with questionable legitimacy, there are also colleges and schools all over the country that grant legitimate degrees, diplomas, and certifications in various fields of Conflict Resolution. However, since there isn't a set protocol for vetting a Conflict Resolution professional, these "letters" often are as meaningless as a degree in "social sciences." Sure, there is a substantial knowledge base. However, there is not anything that propels one through a socially and governmentally approved vetting process as compared to other professions. Therefore, the certificate and degrees are essentially whatever the holders make of them and whatever value the employer, or school system, sees value in.

A quick survey of the US states shows some systems do not have guidelines for certifications, some allow their individual counties and cities to require certifications, and most states only require certification in a small number of fields. For instance, the Supreme Court of Florida only regulates certain fields of mediation while leaving others (i.e., commercial, elder, community, etc.) to be handled by non-profit entities, local government, or no regulation at all. Moreover, the Florida statutes regulating court mediators allow non-mediators to mediate in regulated fields so long as both parties agree and the mediators conform to Florida statutes on mediators. Therefore, it is possible for a person to mediate a case without any formal training.

Concerning Restorative Justice, the Florida statutes allow each circuit's elected State Attorney's Office to offer Restorative Justice Programs for youthful offenders. It never says what the credentials must be or places regulations of Restorative Justice professionals in the realm of any given office. As for arbitrations, certain persons can be arbitrators while others can only serve on arbitration panels. Even here, it is up to the chief justice of each circuit to determine if arbitration is allowable or if an arbitration panel can be used. Moreover, this is just in Florida. Now, imagine having forty-nine other states, plus all of the other US possessions and territories, as well as the District of Columbia, and one can see how crazy and haphazard relying on the government for guidance on credibility and licensure can be.

Ultimately, it will be up to the school or the district to determine what the overseer requirements shall be as well as what the requirements shall be for collaborative partners (i.e., teachers doing circles, panels, peer mediation practitioners, etc.).

Naturally, one would want to have the overseer candidates be able to express either an educational background or professional past in the field of Conflict Resolution. I believe that the key is for the candidate to be able to express this to the school for consideration. After all, does not having a degree in something preclude one from consideration if he/she has practical experience actually doing a craft? I think not! In the same vein, I would not recommend that one get caught up in certifications and licensures. Just because I have a certification in a given field does not necessarily mean that I can transfer that knowledge over to something else.

Remember that Unbroken Circles $^{SM}$ marries multiple types of skills in a relatively new practice called Collaborative Justice. However, in all honesty, much of what this program embraces is Restorative Justice. With that said, most mediators do not know what Restorative Justice Practices even involve and vice versa. When one talks about peer mediation or circles one can have qualified professionals who have no clue what all that entails because it is not a part of their overall Conflict Resolution background.

Any certification or licensure guidelines for an overseer should take into consideration such things. Ultimately, a great deal of flexibility is required. Job candidates must be able to demonstrate/express appropriate skill sets for review and consideration. Naturally, the best solution is to have a trained, certified Collaborative Justice trainer to assist the school or district with the set up.

What I do think should be harped on most of all are the requirements once someone does get the job. In an ideal world, the school or district would set up a certification program that the overseer would have to enroll in to ensure that (s)he has the appropriate training and acumen to do the job. This certification program should also require sufficient continuing education credits so that key identified aspects are continually maintained and honed.

The same should hold true for those collaborative partners involved with the program. A teacher who conducts daily or weekly circles should have to go through a certification program, with a continuing education requirement, to ensure that he/she is always at the top of his/her game when doling out those fundamental services to students. With peer mediation, not only should the peer mediation coordinator be subject to certification and continuing education training, but the student mediators should also have to do the same. Even with panel and Circle Justice volunteers, there needs to be this requirement. Yes, I am sure that coaches, dance instructors, band directors, and preachers will object and grumble about the requirement; all grumbling aside, the need should be established for professionals to deal with an issue as opposed to ill-equipped people hoping with good intentions. Good intentions are not sufficient to handle complex topics and sophisticated methodologies.

# 2.4

## Best Practices

The term, "best practices," is a given set of standards. The key issue for this chapter is how you view, compile, address, and revere these standards. For instance, in New Zealand, these standards are so regulated that they are actually "the law" when handling issues of juvenile crimes in a government-approved panel setting. Here in America, things are much less rigid and, therefore, more open for interpretation with some groups not knowing what their "best practices" policy really is—if they have one at all.

For many people, this chapter is merely talking about a phase of the process that has to be done… just because. A best practice policy for many American workers is something that the higher-ups pass along and the workers soon ignore. In a jaded sort of way, it can be seen by as a way a higher-up justified his/her salary and job title. This is because the American work culture is based on a segregated system where bosses rarely engage with the workers, superiors rarely know what subordinates actually do and encounter daily in their jobs, and the rules vary drastically as to who can do what, with superiors often doing the opposite of what they expect out of subordinates.

With the diminishing value of degrees and other certifications in America, as well as the benefit to the worker for acquiring said academic and professional letters, part of a thriving program has to be a best practices policy that embraces a vetting and training process that looks at both professional experience and education as a part of a cohesive standard. Professional and academic letters should be in a high level of regard so long as they are relevant to the position at hand. In doing so, it reaffirms to future hires, current employees, and others in the community that there is a set standard in place. A standard that includes a vetting process, taking into account degrees, certifications, other academic and professional letters and the practical acumen necessary to the job and its functionality. This standard is an assurance of a given educational and professional benchmark.

In truth, a best practices policy is a serious undertaking. It looks at successes and makes suggestions so that one does not have to reinvent the wheel. In a way, it is evolving and changing very much like a seasoned veteran being in the office, giving pointers on the best ways to handle a given situation.

In the conflict resolution world, a best practices policy is longer than what one would see in another type of business industry or a specific organization. Whereas a traditional business/organization's best practices policy may be a paragraph or two long—a conflict resolution program's policy can be several pages. Indeed, it is the primary reference and guide for all applications of a given program and the first document to research in times of trouble, conflict, or uncertainty.

The utmost reverence must be paid to the establishment of a concise, cohesive, all-inclusive, and well-rounded best practices policy. Moreover, a strong and earnest commitment must exist to its continual updating and maintenance so that its credibility, viability, and importance is not lost.

# Research

Any functional best practices policy must be firmly rooted in academic research. America is drastically behind other countries in many fields of conflict studies. The people drafting the policy needs to take a serious look at policies around the world. This will give them an idea of the form and content needed. New Zealand, Great Britain, South Africa, and Canada have varying standards and rules. Then, academic research in the field should also be incorporated. Topics like Broken Windows and Low Impulse Gratification barely scratch the surface in understanding key behavioral theories and developing what can be a comprehensive and highly effective tool. For this reason, it is advisable to have someone, or a group of people, with a varied conflict resolution and social sciences background, to call upon for guidance from time to time as well as a source for general practical advice. You may also want to contact organizations with similar programs in place.

It is important to look at trends as well as what the critics are saying about certain programs and functions. Issues, such as re-victimization and self-determination are some of the key problems that Conflict Resolution professionals contend with daily. A program concept is made better or worse by how other concepts are utilized and carried out. The critics view allows the researcher to gain new perspective to highlight ineffective methodologies and identify potential pitfalls.

Always remember, "Truth is a three-edged sword." There are always two sides to every story or issue; however, there is an additional side that people rarely try to seek-out—the truth. The heart of conflict resolution should always be seeking out that third edge; therefore, any successfully researched information should result in a more comprehensive and well-rounded best practices policy.

## Industry Standards

Just as any functional best practices policy must be firmly rooted in academic research, such a policy must also have a firm rooting in industry standards. The problem is that industry standards are determinate upon the situation and functionality of the school and the program.

For instance, the Unbroken Circles [SM] Program was offered for use in a modified form at a private school, which addresses juvenile offenders who are at a high risk of incarceration for previous misdeeds. These students are a part of the Juvenile Justice System of Florida with probation officers and court judgments against them. The school itself must contend with educational standards set forth by the Florida Department of Education, performance standards set forth by the Florida Department of Juvenile Justice, and retention and safety standards set forth by the Florida Department of Corrections. Each office and agency touching the school has its own industry standards that the school must embrace and embody in order to stay in business.

Naturally, not every school works under such strict and multiple guidelines. Depending on whether the school or district is private or public is usually sufficient in giving a different set of industry standards. The locations of schools and districts affects the industry standards greatly since states, and other political subdivisions, have varied rules from other states and political subdivisions. Industry standards vary greatly from school to school or district to district, depending upon: structural organization, school location, directing agencies, rules, responsibilities, policies, services, and unionization of the worker base.

No section can be totally comprehensive of the industry standards needed for consideration in a functional and well-rounded best practices policy. Part of the beauty of such a policy is that it is tailor made for that specific school or district. What is needed in Florida may differ from what is needed in Colorado. Therefore, this section of the chapter only mentions the need to include industry standards so the professional(s) drafting the best practices policy can be aware of the need and best address and integrate these standards into the policy to meet the specific needs and demands of all parties concerned.

## Targeted Programs/Functions

Another function of best practices is to address the core applications and functionality of the program. In everything, there is a need and one or more remedies to fill such a need.

To put things in context, let's think of a small fire. In one's arsenal, there is a thimble of water, a large bowl of baking soda, and a special helicopter on call an hour away to drop multiple gallons of water from a nearby lake. The thimble of water may not be enough and, in some circumstances, may even make the fire worse. The special fire helicopter would surely do the job, but it would deplete the year's budget if deployed for such small issues on a routine basis. The baking soda seems contrary to contemporary logic, but it would best do the job since it releases carbon dioxide when exposed to heat, and, therefore, it would handle the job at hand sufficiently, effectively, and economically.

In Section 1 of this book, you learned which programs are best suited for handling a given conflict resolution function. As you learned, each program or functionality has its own benefits and setbacks. However, from a business perspective, a given school or district may not have the resources to dole out such a service. Whereas, Section 1 told how things should operate in an ideal world and the best way to remedy a given problem, Section 2 directly deals with real world issues of scarce resources and compromise. Yes, it is nice when the ideal and the real world agree and are in sync—but this is rarely the case and should not be seen as the norm.

For this reason, it is important for the designer(s) of the best practices policy to be practical and place the programs offered on a continuum of effectiveness with the functions they serve. In other words, classroom circles may be highly effective as a preventative to having conflicts start, but they would be very ineffective at handling high level offenses where a student is about to be tried and sentenced as an adult. By the same token, panels and justice circles may be great for handling issues where a student is about to be tried and sentenced as an adult, but they would be extremely taxing and costly to use as a preventative to the outbreak of conflict.

Let's contrast this with the status quo of using prison as a preventative to lower level crimes. In America, we now have a policy of "three strikes" and others of similar ilk, where minor level offenders go to prison rather than through diversionary programs that cost less money and have a higher success rate. The goal is to scare the offenders out of committing higher-level crimes. What it does is stigmatize the offender, which further acts to deprive him/her of liberty and property. They lose their jobs, homes, cars, driver license, etc. for serving the prison sentence, paying all of the court costs, and trying to get back on track with their lives. Then, because they now have a felony conviction, for a misdemeanor offense, they cannot find places that will hire them. This causes no incentive for the offenders to change their ways and, if the experts are right, may even desensitize the offender to commit further crimes that are more heinous. Things have gotten out of hand. Some professionals now contend it would be far cheaper to offer criminals a full-ride doctorate degree than to imprison them.

It is for this reason, using the status quo for criminal deterrence as justification and reference for how not to do things, that the professional(s) drafting a best practices policy not make a policy so onerous that it solves problems by bankrupting a school or district with inappropriate methodologies. The program offered must best meet the function that it is to serve in the most cost-effective manner possible.

Over time, the acumen of the staff will improve. Data collection, practical usage of the program, and other considerations will color and drive the updating and refinement of the policy. This is a natural progression. Remember, this is an on-going process that requires routine updating and review. When starting a best practices policy, the drafter(s) of the policy give the school or district the best start possible based on data available— nothing more. Things can, and most likely will, change over time as the knowledge base and user demographics change.

## Results Driven

Intrinsically, the whole purpose of doing all of this is getting a desired set of results. Whether stated or implied, the stakeholders all have a set of results they wish to see from the program, and, therefore, the best practices policy must address the results strives for. However, different stakeholders will have different results that they wish to accomplish. Thus, it is vital the drafter(s) are aware of these demands and includes such desires within the policy.

In the world of propaganda studies, there is a term called glittering generalities that best fits this situation. Politicians, in particular, love to use glittering generalities as they talk about hope and change on the campaign trail. However, they never seemingly talk about specifics. For instance, in order to require hope there is an implication that there is harm perpetrated, a reason to need hope. What is that harm? To imply a need for change then there is also an implication that there is a wrong direction causing harm, injustice, etc. To that end, change from what? Politicians seldom address specifics because doing so would allow the voter an opportunity to disagree with them. Over time, this hurts politicians when they fail to meet the desires of their constituency. In time, the constituency wrongfully calls the politician a liar and cheat. The unspecified issues, revolving around the call for hope and change, cause a diversion between how the politician handled an issue and how their constituency wishes for them to handle the issue.

For this very reason, the policy drafter(s) must think like the stakeholders and leave no expectations unaddressed. Administrators have desires that are different from teachers' desires, students will have desires different from those of parents/guardians, and extracurricular instructors' expectations are different from those of churches and civic groups.

In other words, keeping little Johnny from committing another act of arson is a far different result expectation than having little Johnny come to school every day and pay attention in class. Without specifically calling out any given person, group, or incident, the policy needs to embody such expected results so that the churches and civic groups can expect the results of less juvenile crime while teachers and administrators can expect lowered absenteeism, and lowered numbers of referrals. The policy should be vague enough to meet multiple similar desires while specific enough to say what will happen when such an incident is carried out so that a reasonably called for result can be expected from the program.

When drafting the best practices policy, it is critical to the long-term success of the program that the stakeholders are included and properly polled as to what they expect from the program. Ask them specifically what results they expect from the program. If the results seem unrealistic, then further talks may be required for definition. What may be unrealistic from an administrator's point of view may be critical to a church or civic group and actually doable in the eyes of a seasoned conflict resolution professional once he/she has heard both sides and understands the full expectation. No one group or person should have a final say and the whole process should be one of collaboration.

# Contingency Factors

A functional best practices policy must also take into account contingency factors. For instance, in 2006, multiple school systems in Florida experienced a decline in student populations because of market forces at work. This caused the affected school systems to shift gears from rampant growth to drastic cutbacks. However, for school districts that failed to properly plan, further complications ensued once student populations rose, as market forces again changed, caused by the displacement of workers, resulting in them bringing their families back into Florida in droves.

Naturally, no one can plan/expect every contingency. There is the very legitimate argument that some issues are beyond the capabilities of the program to plan.

Past, present, and future student body demographics is one way to plan for contingencies. For instance, issues such as religion, ethnic/cultural heritage, family make up, standard of living, and what I call "X factors" all can be one component to examine in the planning process.

Religion is a topic that many Americans like to refrain from examining. However, changes in religious tastes also translate into a change in beliefs, actions, and resources. In Michigan, the state has received an influx of Muslims. These new students and families have values and cultures vastly different from the Judeo-Christian culture that founded our nation. In New York City, the gambit of religions range from Jewish to Catholic to over a dozen other major faiths. Each area has its own faith(s) that are predominate and affected by changes in society, and economics (i.e., people of other faiths moving in to get jobs and/or locals moving out to find jobs).

In my home turf of Santa Rosa County, Florida, there was a rather unfair court settlement between the School Board and the American Civil Liberties Union, which killed much of the religious infrastructure that assisted local schools and programs. Knowing which resources to count on and predicting which future resources to recruit is vital. In Santa Rosa County, there were a variety of other groups and resources that assisted the school district, but they still could not meet the breadth and depth of services that the churches had routinely provided to the schools. This deficit of services continues today as secular partners try their best to meet demands. Such considerations must be evaluated and addressed in the planning process so that no one is caught off guard. One way to look at this is by properly and routinely surveying the religious and political landscape.

Ethnic/cultural heritage is another huge issue for schools. For instance, before 2001, both the States of Tennessee and Florida had state recognition programs in place for non-federal treaty American Indian tribes. These tribes enjoyed a sort of quasi-state government functionality where certain federal rights, directly denied to them by the federal government, were granted to the tribes by the state government. These issues involved the ability to craft items as American Indian made, intervention by the tribes in child welfare act cases, the right to peacefully assemble as Native Americans, and more. State recognition itself became a national cry from outcast indigenous peoples seeking basic remedies and protections with states like Alabama, Virginia, and others answering the call to protect their indigenous citizenry. Founding families of these states, which had historically hid their heritage, were finally coming out and claiming who they actually were. Old stories, almost forgotten were shared with students by local tribes. Things were truly turning around for the native peoples in a positive direction.

However, in time, irrational and unfounded fears that the state recognition would cause the growth of casinos, reservations, and other "undesirable" aspects, caused ignorant masses to push for the laws to be changed. In 2001, both Tennessee and Florida repealed their state recognition laws. Since that time, thousands of students have lost out on protections and services. Authorities incarcerated one Florida artist for making shell gorgets (jewelry) in his family's tradition. The chances of an American Indian male going to jail or prison in Florida jumped to nearly 93%. High scoring, low-income minority students on track for full-paid scholarships had to abandon their hopes altogether as both minority and merit scholarship programs were drastically cut. American Indian minority-owned businesses changed their designation with the state and lost untold billions in contracts and projects afforded to other minority groups. To make matters worse, federal-treaty tribes, like the Cherokee Nation in Oklahoma, started a practice, of questionable integrity, where they devoted millions of tax dollars into a full-on legal campaign against non-federal treaty tribes charging every non-protected tribe with the made-up crime of "stealing sovereignty." As a part of this prosecution campaign, Cherokee Nation officials made it a point to list every non-protected tribe as fraudulent tribes, sought federal remedies, and even sent lobbyists into states to stop, thwart, and reverse state laws allowing for the recognition of unprotected American Indian citizens. This caused non-protected tribes to vest much of their resources into the protection of their peoples' civil rights rather than raising the lifestyle quality of their peoples and protecting a dying culture that future generations may not be able to one day inherit.

The American Indian issue is just one of a plethora of issues that affect minority communities all across this country. Each has a story and an issue that it is facing. Some are doing better than others are. A critical consideration is the level of representation that a racial/ethnic group has in a position of power. Jeb Bush, the same Florida Governor who signed away American Indian rights in 2001 is ironically married to a Hispanic woman. He personally pushed for billions of tax dollars allocated to Hispanic-specific programs and charities. For minorities, it is not which political party is in power, but rather how many of "us" there is in the political system to address a perceived and/or neglected issue properly.

Consequently, it is important to know what the makeup of the school's actual ethnic/cultural student body is so that proper time and resources are devoted to the situation. After all, schools before the 1980s had American Indians, but these students did not claim it for fear of reprisal by an onerous system and handed down stories of governmental abuse. The change in laws changed the demographic reporting—not the actual makeup of the student body. However, when Cuba started exiling citizens, the actual makeup for the Dade County area schools did change. In a world where multiple racial/ethnic heritage is a viable answer for reporting—it is critical to chronicle properly all of the various races/ethnicities a person has.

Knowing real change from perceived change is crucial since ethnic and minority issues have always been a hot button topic in America with pivotal changes in policy seemingly made overnight. In addition, since billions of dollars are appropriated each year, in almost every state, for minority and ethnic-based program, it is vitally important to stay ahead of the curve in this issue and the multiple political pushes that happen each year surrounding minorities and ethnicities. Remember, the term "equality" may be a nice thought used for invoking patriotism on a US stamp, but that does not mean it is a right protected by the Constitution. Whether one likes it or not, the stone-cold truth of America's economic, governmental, civic, and legal structures is that there are people with more rights, and more advantages than others. Do not let political idealism stand in the way of realistic practicality when developing a meaningful best practices policy.

Family makeup is another vital area of concern for planning. Any teacher, Sunday school teacher, or student, boys/girls-based group leader will tell you that the change in the family makeup has a direct effect on both the kids and society. Since I am involved in a boy's group called the Royal Rangers, I gave a speech on the impact of the family makeup on students. As I noted in the speech,

> An article in the Journal of Research on Adolescence (2004) said that males raised in a fatherless home, and without a positive male influence in their lives, are twice as likely to go to jail or prison. According to US Department of Health and Human Services, approximately 63% of youth suicides in America are attributed to the lack of a positive male influence in the life of a child from a broken home. The Center for Disease Control says that 85% of all behavioral disorder cases in children come from broken homes. The National Principals Association did a study on the state of America's high schools and found out that 71% of all high school dropouts came from a fatherless home that lacked a positive male influence. The American Sociological Review (1991) had an article noting how children from fatherless homes and without a positive male influence, had lower academic expectations and reported lower academic expectations

from their parents. Indeed one finds that identity confusion, aggression, poverty, and a host of other profound issues that are destroying our society and culture can be directly attributed to one thing—the lack of a positive male influence in the life of a child.

Of course, as a leader of a ministry program for boys, the speech focused on how boys are affected. However, these same results and other issues, such as higher divorce rates and lack of self-esteem, are attributable to girls without a stable and positive male influence as well. Then again, in talks with other Royal Ranger commanders, I heard of one boy whose family divorced and the mother got custody as the father left. The only way the boy got a meal was if the Royal Rangers' commander fed him. Later, the mother married and divorced again, leaving the boy behind. Through stepparents, step-grandparents, grandparents, etc., the boy switched from house to house with no one having legal custody. Taking the child to the doctor was practically a nightmare!

Such issues are now commonplace for children. However, in the 1980s, this issue was merely a growing problem. Again, it is a social trend that the plan developer(s) must take into account. For instance, approximately twenty years ago, there was a brief, but profound, trend for Baby Boomers to have children later in life. This caught schools off guard due to improper planning. In today's contemporary society, out-of-country and homosexual-couple adoptions are growing more prevalent, and many schools are failing to consider and plan for this. The goal of this process ultimately is to properly plan and forecast without placing judgment. For the planner and developer, they must see issues as issues and trends as trends without passing judgment or attaching a stigma to the situation. A divorce to preserve a family unit's integrity is still a divorced, single-parent family. It has the same issues and effects on a child as a divorce done because the parents wanted to see other people, drug use, monetary problems, or any other cause of divorce in America. The goal of accounting and planning in an unbiased manner is to let the school or district know which services to develop, improve upon, and strengthen. It affects not only planning but also training and implementations. Because of political correctness, many wish to shy away from this issue. However, if one sees an issue as an issue and facts as facts, there is no need to bypass a problem with a cool, unbiased, non-judgmental approach.

Standard of living is also another timely issue. The top reason for divorce in America is finances. Ironically, experts have pointed out that—with tax credits, child support payments, alimony payments, carried over debt, and other considerations—financial issues are not resolved from divorce and even made worse. However, it isn't only about single parent families. Minorities, on average, tend to make lower wages when all other considerations (i.e., age, education, gender) are equal. Even then, some minorities make far less than other minorities. Based on location, income can vary drastically from county to county and state to state.

Communities with a high military population tend to have a higher than normal educational level in their worker base while paying out lower than normal salaries. The notion of under-employment is an issue that liberals and conservatives choose to promote or deny whenever the climate suits their need.

As stated previously, out-sourcing to Third World countries is having a long-term effect on families as the spending power of the dollar is deflated (i.e., the cost to purchase a given item is higher now than it was previously but the income of the family has not changed). Businesses suffer when taxes are raised and mandates are given without justification or appeal. In parts of the country, dairies and distributors were hurt when the federal government ruled that milk was as toxic to wildlife as petroleum. In Atlanta, Georgia there was a publication of foreclosed upon properties, which was over two inches thick, placed by the taxing authority just shortly after the real estate market popped.

Such concerns can affect not only taxes coming in but also how societies react. For instance, in Atlanta, logic would dictate that as higher-income, non-minority groups left the state, trying to find work there would be an increase in the percentages of low-income and minority demographics. This would naturally place strains on the school system. In areas hit by recent federal restrictions on dairy production and distribution, the added monumental costs of producing milk, and milk-based products, at an affordable price, caused many people to lose jobs. Children raised in dire poverty are more likely to act out. This will cause a need for more services. Keeping abreast of the political-economic landscape of society, allows the school or district to stay ahead of the curve and be ready to supply the need for extra services and training when it arrives.

Early in my career, I used to write a social column called The X-Factor where I addressed key socio-cultural elements that the contemporary media was failing to address. One such "X factor" may be the rise in Sovereign Citizen families. People representing the Sovereign Citizen movement have an unfounded belief that there is a paper version of them and a real version of them. Thus, they are immune from the law because the real version of their persona is immune from the paper version that mandates they have a driver license, birth certificate, etc. This group is becoming a national plague with one group actually stealing a mall in central Florida by filing false foreclosure documents in court, putting chains around the doors, and barricading themselves in the mall itself.

Other "X factor" issues involve gender confusion or transgenderism. As noted previously, the ACLU and the Santa Rosa School Board ended up in court because of a male student who was living as a female. The public school was extremely religious, and so it was religion, not policy, which the ACLU attacked when they filed suit.

Of course, "X factors" do not have to be as severe as the case for Sovereign Citizens or the civil liberties suit filed because someone wanted to live his life as a person of a different gender. Yes, the issue of gay/lesbian/bisexual/transgender student populations rising is one to track because it might change demographic needs. Anarchist groups, gangs and other issues should be monitored.

Historic trends in drug abuse are important because drugs of unique eras have brought different cultures and different problems. For instance, whether one agrees or disagrees with the legalization of marijuana—the pothead culture of the early 1970s school system is a drastically different makeup from the cocaine and heroin culture of the 1980s, the methamphetamine culture of the 1990s, and the newly emerging drug cultures of today. The majority of people imprisoned in our time are connected to drug offenses. These people cannot get federal aid for school; however, a person convicted of killing someone is able to do so.

Ultimately, an "X factor" element is an issue that affects students, their families, classrooms, and communities and that it is seemingly taboo. Just because it is socially taboo does not mean that a school or district will not be affected by it; it should be addressed and taken into account in the planning of a comprehensive policy.

Just as there are social, economic, and "X factor" elements at play that should be taken into consideration, there is also another element that should be looked at—the laws of the land.

For instance, the Unbroken Circles [SM] Program relies heavily on Restorative Justice Practices. In Alabama, Colorado, Florida, and other states, there are laws that allow for some use of Restorative Justice Practices under certain situations. In the case of Alabama, inmates in adult prisons are prohibited from contacting their victims. This negates the whole purpose of Restorative Justice. In Florida, however, Restorative Justice Practices allow victim contact with juvenile offenders. According to the statute, the elected State Attorney for each circuit may decide to establish a center that is devoted to handling Restorative Juvenile Justice cases. However, just because there is a law allowing something to take place, does not mean that such actions will occur.

As a recent survey of State Attorney Offices in Florida has shown, many elected officials are so reluctant to the idea that they would not even answer questions involving the development and implementation of such a program.[1] The silence from these elected officials was deafening, with only two elected officials agreeing to answer questions. Of the questions answered, these offices indicated that they would rather prosecute or use Teen Court and arbitration as diversionary methods, rather than using any Restorative Justice option afforded by Florida law. [2]

Indeed, there often is no need for officials to go "outside of their wheelhouse" when they are elected solely to prosecute citizens. Besides, why would elected officials take money out of their budgets when other methodologies are in place? For instance, Teen Courts have funding from speeding tickets and other fines to fund them, and they give immense prosecutorial power back to the State. Arbitration (a system mimicking a court where usually an attorney acts as judge) has preference in some circles because it has officiated through a private company with the costs often paid out by the offenders as a part of their court fines.

The key to proper planning is to not only know what programs exist but also what programs are used or preferred by officials. For instance, the Florida Supreme Court regulates Dependency Mediation certification. A person might spend thousands of dollars to get this certification, but it is pointless if the circuit one operates in does not use it. Again, using my home state of Florida, they reserve arbitration certification specifically for attorneys. There is an option for mediators to serve on arbitration panels, but alas, there are few mediation panels used in the state. In addition, a survey of other states, with similar laws, shows a congruency in the demonstrated trends of the day.

Knowing which options are used and which are available allows the school to frame a plan. The plan allows the users of the program to know:

a) What functions are allowed by law?

b) How the school is diverging from traditional practices?

c) What the landscape is politically?

d) How bad things can get for an offender should he/she have to go outside of the conflict resolution program established by the school or school district.

## Annual Review

The annual review process is, for many people, like going to the dentist—unavoidable that is usually unpleasant and even dreaded. However, the information gleaned from an annual review is vital to the longevity of a comprehensive conflict resolution program.

From a functionality perspective, the first question in the review process should be, "What successes has the program seen?" This is followed by the question, "What failures have the program encountered?"

The two questions frame the bulk of what the vast majority of users and stakeholders want to know about the program. Remember that being results driven is a primary purpose of the program. Inclusion of multiple stakeholder desires in the planning phase allows reviewers, in the reviewing phase, to give context by addressing those desires head on with actual results. For example, a review may report that the program experienced an 86% decline in student referrals, a 62% increase in overall grades, and a 35% decrease in absenteeism. This data may be something administration will use for further evaluation and support of the program. By contrast, a local church or civic group may look at a trend where a 7% increase occurred over a two-year period in the escalation of offenders to higher levels of the program. This alerts all parties that a revision to the plan is needed.

Using stakeholder input, an evaluation program needs to be in place that tracks the program's impact to the school. Such considerations may be the grades and comparison of any changes in final grades. In Florida, the FCAT test is so important that "A" students at defined levels are denied the chance to advance to the next grade level if they fail certain parts of the test. Schools are denied funding based on student performance. Therefore, critics claim that public school districts are purposefully teaching the FCAT rather than giving children the education needed in a free market system. For this reason, major test scores, for tests like the FCAT, are a critical piece of data that stakeholders would want to track. Other issues might involve absenteeism, tardiness, and even bullying. Other stakeholders may be interested in the number of referrals from fights or substance abuse referrals. Essentially, whatever is being tracked, it needs to be data critically important to the stakeholders.

One area that most people never want to look at is one where there is no change. Some view no change as a level of perfection. Others see no change as an area of stagnation. Still others see no change as being a barrier to overcome. The problem is that based on one's point of view, differences of opinion can vary based on just one outcome. I contend, however, that knowing where the areas of no change are, allows a discussion to ensue.

Is the area of no change on drug use because the school has maximized its effectiveness, because the school has underutilized its effectiveness, or that it has made no impact? The answer to this can lead to massive changes in training, program structure, and funding. The concept of "no change" isn't a failure, success, or impasse. Rather, it is an improbable statistical anomaly that warrants further investigation.

Once all of these factors are considered, then and only then, can the plan look to ways of evaluating any remedies or plan revisions to affect immediate goals. Remember, annual evaluations should affect and focus primarily on the immediate and not the intermediate or long term. Historical data from annual reviews are the primary basis for any remedies and plan revisions for the intermediate or long-term. However, longer-term goals involve the issue of trending data over long periods of time. Therefore, the annual review should only look to the immediate and state what currently needs fixing.

A good example of this is to look at a hypothetical situation where the local churches are calling for the school to work on discipline more as they are seeing a rise in the number of juveniles being disrespectful to adults and senior citizens. If a recent review shows that the number of school referrals increased by a given percentage, then the school and other stakeholders may want to look at immediate remedies and plan changes to fix the problem. For example, if a recent plan change called for cost reduction and resulted in less training, this could then be posited for review of cost effectiveness for desired results. The key is to always remain collaborative and on point.

# Periodic Re-Focusing

The annual review process is great for looking at the immediate successes, failures, and points of no impact to see what needs addressing to achieve those short-term goals. This same review process is also a data collection tool so statisticians can trend the data and pull out patterns. Such data collecting and formulation is vital for a process called the periodic review and re-focusing phase. A re-focusing happens on a rotating cycle of every five to ten years and specifically deals with intermediate and long-term goals.

In essence, this review and re-focusing phase is much like the annual review but it ignores the immediate needs and instead looks to the intermediate and long-term needs. To do this, it is important first to determine when the cycle, or cycles are that the re-focusing review will take place. For smaller schools, it may be more cost effective to do only one re-focusing review every seven years. However, for schools with greater resources, it may be beneficial to have two reviews done with the intermediate re-focusing review convened every five years and the long-term re-focusing review done every ten years. Essentially, it is all up to the school to determine the cycle and number of reviews required.

The key is to evaluate intermediate and long-term goals properly and make adjustments based on collected historic annual data. Where an immediate goal may only be for the upcoming year, an intermediate goal will usually look three to five years, or more, into the future. Long-term goals surpass intermediate goals by forecasting ahead seven years to ten years or more. By nature, and design, goals for intermediate and long-term purposes should be on the macro level that warrants the time and energy devoted to reviewing it on a longer-term cyclical basis.

A great example of an intermediate goal is the establishment of a Conflict Resolution wing to a school. Such a wing needs to look at future expansion plans, curriculum development plans, and need. Naturally, having such a wing would foster greater interest in Conflict Resolution and give the school an area for training, handling disputes, testing new methodology theories, etc. Moreover, the creation of a Conflict Resolution wing would create a sort of rudder to help steer the school in its long-term goals.

What might these long-term goals be? Essentially, a long-term goal can be any lofty vision or purpose that best serves the school, the district, and the involved communities. For instance, using the Conflict Resolution wing as the intermediate goal achieved, the long-term goal might be to develop such a wing to the establishment of a vocational training program where participants earn certification, once they graduate, to become mediators handling issues of commercial disputes, divorces, civil law suits, political/diplomatic disputes, or juvenile disputes. The school might even wish to establish a program where students go into the community to train other schools, businesses, and civic/church groups. Much akin to Advanced Placement and Dual Enrollment programs, the school might wish to partner up with a local Conflict Resolution college/university to offer students a chance to get free college education while attending high school classes.

Invariably, the opportunities are endless. Moreover, as stated previously, the process is a near mirror image of the annual review process with similar issues like tracking successes/failures, looking at impacts, and making revisions to fundamental basics. Moreover, having intermediate and long-term goals and re-focusing reviews gives a sense of reverence and respect to the program. It shows a commitment by all concerned that Conflict Resolution is a worthwhile endeavor worthy of growing and fundamentally altering the school, the district, and the community in a positive way.

# References

1.   Johnson, K. (2012). *Neighborhood Restorative Justice Center: State Attorney Survey.* Author Survey of the State Attorney Offices of Each Circuit in the State of Florida. Ken Johnson:Milton, FL

2.   Office of the Hon. Norman R. Wolfinger, State Attorney for the 18th Judicial Circuit of Florida, 2012. Office of the Hon. Bruce Cotton, State Attorney for the 19th Judicial Circuit of Florida, 2012.

# 2.5

## The Importance of Training

No plan or program is any more effective than its training. Training allows the perpetuation of any program. It is also the fortification of the program and the instilment of essential core values.

Think of a program as being a chain to work with and training being the maker of the chain. If two-thirds of the links of a chain can pull forty pounds, and another one-third can pull twenty pounds, how much can the overall chain pull? The answer is twenty pounds. That is because the weakest links will give out before the other chains even have a chance to actualize their full potential.

As I said earlier in this book, this program was inspired by my playing with rubber bands—not chains. However, the same principle still applies since a rubber band has different thicknesses and even nicks that can cause the overall structural integrity to falter without revealing its full and true potential. This plan goes one-step farther in realizing that some programs will "break" because the faltering program was not intended to hold in the problem exclusively, but merely its job was to slow down and negate some of the harm so that another program could reach its full potential in helping a troubled child. Yet, without sufficient training, programs are more subject to unforeseen breakdowns which might cause other programs to prematurely, and unexpectedly, fail to resolve a program. Each time a lower level of this program fails, and a problem escalates, the overall costs of the program are increased. Also increased are the chances for further unmitigated harm and damages. Therefore, I cannot overemphasize the critical importance of a diligent and effective training program.

# The Trainers

In Chapter 2:3, we talked about the need for a professional, or group of professionals, to oversee the program. Oversight is an administrative function that is an inherently different function from the act of training. An administrator may do the work of the office (i.e., training) from time to time, but their main function really is to review, evaluate, tweak, and report on the functionality of the program. They are the overseers of the process. Trainers, however, are the actual workers. They have their hands messy in the actual work of the process. Therefore, please do not confuse previous discussions about administrators of the training functionality with actual trainers.

Recall in Chapter 2:3, we talked about facilitators and people acting as facilitators. In that chapter, we discussed school resource officers, guidance counselors, teachers, and even trainers as facilitators. However, a facilitator is merely a trained individual, acting as a neutral, who facilitates a given program. Ideally, it would be nice for a school or district, to have a group of facilitators to handle issues as they arise. Just remember, a facilitator's function is to carry out a specific process. They are also doing the work of the program, but they may not be the ones doing the training. Instead, they are the receivers of the training. Therefore, a trainer has a totally different function that we have yet to address.

To start, the first step in setting up an effective training program is to find trainers. It is best to have someone actually trained and certified in the Unbroken Circles <sup>SM</sup> Program to do the initial training. This, however, is just to get the school(s) started off on the right foot. After a year or so, to maintain the vitality of the program, effective in-house trainers are called for. This will lower program costs, as they address issues of concern unique to the school or district, routinely review the effectiveness of the program, help tweak the program as needed, keep a continuity flowing regarding the program, and offer remedial training to those individuals needing further help in grasping and facilitating the program.

However, before any school or district can begin this process, a critical question begs addressing, "Who are going to be the trainers?" Naturally, the first response any school is going to make is to utilize a teacher. After all, as was discussed in Chapter 2:3, teachers can be either part time or full time administrators for the program. I also suggested that they might serve as facilitators for the program. However, this is usually the wrong response in regards to actual trainers. In fact, as a culturalist and Conflict Resolution specialist, my experience indicates if one's first response is one's best response—one has failed to fully look at the problem and come up with an effective solution. Training is a full time obligation even if the school or district chooses to have a part time administrator. Ultimately, trained teachers need to be in the classroom teaching core subjects. Trainers need to be on campus equipping the teachers with the skills and resources they need to carry out the program best as collaborative partners and facilitators.

Another, more secondary, response may be to use a teacher aide, parent, administrator, an office assistant, or even a counselor for a trainer. Again, the problem is that secondary responses are very much akin to first responses in that they are not generally the best solutions to a problem. Remember, you are wishing to change the culture of your school or district. Any culturalist will tell you that, while some immediate results are evident with any culture-changing program, it takes a minimum of ten years to change the culture of a given organization permanently. Parents are not going to stay around with a school for ten years. In addition, if you use staff, the person doing the job will have to spend ten years of their career just doing this one job. Most staff will not see a trainer position as being advancement for their career unless they truly have a desire to work in this field and grow it. Indeed, unless there is a love for this position, most people will more than likely see the job as being more work than there is payoff. Let's face it; it's just the nature of the beast to feel this way since trainers have to constantly be in training classes themselves. Often they find themselves researching the newest data in their free time and trying to find innovative ways to solve common and chronic problems to which there is no obvious solution. In addition, they must do all of this in a calm and friendly manner where they are perceived by others to be in total command of the situation at all times.

The best solution to the immediate need is to hire qualified trainers who are outside of the educational system but have a love of the program. Think of these people as being at par with secretaries, school resource officers, and other critical office staff who may not have a degree or training in childhood education as a part of their overall background.

The term "qualified" is a precarious one however. As I noted in Chapter 2:3, with this book I oft times speak in generalities so that your school or district may speak in terms of specifics. I also noted in that chapter, it is up to the school or district to determine what qualifications one must have. Naturally, it would be nice and beneficial if they are certified as a trainer in the Unbroken Circle $^{SM}$ Program. However, this will not always be the way that the school or district will want to go.

If I can make any suggestion, I would first make sure that the candidate expresses sufficient communication skills. In other words, can they learn about something very complex and teach it to others in a step-by-step, thorough, and easy to understand way. If a person has such a skill, then practically anything else can be something that they learn on the job or in the classroom. So, like restaurants do with chef applicants, instead of having applicants send in resumes telling what all they should know, set up a test to find out what they really know. Have them read about something, give them a few minutes, and then have them train a panel on the subject.

Remember, a program is only as strong as its weakest link. The trainer is that longevity of the program. They are the builders of the program. Ultimately, they are the maintainers of the program, so do not neglect their importance!

**Training Materials**

If trainers are the makers of the workers, then training materials are the tools needed for the workers to do the work. Additionally, so often, schools in financial crisis neglect training materials in the hopes that staff will rise to the occasion to fill the need.

The problem with Conflict Resolution and Restorative Justice training materials is they are so varied, they follow so many different schools of thought, and often their updating is questionable at best. For instance, there are Restorative Justice Professionals, like myself, who see the process as being a distant relative of mediation. Others see it as being as different as birds and fish. Some wish to have the latest data while others like to set forth good footing that has been time-tested and proven to work. I cannot tell you which is better or more valid. All I can offer is my opinion and give you firm reasoning for my opinion. The same is for schools and their districts when it comes to which "flavor" of Collaborative Justice they like and how updated the materials need to be.

Part of the job function of a Restorative Practices Office should be determining what styles of Collaborative Justice fit best with the school or district and then determining how updated and revised the materials should be. This complicates matters because who makes the call when it comes to updating and revising materials and training curriculum? Are the trainers also the writers and updaters of some of the curriculum? If so, how much of the school's or district's resources are tied up in this process? In addition, to what end is this revision and updating necessary? One must be careful that the training always benefits the ones receiving the training rather than the updating and revising being a tool to grow a bureaucracy.

**Training Perks**

One of the reasons many training-intensive programs fail is because there is no justification for the workers constantly to be undergoing training. For instance, a government agency called in all of its workers for sexual discrimination training. There, the workers learned how to properly hug and such. At the end of the training, the attendees received a certificate. The training caused more harm than good because there hadn't been an issue of sexual discrimination. Additionally, the workers felt put off because they never had an issue of sexual discrimination; they now had double the work to do because they had to neglect their primary job for this training, and when it was all said and done, they did not receive any sort of raise or benefits from undergoing the training. As I told the HR person, "I am glad to see you back in the office. I know you have been busy the past couple of days teaching your workers how properly to sexually harass someone. Hug?"

This is not to say that all training-intensive programs will fail. Some do things right. For instance, I remember a relative of mine complaining about having to go to training. When I inquired, I found out that the government agency was paying for food, travel, and lodging and they were going to give my relative raises each time a training module was completed. To that, I responded, "So, where do I sign up? I will spend the next year in training if they are going to pay all of my costs and then give me multiple raises for someone else to do my job while I am in a classroom!"

As you can tell, I have a sort of twisted way of looking at things. Going too far one way or the other often times will result in the ultimate destruction of an otherwise stellar program. Benefits should be doled out sparingly and in an appropriate manner. In regards to the relative receiving payment for training, she is now a supervisor over her division. Per the program training module, new classes were only offered once she had sufficiently shown practical work experience in order to warrant further advanced training. Thus, that particular training program was effective. Had they not required actual work to warrant the training, then it would have been just another failure as it imploded upon itself with high costs and low worker productivity. Thus, an appropriate marriage must exist between the necessity for training and the actual necessity of the work being done.

Keep in mind that workers typically hate training. Very few people are going to say, "Oh goodie! Training! I'll make cookies…it'll be fun!" Therefore, training needs to have perceivable benefits which employees can appreciate. This, however, is hard since not everyone has the same goals or appreciates the same rewards. For instance, some people want to have a title so they look important and valuable. Others, like myself, could care less about the titles and awards and would rather have a hefty raise. The job was originally sought out to make money—a purely capitalist approach.

Some of the benefits of training may be things like making the training a part of the condition for employment. While I may desire compensation for more training, I am more than happy to undergo training if it means I will be fired if I don't take the class. A little less hostile may be the benefit of greater job competency. Greater job competency makes one feel more in command, it sets the worker apart from other less-skilled workers, and it can ultimately lead up to future rewards and advancements. Monetary benefits are also a perk that can be associated with training. Who doesn't like more money? Having an easier job is yet another perk tied to training. If I can do my job better and more easily, it will take off stress and ultimately make me a happier person—and what is the real cost of one's happiness? Having a certification tied to a job is also very nice. If anything, it bulks up the resume so that one can seek out future advancements in his/her career field. Status is another thing tied to training. For some reason, people love to have that level of separation that says,

"I am just a little bit better because I did this or that." Of course, opportunity for advancement is a major player when talking about perks tied to, and actualized because of, training. Who doesn't want the chance to advance and do well in a job?

The key is first to find out what your employees see as a benefit or a perk. As I said before, we all value different rewards differently. For me, I can have a filing cabinet full of awards and certifications, yet they don't matter to me until I have more money resulting from it all. For others, they would trade in a hefty raise for a colored piece of paper in a frame and a seemingly meaningless title. In my world, it is craziness, but to them, it could be the acceptance they never had. So, who am I to down play it even though I cannot understand it? For the developers of the training programs, it is vital, however, to be aware of what motivates the crew and where they see rewards. Once you know this, you can set up a plan that properly balances training with real world application of knowledge, doling out rewards in an appropriate manner so the participants all feel better benefited from the experience.

## Program Standards, Review & Enforcement

While a great portion of this chapter has concerned itself with the issue of training, there is still another area which needs addressing. I am talking about the development of the program standards as well as the associated review and enforcement thereof.

Again, this chapter does not talk about specifics. That is for your school or district to figure out. Instead, I will ask questions that need to be asked and give some direction so the school or district can make those specific decisions that make for a vital and tailored program to address the special needs of each.

One question is, "What are the set requirements of the program?" Now, for some, this is an easy question. For others, you might as well have asked them how a space shuttle gets to the moon. However, remember the work you have already done in Section 2 of this book. Already, you should have begun to set a plan in place that makes answering the question a little easier. For instance, since bullying is relevant in our schools today, one would think reducing bullying by 10% in the first year, and by 30% over the next five years, might be a set requirement of the program that will color the training, facilitation efforts, and focus of the program. Teen pregnancies account for about $10.9 billion in costs to the US government each year; therefore, it might be critical to the school to address inappropriate and dangerous behaviors. Ultimately, what I am saying is that the school is well aware of the problems, this book has already made a call for benchmarks to be set, and now it is just a matter of actually saying it all out loud, as well as putting it on paper.

Along the same line, we have already discussed the need for continuing education requirements. Therefore, now would be an appropriate time to ask the question, "What are the set educational requirements for the program?"

Once done, a few more questions beg to be asked. Who all will be in charge of the review of the program? Will it be PTA/PTO members and representatives? What part will administration play in this? How much of a part in this should the School Board play in the review of the program? Should there be a special committee made up to review all, or part, of this program? Who will make up such a committee? Does the Restorative Practices Office get to weigh in on the matter any? Again, in regards to these questions, the specifics need to be made a part of a written requirement of the program.

As we have talked about before, the gathering of statistics and data is vital. However, different offices within the school or district have different uses for the data. For instance, I have suggested that the Restorative Practices Office of the school or district do its own data collecting. Yet, for the purposes of program review, I am not so sure that data exclusively acquired from this office should be solely used in the review process even though I would support it being used with other data from other offices. Naturally, each district and each school is different and has different variables that will lead them to a given solution. So, this leads to other questions such as, "Where does the data come from that will be used in the program standard development and review processes?" "Who will be in charge of collecting such data?" Moreover, the question begs addressing, "How will the data be used?"

What about a certification process for the program? We have talked about it already on multiple occasions in this book. Its consideration and development has been called for. So, questions are asked like: What are the established requirements for each level of certification? How many levels of certification will there be (i.e., Circle Keeper, Peer Mediation Facilitator, Student Peer Mediator Certification, Circle Justice Facilitator, Trainer)? When do the holders of such certifications have to renew their credentials? Who notifies them? How are they notified? What is the complaint policy should someone potentially violate a condition of certification? Is there an appeals policy in place? Are the penalties fair and readily displayed to eliminate confusion? Again, all of this should be part of the written program standards and review policy of the school or district.

It may sound simple. It may sound repetitive. It may even sound unnecessary. However, these questions should be answered as a formal part of the standards and review process and are critical to the vitality of the program. Additionally, as I said already, much of the work has already been called for in previous chapters. Therefore, all one is doing in this stage of the game is formalizing what should already be known.

# Program Audit & Review

Let's talk about audits for a minute. Part of any review process involves the auditing of records. For many Americans, we like to think of an audit as being only about the monies and making sure that all of the monies are going in the right place. However, nothing could be further from the truth. All great audits look at the policies, procedures, stated objectives, and actualized results and then a solution is proposed to keep the program or organization in the right direction.

Here, again, we have already covered much of this in previous chapters. However, it is important to finalize the answers to seemingly simple questions. I say seemingly simple since they were once hard and should now be easy since they have been covered.

One such vital question should be, Who is tasked with the audit and review of the program? This will invariably lead to follow up or quantifying questions such as, Is it a School Board member? Do we need a special panel for such a task? If so, who makes up such a panel? Again, these vital questions must be formalized in writing. Personally, I like the idea of a special panel with at least one School Board member, PTO/PTA member, a Circle Justice partner (i.e., church or youth athletic partner), a Conflict Resolution/Restorative Justice/Collaborative Justice specialist, and a CPA as members. This allows stakeholders to be involved and allows the school to utilize the benefits of a diversified knowledge base to ferret out any potential problems that may exist.

Along the same vein, I think that audits and special reviews of this type should be separate from other reviews. While some schools or districts may decide to ignore my counsel on this matter—it only makes sense that something this involved be yet another layer of review and accountability to maintain the overall integrity of the program.

Frankly, I like a large audit of programs. Detailed audits of this nature are called forensic audits in some settings and applications. Such an audit not only looks at the finances, policies, and procedures of a program but also looks at the statistics that the programs, procedures, and policies are built upon. As the old joke goes, "5 out of 4 statistics given are made up." While I am not saying that schools today deliberately make up statistics, it is still very easy to twist data to make an assertion that, on its own merit, might otherwise be baseless. You can have the best program in the world, and all it takes is one person with an agenda to mess things up. Knowing that everything is being looked at just helps to assure all involved that the program is safe, secure, and meeting the claims and demands that it embodies.

Another thing that most people will disagree with me on is that I like the idea of an overall cost and benefit being associated to the school by the program. If the program is costing $3 million to the school but is saving the school $12 million, then attribute such a benefit to the program saying that it saved $12 million to parents and taxpayers alike. Similarly, if the program cost the school $3 million, and then it caused another $9 million due to failed programs, then attribute that cost of $12 million dollars where it is due. Let's face it; education today is a high stakes endeavor. In states like Florida, not having students pass certain tests can ultimately cost the school millions of dollars and adversely affect timely graduation. If a program is enacted to lower tardiness, lower absenteeism, lower violence, and improve grades —by golly, I think that it is only fair to everyone depending on the program to see just how well it is working and where the benefits and costs are seen with it.

With that said, I have no problem in the findings from such an audit and review being used for the purposes of budgeting, as evidence for consideration in subsequent reviews, publication to the public and media about the success of the program, etc.

I expect different reactions from school districts. Some will adopt this and others will ignore the program. Ultimately, the review, audits, policies, procedures, etc. of the program are for the people working the program. The program itself is just a tool for the people to work with. Success and failure are a uniquely human characteristic.

# Conclusion

This book should have made things painfully clear to you, the present system of handling juvenile and youthful offenders has faltered to a state of near disrepair. In addition, I noted how there are no other commercially available programs on the market that marry the concepts and practices this way. In the whole of Collaborative Justice, this book is a cornerstone upon which a new way of thinking may begin.

This book gives you an opportunity to take a stand and change the tide of things to come. My critics don't like me very much—but they do respect me. What I preach is heresy to their ears. Mediators say that Restorative Justice is just a fad and cannot hold its own—despite countries all over the world proving this assertion wrong. Restorative Justice professionals say that I am wrong and that Restorative Justice's place is in transforming conflict rather than resolving it; yet they still embrace victim-offender mediation (VOMA) and other Conflict Resolution practices inherently Restorative Justice. Indeed, as they have argued against me, the perceived boundary line between the two have blurred as mediators study transformative mediation, and Restorative Justice facilitators tout programs that involve community mediation principles. All of this has formed a new idea of collaboration of the Conflict Resolution arts into Collaborative Justice.

Let the critics say what they will. Now, it is up to you to determine if the facts and figures, theories and practices, and problems paired with solutions presented in this book provide you with a compelling enough case to attempt to rise up against the status quo and do something possibly paradigm-changing in the lives of children. As I have said before, just implementing one part of the program can still make a meaningful change. It is not an "all or nothing" matter but rather I have given you tools to tailor your own school's destiny.

I have spent six years of my life working to make the Unbroken Circles [SM] Program what it is. I spent another year assembling this knowledge, re-checking the data, and looking for the latest data, just to give the secrets of this program to the world

A Buddhist monk once told me that, in his faith, when a person is at his wit's end, he takes a piece of cloth, prays over it, and flies it as a flag so the prayers are carried on the wind to one day land on fertile ground as seeds of hope and inspiration. I can also remember an art teacher who once told me how ancient artists used to burn their paintings, music, and poetry in order for the smoke to rise up and inspire others with even more genius works. In a way, I guess, this book is like my Tibetan prayer flag or my artist's bon fire where I am releasing something that I am so intimately familiar with so that others whom I have never met before might have benefit of it.

Ironically, as I strove to complete this book, I had a number of people express to me their concerns about liability issues. I guess anything and everything these days is a liability. In a way, liability is as culturally significant to this generation as the Vietnam War was to my father's generation where people almost pummeled each other racing to a microphone to say, "This could be another Vietnam!" Yet, as I have said before, I see things in a little different fashion than others. Therefore, rather than shutting them down, I try to listen with earnest sincerity as they tell me their concerns. More often than not, they tell me that they are worried that if the program is mismanaged, I might end up in court as a part of a lawsuit. To that, I usually smile and reiterate that, in the end, with all things considered, I can assert with absolute certainty and confidence that a well-developed program, like Unbroken Circles <sup>SM</sup> will not fail the schools.

Indeed, as this book has come to its end, I have found many things comical. For instance, it has been my experience that it is common practice with these types of chapters, where an author, after spouting off all of his beliefs and assertions, will note how he changed his mind while writing his book. At the end, he is telling you that everything you have read is flawed and wrong and cannot be trusted. I find it hilarious and unique to our free market system that the desire to sell a book trumps the desire to pass along good knowledge. Frankly, I cannot, and will not, offer that disservice and disrespect to you. Instead, if there is any new-found revelation for me to share, it is to inform you that writing this book has only quickened my resolve and made me more convinced that this program is necessary and well needed in the American school system.

I say this with firm resolve because God has been good to me. I know that isn't the politically correct thing to say in a book about education-based programs. However, it is the right thing to say. Let's face it, I could have become hard and bitter at all of the hurt and strife that I have seen. Instead, a calm hit me that is contrary to my very nature, and I found a resolve that defied all reasonable logic to seek out a solution to a need that no one seemingly cared about. When I was willing to give up, teachers and opportunities sprung up in my path to spur me on. Even toys, like rubber bands, became unexplainably abundant in my life so that I had no other choice but to play with them and become infinitely familiar with their functionality. I knew what I wanted, but the footing and route of my path was rarely known to me. The old adage that, "you've got to go through Hell before you get to Heaven" really is true for me. It hasn't all been roses and laughter on this journey. I have seen the worst that our culture can offer. People whom I looked to as professionals scoffed at my ideas because they ran contrary to their own agendas and dogmatic beliefs. In addition, if I could see into the future now, I am sure that even darker times are on the horizon, as critics on all sides will have a field day picking apart this book and trying to find fault. Nevertheless, in the end, I know the gift that I now can share which will make life better for America's youth. I have arrived at the destination to which I have trekked.

I began this book by thanking you, so it is only fitting that I want to end this book by thanking you. It is one thing to pick-up a "how to" book, and it is quite another thing to see it to its end and actually act on what was taught. I have done what I can to give you the tools that you need. I have given you every warning and sage advice that I can muster. All I can do now is ask that you please be a light of hope to a young person in need by carrying this program to your local school or school district.

# Appendix Section

## APPENDIX "A" – SAMPLE
INSTRUCTOR CONFLICT RESOLUTION NEEDS QUESTIONNAIRE FORM

Dear Teachers:

The need to resolve conflicts in the classroom is paramount to keeping safe and happy schools. Schools all across the world are utilizing circles, peer mediation, mentorship, and other restorative practices with great success. Of these successes, school districts have been able to lower the number of drop-outs, improve grades, and keep at-risk youths out of the criminal justice system.

We feel that the art of conflict resolution is at a point where it has been proven safe and effective in the school system. Moreover, we feel that a program based on restorative practices is beneficial to our schools.

Therefore, we ask that you please fill out the following form so that we can tailor the program to the needs of OUR teachers and students in lieu of buying a commercial module that may or may not properly address all of our needs. We will need all questionnaire forms in by the ___ day of _____, 20__.

Your cooperation in this exciting program is greatly appreciated!

Sincerely

(Name/Title of Administrator or Program Director)

\* \* \* \* \* \* \* \* \* \* \* \* \* \* \* \*

1. Generally speaking, how much time do you spend dealing with behavior and inner personal conflicts between students?
   A.   Less than 10% of the day          B.   10-30%
   C.   30-50%                            D.   More than 50%

2. On a scale of 1 to 10 with 1 being the most popular method, how often do you use the following to resolve conflicts? (Note: Each item is a standalone topic to rate; therefore, you may have more than one topic that you can give the same rating to.)
   ___   Refer student to principal          ___   Refer student to dean
   ___   Refer student to resource officer   ___   Give detention
   ___   Send note to parent                 ___   Give discipline assignment
   ___   Separate them from class            ___   Let students work it out
   ___   Act as a mediator                   ___   OTHER: _____

3. Do you feel that your current methods of handling disputes and problems are effective most of the time? ___ Yes ___ No

4. Would you be willing to try new options if they could reduce the negative aspects of classroom disputes and increase student performance? ___ Yes ___ No

5. Please list how often you have had to deal with the following problems:
   (Use "V" for "Very Often, "O" for "Often", "R" for "Rarely", and "N" for "Never")

| | | | |
|---|---|---|---|
| __ | Talking out of turn | __ | Public Displays of Affection (PDA) |
| __ | Shoving, mild aggression | __ | Name calling |
| __ | Racial, ethnic, religious tension | __ | Bullying |
| __ | Poor sportsmanship | __ | Fighting |
| __ | Cliques/Gangs | __ | OTHER: _____ |

6. When do you observe most conflicts happening? (Please circle all that apply)
   A. Before school          B. Before lunch
   C. At lunch               D. After lunch
   E. At P.E.                F. Between classes
   G. After school           H. In class
   I. On the bus             J. OTHER: _____

7. Where do you observe most conflicts happening? (Please circle all that apply)
   A. At the bus ramp/(un)loading area   B. In the hallway
   C. Lunchroom                          D. Classroom
   E. Gym/Field                          E. OTHER: _____

8. Have you ever heard of Peer Mediation before today? If so, what is your perception of it?

9. Have you ever heard of Restorative Practices before today? If so, what is your perception of it?

10. Do you feel that the school is ready for a Peer Mediation of Restorative Practices program? Please explain why you gave this answer.

11. What are your expectations from such a program?

12. What are your fears or concerns about such a program?

13. Any additional comments or suggestions?


Teacher Name: _____ Class:_____ Grade Level: ___

## APPENDIX "B" – SAMPLE STUDENT NOMINATION FORM

Dear Teachers:

We are seeking nominations to assist us in selecting students for a peer mediation program at our school. We wish for this group to be diverse in backgrounds and representative of the makeup of the student body. Students nominated to this position do not have to be high achievers or even leaders. Rather, we are looking for students who are empathetic of others, fair, impartial, confident, organized, and who exhibit good communication skills.

Once selected, the student and parent(s)/guardian(s) will be notified. The student will then undergo a rigorous training program to prepare him/her for the issues that he/she will encounter.

Your assistance with this aspect of the program is greatly appreciated.

Sincerely,

(Administrator/Program Director Name and Title)

---

**PLEASE FILL OUT AND RETURN TO _____ BY ___/___/___ .**
**THANK YOU!!!**

Student Nominee 1 _____     Grade: ____
Home Room Teacher _____

Student Nominee 2 _____     Grade: ____
Home Room Teacher _____

Student Nominee 3 _____     Grade: ____
Home Room Teacher _____

Student Nominee 4 _____     Grade: ____
Home Room Teacher _____

Student Nominee 5 _____     Grade: ____
Home Room Teacher _____

Student Nominee 6 _____     Grade: ____
Home Room Teacher _____

Student Nominee 7 _____     Grade: ____
Home Room Teacher _____

## APPENDIX "C" – SAMPLE STUDENT NOMINATION LETTER

Dear (Name of Student):

Congratulations! The faculty and staff of _____ School have nominated you to be a peer mediator in our peer mediation program.

With this honor comes great responsibility. You should seriously consider whether to accept this position since it requires a great deal of maturity as well as time.

Peer mediators undergo rigorous training sessions and handle issues of a sensitive, personal, and most times, confidential nature. Indeed, the training that our peer mediators receive is not unlike the training that adult, professional mediators receive to handle court cases, business disputes, international disputes, and other issues.

Enclosed with this letter is a Permission Letter and Letter of Acceptance. If you and your parent(s)/guardian(s) decide to accept this position, please fill out these forms and return them to Mr./Mrs. _____ in the _____ office by ____/____/____.

Congratulations again on receiving this high honor.

Sincerely,

(Administrator/Program Director Name and Title)

# APPENDIX "D" – SAMPLE PARENT PERMISSION LETTER

Dear (Name of Parent/Guardian):

Congratulations! We are pleased to inform you that _____ has been nominated by the faculty and staff of _____ School to be a peer mediator in our peer mediation program.

Peer mediation is a form of conflict resolution where students are trained to handle interpersonal conflict issues under the close supervision of a trained, adult mediation facilitator. Peer mediators are not arbitrators. Rather, peer mediators are impartial parties who help opposing sides to resolve conflicts and solve problems.

Peer mediation is very safe. Effective peer mediation and conflict resolution programs have been used in thousands of schools in the US, Canada, South Africa, Australia, New Zealand, and Europe. The training that the students receive are life skills that many colleges have identified as being crucial to future success in the work force.

We hope that you will consider allowing _____ to participate in our program by signing the permission slip below. _____ was only nominated because the faculty and staff felt that (s)he was of a high enough caliber to handle the responsibility of the position and that such a leadership position would only help your child to excel for years after his/her academic career at our school.

Again, congratulations to your family for such an honor. Please feel free to call me if you should have any questions.

Sincerely,

(Administrator/Program Director Name and Title)

\* \* \* \* \* \* \*

I, _____, give my child, _____, permission to participate in the peer mediation program at _____ School.

Signature: _____     Date: _____

## APPENDIX "E" – SAMPLE STUDENT ACCEPTANCE FORM

DATE: _____

I, _____, hereby agree to participate in the peer mediation program at _____ School.

I understand that I must undergo a rigorous training program in order to participate. Once I have fulfilled this requirement, I will be required to take an oath of office. Only after I have completed the training session and taken the oath of office will I become a CERTIFIED PEER MEDIATOR.

I understand that with such an honor will come the duty to be fair, impartial, and confidential. I understand that this is a public trust. Moreover, I understand that at anytime I may be ejected from the program should I violate the guiding rules and policies of the program.

Signature of Student: _____     Date: _____

Signature of Parent: _____     Date: _____

- - - - - - - - - - - - - - - - - - - - - - - - - - - - - - - - - - - - - - - - - - - - - - - - - - - - - - - - - - - - - - - - - -
## FOR OFFICE USE ONLY
- - - - - - - - - - - - - - - - - - - - - - - - - - - - - - - - - - - - - - - - - - - - - - - - - - - - - - - - - - - - - - - - - -

| | |
|---|---|
| **Date Received** | |
| **Tentative Training Date** | |
| **Tentative Training Start Time** | |
| **Tentative Training Completion Date** | |
| **Parent/Guardian Permission on File?** | |
| **Training Completion Date** | |
| **Training Test Score** | |
| **Student Certified as Peer Mediator?** | |
| **Date Student Certified as Peer Mediator** | |

Signature of Program Director _____     Date: ___/___/___

Printed Name of Program Director _____

## APPENDIX "F" —SAMPLE PEER MEDIATION OATH

I, _____, hereby swear (or affirm) to help the students of _____ School to settle their differences in a peaceful manner.

I will always strive to be truthful and fair, never seeking to do harm, always pursuing the goal of peaceful settlement with the utmost care and confidentiality.

I acknowledge that I am the guardian of the process and keeper of the confidence. The disputants are the authors of their own conflict and must, therefore, jointly work to end their conflict. The process must be self-directing by the disputants; therefore, I will not let anything break or bend this process to harm or help another. I will never let the revelations of any mediation session go public.

I vow to undertake the role of a leader in this school. In as much, I will fashion my behavior and hone my skills in a way to command respect and recognition by my peers as an empathetic and compassionate leader as well as a source of wise counsel.

I will hold true to the axiom that the truth is a three-edged sword where each side of a dispute usually has its own perceptions but the truth is traditionally found being hidden somewhere in the middle of these perceptions. The truth shall be my lamp and guide as I work to help others to resolve their conflicts and be made as whole as is possible by the process.

By my word, by my heart, by my honor, I shall quicken these words and make them not empty or hollow but rather policy and creed made manifest in my daily life. By my honor, I hereby assert that I accept this great privilege and this great burden and make it a part of who I am as a person.

Signature of Student: _____     Date: _____

Printed Name of Student: _____

ATTEST:

Signature of Director: _____     Date: _____

Printed Name of Director: _____

# APPENDIX "G" —SAMPLE PEER MEDIATION REFERRAL FORM FOR TEACHERS

DATE: ____/____/20__          TIME: ____:____ ___M

REFERRED BY: _____

URGENCY OF THIS MATTER:     __ Earliest convenience     __ Tomorrow

                            __ ASAP                    __ Today

1. Names, grade levels, and homeroom teacher names of students in conflict:

   ........................................................................

   ........................................................................

   ........................................................................

   ........................................................................

   ........................................................................

2. When/where did the conflict occur?

   ........................................................................

3. Please describe the nature of the conflict (i.e., fighting, gossiping, etc.):

   ........................................................................

   ........................................................................

   ........................................................................

4. Are the student(s) aware of being sent to peer mediation?

   __ Yes __ No

5. Any background history or additional comments?

   ........................................................................

   ........................................................................

   ........................................................................

   ........................................................................

*Please drop form off to _____ or the nearest referral lockbox located in the Teacher's Lounge, Library, Cafeteria, and Main Office. We check the referral lockboxes twice a day at approximately __:__ AM and __:__ PM. If you this is an urgent matter, please drop this slip off at the Restorative Practices Office.*

*Thank You!!!*

## APPENDIX "H" —SAMPLE PEER MEDIATION REFERRAL FORM FOR STUDENTS

DATE: ____/____/20__          TIME: ____:____ ___M

REFERRED BY: _____

URGENCY OF THIS MATTER:     __ Earliest convenience          __ Tomorrow

                            __ ASAP                          __ Today

1. Names, grade levels, and homeroom teacher names of students in conflict:

   ..................................................................................

   ..................................................................................

   ..................................................................................

   ..................................................................................

   ..................................................................................

2. When/where did the conflict occur?

   ..................................................................................

3. Please describe the nature of the conflict (i.e., fighting, gossiping, etc.):

   ..................................................................................

   ..................................................................................

   ..................................................................................

4. Is the student(s) aware of this peer mediation referral?

   __ Yes __ No

5. Do you assert that you are not using this as a way to get out of class?

   __ Yes __ No

6. Do you feel harmed, threatened, or intimidated by this student?

   __ Yes __ No

7. Any background history or additional comments we should know about?

   ..................................................................................

   ..................................................................................

*Please drop form off to you teacher, librarian, cafeteria monitor, or to the main office. If you this is an urgent matter, or if you fell at harmed or threatened, please immediately report this matter to the Dean's Office.*

*Thank You!!!*

# APPENDIX "I" - SAMPLE MEDIATOR'S NOTE SHEET & PROCEDURES SHEET

*Case No.* _____

*Date:* ____/____/20____          *Time:* ____:____ ___M

*Name(s) of Mediator(s):* _____

NAME OF PARTICIPANT 1: _____

NAME OF PARTICIPANT 2: _____

NAME OF PARTICIPANT 3: _____

NAME OF PARTICIPANT 4: _____

## POINTS OF CONFLICT:

## POINTS OF COMPROMISE/AGREEMENT:

# MEDIATOR PROCEDURE CHECK LIST

**(Peer Mediator Should Read Aloud to Parties, as is Applicable)**

1. Introduce yourself.

2. Welcome each party to the peer mediation process and ask them their names and grades.

3. Explain what your role is as a mediator, how the process works, and what is expected of them.

4. Have all parties agree to some ground rules, to wit:

(Read aloud to parties involved)

A. Each party must earnestly try his/her hardest to solve the problem.

B. Each party must be truthful at all times.

C. While it is okay to show emotions, each party is expected to be civil to each other at all times.

D. Listening is just as vital as talking when dealing with Conflict Resolution. Therefore, each party is expected to listen to each other and not interrupt the other person. For this reason, parties will be given a pen and paper to jot down any points that may have come to mind while the other party is talking.

E. By participating in the peer mediation process, all parties involved earnestly must work towards a meaningful solution to the conflict

F. Will sign a written agreement once a solution has been agreed upon

G. Each party takes full responsibility for carrying out the agreement

H. With exception to the Dean, Principal, School Counselor, Law Enforcement, and other officials of similar ilk —the contents of what goes on in this mediation session are to be kept confidential and not used or divulged to any other party unless both parties mutually agree to either a partial or full disclosure.

I. The process is voluntary. If either party wishes not to proceed any further, during the course of the mediation, he/she may do so. This is called an "impasse." Traditionally, the mediation session is stopped and the conflict is then handed over to the authority traditionally tasked with handling the problem (i.e., Deans Office, Principal).

5. Parties involved in the dispute are to speak directly to each other as they discuss their issues, feelings, needs, wishes, and hopes.

6. Tradition suggests that the mediator start with the student who has brought the conflict to mediation. However, the party wishing to speak first, even if he/she did not bring the issue to mediation, has full right to speak first. Make sure to ask each party what has brought him/her to peer mediation.

7. Be sure to listen and take notice of the content and feelings being expressed by both students. Jot down any important points that you feel may need to be addressed or clarified.

8. Rephrase what the party just said and clarify what the party is trying to convey. Use phrases such as, If I understand you correctly…, I can see that you are angry… Is this what I heard you say...? and Are you saying that...?"

9. When necessary, strive to keep the parties on topic by saying phrases such as, "I need you to stay on the topic" or "Is there anything else either of you want to share about...?"

10. Ask clarifying questions and summarize the concerns and issues. You may wish to use clarifying comments such as, "Is the main concern...?" or "It sounds like you agree (or disagree) that...."

11. It may be necessary sometimes to have what is known as a "caucus" or private meditation session between an individual party and the peer mediator. For fairness, if this is done, both parties should be allowed a caucus session with the mediator. Caucuses are only used at times of gridlock, when the parties are becoming too emotional, or when it appears that one party is not being forthright in the session. To conduct a caucus, tell the parties that you think it is time to caucus, explain what a caucus is (a private, confidential meeting between a single party and the mediator), get their agreement to enter into a caucus, ask one party to sit outside at a designated area, and then caucus with the party you wish to speak with. Before sending a party outside or calling-in another party, get either a full, or a partial, disclosure to speak with the other party about what took place in the caucus. Do not speak about anything that happens in the caucus without permission first.

12. Have the parties brainstorm to find ways to solve the problem. Ask them, "What are some of your ideas on how to solve this problem?"

13. Look for certain areas of agreement and then present them as possible solutions with questioning such as, "Let's see, it appears that you both are in agreement     that … so would … work for you (and you)?"

14. Help both parties make a plan of action by having them jointly decide what efforts they want to use to try to solve the problem. Start by identifying what steps need to be taken, prioritizing which steps of the plan are more critical, note which obligation belongs to which party to do, note when the obligations should start/finish by, and write down this plan and solution in an agreement.

15. Help both parties to incorporate into the plan consequences, should either party not follow through. Also, help the parties prioritize the importance of the infractions and pair them appropriately with the mutually desired consequence.

16. Have both students sign and date the agreement. Put the original in a file and make copies for each party to take with them.

17. Congratulate parties and shake hands with each other.

## APPENDIX "J" – SAMPLE PEER MEDIATION AGREEMENT FORM

*Case No.* _____

*Date:* ____ / ____ /20____          *Time:* ____ : ____ ___M

*Name(s) of Mediator(s):* _____

        **NAME OF PARTICIPANT 1:** _____
        **NAME OF PARTICIPANT 2:** _____
        **NAME OF PARTICIPANT 3:** _____
        **NAME OF PARTICIPANT 4:** _____

We, the undersigned, hereby state that we entered into peer mediation on this ___ day of _____, 20___, and that we voluntarily agree to the following:

_____

_____

It is the duty of _____ to do _____ by ___/___/___ .
It is the duty of _____ to do _____ by ___/___/___ .

If either party fails to fulfill his/her part of the agreement, he/she must first notify the other party and give a full explanation as well as to propose a peaceable solution. If that should fail, then _____ will happen as a consequence. If this then fails, _____ will happen as a consequence.

We further state that we enter into this agreement willingly and should any party not be abiding by these provisions, we hereby agree to return to mediation for further conflict resolution.

SIGNATURE OF PARTICIPANT 1: _____
SIGNATURE OF PARTICIPANT 2: _____
SIGNATURE OF PARTICIPANT 3: _____
SIGNATURE OF PARTICIPANT 4: _____

           SIGNATURE OF MEDIATOR: _____
           SIGNATURE OF ADVISOR: _____

# About The Author

Ken Johnson is better known as "America's Culturalist." He is a Social Scientist (a.k.a. Culturalist) as well as a Collaborative Justice professional with numerous op-ed columns and articles to his credit. Community and culture are important to Ken. He is a very active and proud, seventh generation Floridian living in Santa Rosa County, Florida. A former substitute teacher and continuing education instructor, he also has fifteen years of practical working experience in the criminal justice system.

Ken has special training as a Restorative Justice facilitator through the University of West Florida, College of Professional Studies. He also holds special certification through the Florida Supreme Court as a Certified County Court Mediator. Ken serves on numerous boards and panels for non-profit and government agencies. For his good works, he was commissioned as a Colonel of Kentucky. In addition to his experience and certification, Ken also holds a BA in Social Sciences from the University of West Florida as well as an MBA from Saint Leo University.

Ken currently lives in the western Florida Panhandle with his wife. They have family and friends nearby. He has a little dog that loves to sit on his lap as he works, causing Ken to make typographical errors. Conflict resolution is a passion for him as is bettering the lives of young people in America.

CPSIA information can be obtained at www.ICGtesting.com
Printed in the USA
LVOW02s0841200915

454921LV00003B/5/P